Governing for Health

Governing for Health

Advancing Health and Equity through Policy and Advocacy

FRAN BAUM

OXFORD
UNIVERSITY PRESS

OXFORD
UNIVERSITY PRESS

Oxford University Press is a department of the University of Oxford. It furthers
the University's objective of excellence in research, scholarship, and education
by publishing worldwide. Oxford is a registered trade mark of Oxford University
Press in the UK and certain other countries.

Published in the United States of America by Oxford University Press
198 Madison Avenue, New York, NY 10016, United States of America.

Library of Congress Cataloging-in-Publication Data
Names: Baum, Frances, author.
Title: Governing for health / Fran Baum.
Description: Oxford ; New York : Oxford University Press, [2019] | Includes
bibliographical references and index.
Identifiers: LCCN 2018023168 | ISBN 9780190258948 (pbk. : alk. paper)
Subjects: | MESH: Health Policy | Environmental Policy | Government
Classification: LCC RA427.8 | NLM WA 525 | DDC 362.1—dc23
LC record available at https://lccn.loc.gov/2018023168

9 8 7 6 5 4 3 2 1

Printed by Webcom, Inc., Canada

Contents

Acknowledgments

BOOKS ARE NEVER just the product of individual thought. So it is with *Governing for Health*, which draws on the 35 years during which I have researched, taught, and thought about the social determinants of health. Friends, work colleagues, comrades in progressive health struggles, and students have shaped my thinking over the years and are too numerous to list here. Thus I restrict myself to those who have helped directly with this book in the past two years.

Connie Musolino has been a brilliantly efficient research assistant and made the process of producing this book much easier. Peter Sainsbury was generous in providing insightful comments on the chapters on urban planning and environment, as did Rob Hattam on the education chapter. I tweeted the wellness manifesto and received useful comments from fellow tweeters and particularly helpful comments from Jon Jureidini, Melissa Raven, Melissa Sweet, and Emma George.

Concomitant to writing this book I have been co-director of the National Health & Medical Research Council Centre of Research Excellence (CRE) on Social Determinants of Health Equity. Through CRE activities, I have been involved with colleagues in many detailed and thought-provoking discussions about aspects of governance for health. I thank them all for these enriching sessions. A special thank you to my co-director Sharon Friel. We share a passion for social determinants and have worked together for many years to create structures within which progressive research can happen, and we became firm friends through the process. I have a network of wonderful overseas research collaborators who enlarge my thinking beyond Australia. Jennie Popay, Ron Labonte, and David Sanders have been important in shaping ideas for this book.

My colleagues at the Southgate Institute for Health, Society and Equity have all enriched this book. Recently I have worked particularly closely with Toni Delany-Crowe, Matt Fisher, Toby Freeman, Tamara Mackean, Colin MacDougall, Kathryn Browne-Yung, and Anna Ziersch on issues of policy and governance, and I thank them for their contribution to my thinking which shaped ideas in this book.

My research always engages policymakers and I am grateful to those who have taken time out of their inevitably busy and politically driven lives to join our advisory groups and to help me understand the realities of the policy world and how it shapes the opportunities for governance for health. I am particularly grateful to Carmel Williams (SA Health) for our ongoing partnership and her willingness to describe her policy world to me in frank and open ways. Sir Michael Marmot and the Hon. Monique Begin, with whom I served on the Commission on the Social Determinants of Health, continue to inspire me with their ongoing commitment to healthier and equitable societies.

I am grateful to Chad Zimmerman Senior Editor at Oxford University Press for being enthusiastic and encouraging about this book. Chloe Layman, Assistant Editor has been very supportive and the editing from Dorothy Bauhoff extremely helpful in ensuring clarity.

My passion to ensure that one day we live in a world that is governed for health is always rekindled when I spend time with my comrades from the People's Health Movement. I am grateful for their inspiration and commitment.

My deepest gratitude is to Paul Laris, my husband and best friend. Not only did he read and critique every chapter, he also offered every encouragement and the best in companionship and love while I was writing this book.

I dedicate this book to my grandchildren, Anika Laris and Riley Goff-Laris, my great-nieces and -nephews, Libby and Abby Thornton, and Maisa and Lasse Leikas, and all of their generation who deserve a sustainable world governed for health.

Fran Baum
Henley Beach, South Australia
May 2018

Governing for Health

1

Introduction

. . . health, which is a state of complete physical, mental and social wellbeing, and not merely the absence of disease or infirmity, is a fundamental human right and that the attainment of the highest possible level of health is a most important world-wide social goal whose realization requires the action of many other social and economic sectors in addition to the health sector.

—WORLD HEALTH ORGANIZATION (1978: 2)

I WANT TO persuade you that a shift to governing for health, equity, and well-being, rather than profit, is vital if we are to continue to improve life expectancy and survive as a species on this planet. Our planet is living through dramatic times. The good news is that humans are living longer than ever and fewer people are living in absolute poverty than in the past. The bad news is that we are becoming less equitable, some people's life expectancies are declining, and we are using up our planet's resources at an unprecedented rate and are warming the climate to a point that will soon mean that life as we know it will be unsustainable. The planet will continue to orbit the sun, but it could be a planet without people. The cause of these reverses in human and planetary well-being is that we have allowed an economic model of life to dominate our imaginations so that money and growth are valued above all else. The pursuit of wealth has become the most desired thing. This has meant that we are becoming less equal, less fair, and less sustainable, and, for some groups, less healthy. The unimagined wealth experienced by a very small proportion of our planet's population has been accumulated through despoiling the natural capital of the world—the air, oceans, lakes, forests, wetlands, marshes, savannah, and deserts. Millions of years of evolution have been wiped out in the interests of very short-term profit taking. In most sectors of our society, decisions are made in favor of profit, rather than in terms of what is good for our collective health.

It is against this background that governing for health and well-being becomes so vital. We have entered the Anthropocene age in which human activity is shaping the planet's environment. Unless we govern that activity and ensure that it is directed at creating the conditions for health and well-being, it will pose a direct and increasing threat to our health. Such governance will require a fundamental rethinking of what we value as a species and how we are going to reverse and repair the damage done to the planet. Our survival depends on a shift to a world in which community, society, more equitable sharing of resources, and conservation of the planet matter much more than money and the economy. This shift will be good for human health and will create a future in which older people feel satisfied that they are handing over a sustainable legacy, and younger people feel excited by a sustainable and healthy future, full of opportunities and potential. In the 1960s there was a widespread assumption that things would continue to get better. However, in the 1970s and 1980s the world chose the path of neoliberalism, and optimism was squeezed out of our vision.

Governing for Equity

In the first two decades of my life I was fortunate to be the recipient of considerable support from the state. The British National Health Service saved my life. I needed a blood transfusion at birth and Mum always told me how lucky I was to have been born at a time that health care was free and accessible. Then I had a great public education. I went to a state-funded nursery school from age three and was able to develop good skills. My state primary school provided me with good basic education and some frills such as weekly drama classes. My secondary education was good enough to see me win a place at university. I was the first in my family to complete high school, let alone go to university. What's more, my local authority in the United Kingdom not only paid all my fees, but also provided a means-tested maintenance grant, which meant, because my parents didn't earn much, I had enough to live on. Once I'd graduated, I bought my first house with the help of a state grant.

Thus, in many ways, I'm a product of an interventionist, redistributive state. It worked well for my generation of baby boomers. We grew up with a sense that not just our parents but the broader society would look after us. It would give us a hand up and take an interest in our collective welfare though a myriad of policies. There was a greater sense of "we" and "community" and collective consciousness. I suspect that this solid base of feeling cared for may have encouraged our youthful rebellions in the 1960s and early 1970s. How could we make our society even fairer and more collective?

The period of my childhood was characterized by economic growth and growing economic equality in Organisation for Economic Co-operation and Development (OECD) countries. As a young history undergraduate, I can remember a certainty that the future would be better: more equal, healthier, and sustainable. History also taught me that while individuals appear to have agency over their lives and health, many aspects reflect the circumstances and time in which we are born. Here are some examples. A young man moving from rural England to rapidly industrializing Manchester in 1828 would face a life expectancy of around 28 because of the horrific living conditions in newly industrializing cities. The election of the Nazis in Germany in the 1930s had dire consequences for Jewish people, those who were leftist or gay, Roma people, and those with a physical or mental disability. A 30-year analysis of the influence of austerity and prosperity-related events on suicide rates in the period 1983–2012 in Greece found a rise in total suicides by 35.7% after austerity was introduced in June 2011 (Branas et al., 2015). In Ireland a 57% increase in men's suicide in Ireland was attributed to recession and austerity between 2008 and 2012 (Corocran, 2015). Workers in the Wittanoon Asbestos mine in Western Australia in the 1950s had no idea of the long-term adverse impact of asbestos on their health. Syrians in the past five years have faced terrible threats to their life and survival. Refugees around the world have been displaced by circumstances beyond their control. The historical instances go on and on. Whether or not we are healthy and how we live are primarily to do with the social and economic circumstances in which we are born, live, play, and work.

This realization, and the fact that more policymakers need to appreciate this, motivated me to write this book. A healthy, sustainable, and equitable society will not result from the uncoordinated actions of individuals, but from planned and systematic action by communities, governments, and international organizations. Living a healthy, fair, and sustainable life should be the birthright of every child born on planet Earth, and achieving this outcome the aspiration of every government. Yet, despite continued and persistent economic growth over the past half century, our world remains unhealthy for many, and is becoming less fair and sustainable. It doesn't have to be this way. Collectively we have sufficient resources to ensure health, fairness, and sustainability. What we lack are the govern-ance processes to ensure that these attributes are top priorities and have at least equal consideration with the goal of economic development. So this book will use evidence to highlight the actions that can be taken by governments and their public servants to maximize the chances of citi-zens leading long, healthy, productive, happy lives. In this book I point to the existing strengths of the "nanny state" in making our lives better, and also show how public services can be improved and adapted to different needs through relational governance and participatory and deliberative democracy.

Whether to govern for sustainable health or for short-term profit is a theme that runs through this book. In every chapter this dilemma emerges. The book's overall contention is that governments too often opt for the policies that will ensure profit for some, justifying the decision with the expectation that economic growth will bring benefits for the entire population in its wake. But wealth has not trickled down to the many—rather, it floats up to the few. The experience of the last decades has shown that while life expectancy has continued to increase in most countries, inequities have grown very significantly, and chronic disease rates are growing globally. In addition, there are now instances in the United States and the United Kingdom where life expectancies are static or declining (Marmot, 2018). From World War II until the 1970s the world became more equal, but this achievement has been largely squandered. Now the wealth of the world has become obscenely unequal. Credit Suisse (2017) reports that the forty two richest men in the world own as much wealth as the poorest 3.7 billion people, Oxfam (Hardoon, 2017) further report that the incomes of the poorest 10% of people increased by less than $3 a year between 1988 and 2011, while the incomes of the richest 1% increased 182 times. There is evidence that societies that distribute their resources less equally also do worse in terms of a range of measures of health and well-being (Wilkinson and Pickett, 2009).

Healthy Environments Create Healthy People

Health and how equally it is distributed are good markers for how well we are doing globally and within nations. The institutions we establish, the values that drive them, the people within them, and the priorities we choose are the driving forces behind health and its distribution. But, I can hear some readers saying, surely people make their own choices that determine their health? Of course, individual choice has some effect, but overwhelmingly the social and economic structures within which we all live and our opportunities to live in healthy environments determine how long and how well we will live, as the preceding examples of how environments constrain individual agency demonstrate.

This means that governing for health is vital for the well-being of all. This goes for all government sectors, as every one of them has an impact on our health. Whether this impact is positive or negative is determined by the policies and decisions made within each sector.

Determinants of Health and Health Equity

Figure 1.1 shows the ways in which the health of individuals is shaped by layers of influence from lifestyle, through social and community characteristics, the conditions of everyday life (including educational opportunity, employment, and the availability of services) and then social, economic, and environmental conditions. Together these make up the social determinants of health. The Commission on the Social Determinants

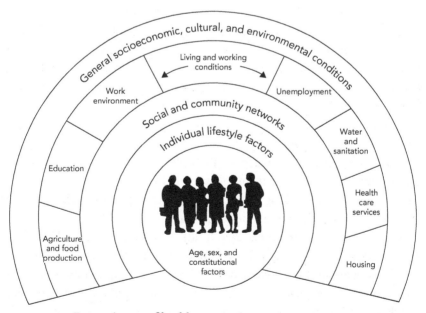

FIGURE 1.1. Determinants of health.

Source: Whitehead and Dahlgren (1991). Used with permission from Institute for Futures Studies.

of Health (2008) saw these determinants as both the conditions of everyday life (including housing, education, employment, and the extent and quality of human services) and the underpinning distribution of power and resources.

The work of this Commission was vital in showing the extent of health inequities and in amassing the evidence on why health is not equally divided but is spread across a gradient in society and between countries. Thus in many rich countries average life expectancy is over 80 years, while in many African countries life expectancy is around 50 years. There are no biological reasons for those differences. They reflect the social determinants of health. Figure 1.2 provides a sociological explanation of these differences, showing that the policy context shapes social hierarchies. These, in turn, largely determine individuals' socioeconomic position in terms of education, employment, and income. Together these factors shape the distribution of health in a society.

Looking Below the Iceberg

How health is shaped by our social and economic milieu is largely invisible—it lies below the surface of the iceberg (Figure 1.3). The links between, for instance, unemployment and poor health are not immediately evident. This leaves the door open for people to point to the tip of the iceberg and blame people for their poor health and short lives, claiming that people indulge in unhealthy behaviors and don't take care of their health. It's much harder to look below the surface of the iceberg and make the link, for example, between increased sales of junk food and rising rates of childhood obesity, or to link increased anxiety and depression to the growth of insecure work contracts.

Yet looking under the surface of the iceberg is exactly what we have to do to solve intractable health problems. This is how many OECD countries have reduced smoking rates. Looking at the tip of the iceberg shows only smokers, who can easily be blamed as irresponsible for smoking in light of the evidence on smoking and cancer. Yet taking a look below the surface shows that there was a powerful tobacco industry working to keep people focused on the smokers' behavior and spending many millions of dollars on lobbying governments to prevent them from regulating the use of tobacco (Chapman, 2008). A "tip" approach to diabetes would easily lead to finger pointing at people with diabetes who don't try to reduce their weight. Yet many factors are driving an increase in diabetes—people may

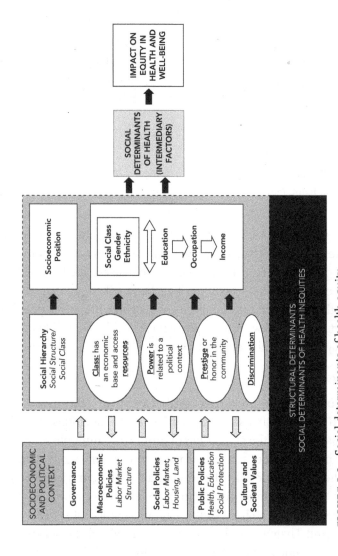

FIGURE 1.2. Social determinants of health equity.

Source: Solar and Irwin (2010: 35). Used with permission of the World Health Organization.

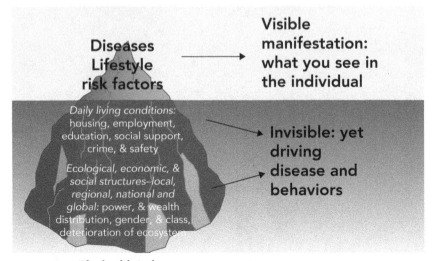

Diseases
Lifestyle
risk factors

Visible
manifestation:
what you see in
the individual

Daily living conditions:
housing, employment,
education, social support,
crime, & safety

Ecological, economic, &
social structures–local,
regional, national and
global: power, & wealth
distribution, gender, & class,
deterioration of ecosystem

Invisible: yet
driving
disease and
behaviors

FIGURE 1.3. The health iceberg.
Source: Based on Baum (2009).

live in an area that is not safe or appealing to walk around, many cities are car dependent and don't encourage walking or cycling, air pollution, the supply of high-fat and high-sugar foods has increased, and healthy food is often more expensive than junk food. This book will argue that when you look below the iceberg at the conditions of everyday life, while people can and do exert agency and work to improve their health and well-being, good public policy can make their efforts far more effective.

The Base of the Iceberg

At the base of the iceberg are the factors that are driving the distribution of resources in the world and so, in turn, drive health inequities. A capitalist economy that relies on the generation of profit from multiple sources and that for the most part does not protect the environment largely shapes our world. In the post–World War II period, many rich countries established welfare and taxation regimes that resulted in reduced economic inequities and improved health. The basis of these regimes was challenged from the 1980s. Margaret Thatcher in the United Kingdom and Ronald Reagan in the United States encouraged the rise of neoliberal policies that have led to dismantling of the welfare states, deregulation of industry and commerce, privatization of assets previously in public ownership, and lower taxation. As a result, economic inequities have grown to a level not seen since the 1920s (Piketty, 2014) and the wealth of the super-rich is soaring to new heights, the once prosperous middle class in OECD countries is under increased pressure, and poverty remains the reality for billions. While there is a growing middle class in middle-income countries, there are also increases in inequities in countries like India and China. Projections suggest that by 2030, if current trends continue, the top 1% will control two-thirds of the world's wealth (Savage, 2018).

Underpinning neoliberalism is a system of governance that many commentators say is directed toward supporting the profits and activities of transnational corporations (TNCs) (Freudenberg, 2014; Korten, 2015). In the 1980s the World Trade Organization (WTO), the World Bank, and the International Monetary Fund (IMF) systematically established a trade regime that favored big business, sold neoliberal policies in the form of structural adjustment packages to low- and middle-income countries, and cutbacks to welfare states in richer countries. More recently, many countries have adopted austerity politics in the wake of the global financial crisis of 2008, even though profits for TNCs have continued to rise and the very wealthiest individuals continue to grow their wealth at a much higher rate than the rest of the global population. Living in a neoliberal world means that it is hard to appreciate the ways in which it has changed the way we think, act, and govern the world. The Marxist geographer David Harvey put it this way:

> Neoliberalism has, in short, become hegemonic as a mode of discourse. It has pervasive effects on ways of thought to the point where it has become incorporated into the common-sense way many of us interpret, live in, and understand the world. (Harvey, 2007: 3)

The extent of inequity and the dangers of the ensuing lack of social trust and decline of solidarity are being recognized by the IMF, which now talks of "inclusive growth" (Lagarde, 2013). The former chief economist at the World Bank (Stiglitz, 2012) has now criticized the growth in inequities that came in the wake of its neoliberal policies. The adverse health consequences of the neoliberal system have also been recognized by a Global Commission established by *The Lancet* and the University of Oslo (Ottersen et al., 2014). The report from the Commission recognized the massive power asymmetries and noted that the global economic and political determinants were central in producing health inequities. They recommended that global governance for health must be rooted in commitments to global solidarity and shared responsibility in order to produce healthy people on a healthy planet.

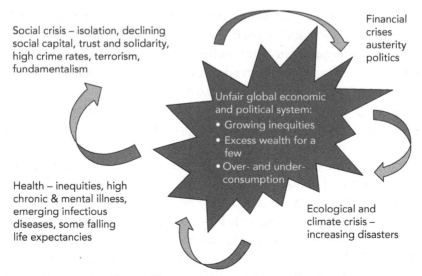

FIGURE I.4. Unhealthy world: governed for profits, creating inequities
Source: Baum

The Challenge We Face

A world governed for profit alone will be unhealthy and will result in financial, ecological, and social crises that interact to affect health adversely (Figure 1.4).

Rethinking how we govern the world is vital to our survival. The stakes are high and require a fundamental reframing of the value of governance, away from one designed to first and foremost promote the free market and profit for a few, to one designed to promote health and well-being for all global citizens. Government has become framed as a barrier and obstacle to people through a generation of neoliberal thought, and such framing has a powerful impact on our actions (Lakoff, 2014). My aim in this book is to reframe government and governance as beneficial and as essential elements of our health and well-being. A summary of the book's main arguments follows.

Map of the Book

The following chapter examines why public policy is vital to governance for health and considers whether individuals or societies are responsible for producing health. Neoliberal ideology is linked to individualism, which holds that individuals are responsible for their actions and that society is nothing more than a collection of individuals. Such views were summed up in Margaret Thatcher's oft quoted phrase, "there is no such thing as society." Then the importance of understanding policy processes as part of governing for health is covered. Finally, meta-policy messages that will be vital to sustaining human and ecological health in the coming decades are proposed.

Politicians are addressed directly in Chapter 3 by setting out the arguments of why they need to govern for health and the barriers they may find to doing so. It provides a well-being manifesto as a starting point for the development of a vision of a society governed for health and well-being. The centrality of power and the need to gain civil society support for progressive change are also examined. Options for more participatory and relational public policy are considered.

Governance for health is unlikely to eventuate without a rethinking of fiscal policies, which are currently dominated by neoliberalism. Chapter 5 proposes ways in which fiscal sectors can become more health enhancing, including by adopting sophisticated indicators of societal progress. Ways in which local (rather than transnational) economic activity can be encouraged are canvassed. Arguments are presented for the public ownership of essential assets and the importance of making the reduction of economic inequity a goal of fiscal policy.

Health, education, environmental and urban planning, and local government sectors are the topics of Chapters 6–9. Cross-cutting themes include the impact of privatization and the continual dialectic within public policy between the arguments for supporting a strong economy with those for maximizing the health and well-being benefits for people and the planet. This includes a discussion of the health sector as both a leader and steward for health governance. Internally, health sectors can do much to promote health, but this requires critical appraisal of the role of medicine and attention to the importance of primary health care and health promotion. They can act as stewards by monitoring equity and advocating and supporting initiatives such as Health in All Policies.

The vital role of education as a determinant of health, together with the need to spread its benefits equally, is examined in Chapter 6. Chapter 7 on urban planning reviews the challenges of creating more ecological and healthy cities. Chapter 8 on the environment sector argues that without significant protection from economic activity, the planet may reach the point where it can no longer support healthy human life. Dramatic action and changing governance priorities are required. The non-economic value of the natural environment needs to be appreciated in the way it is by Indigenous peoples worldwide. Climate change poses major threats to health. So moves to mitigate and prevent future global warming are vital. In both Chapter 7 and Chapter 8, positive examples of good governance for health are provided. The importance of local government to healthy daily living conditions is reviewed in Chapter 9. The ability of cities to improve daily living conditions and take action to protect the environment is recognized more than ever. Global movements like Healthy Cities and the United Nations' New Urban Agenda are mobilizing effective local governance for health. The devolution of a stronger public policy role to local governments presents an opportunity for local communities to take more control over the issues that directly affect their lives.

The crucial role of civil society and participatory processes in good governance is explored in Chapter 10. Examples of effective civil society campaigns and their strategies are described. The ways in which governments can encourage effective participation and embrace the value of strong civil society movements as a part of healthy governance are examined.

The final chapter distills six key lessons for governing for health. The first is that reducing inequities is the central, vital mechanism for building population health. The second lesson is how vital it is to recognize that human health is intimately connected to planetary health and needs to be viewed as part of the broader ecosystem. Next I argue that how we govern is vitally important to how healthy, sustainable, and equitable we are. My fourth lesson is that regulation is a powerful and essential tool of governing for health. Fifth, I make the point that new ways of measuring progress are important. Finally, I note the importance of ubiquitous leadership for health, equity, and well-being.

In a nutshell, this book argues that the human species is facing multiple threats to its health and well-being. The threats interact in the complex systems that make up our ecological, economic, social, and political worlds. Our imagination and governance structures have been captured by a construct called neoliberalism, which now poses threats to our collective survival, let alone health and well-being. The good news is that we do have alternatives to this construct. We can rediscover old ways and learn new and exciting ways of governing ourselves to build healthy, sustainable, and equitable societies.

2

The Power of Policy to Promote Health and Well-Being

Governance for health requires a synergistic set of policies, many of which reside in sectors other than health and outside government and must be supported by structures and mechanisms that facilitate collaboration.

—KICKBUSCH AND GLEICHER, *2012: ix*

GOVERNING FOR HEALTH is about designing, crafting, drafting, and implementing policies that will result in healthy, equitable, and sustainable societies in which well-being is enhanced. These policies need to be present in every sector. They need to both direct government actions toward well-being and provide a regulatory framework for the private sector. This chapter examines the role of values and ideologies in policy, including the extent to which agency or structure determines health, describes policy processes, and finally outlines the important meta-policy messages required for good governance for health and well-being.

Values, Ideology, and Policy

The question of what policies we adopt to govern for health is greatly influenced by our values and beliefs about how individual well-being is best promoted, and what role the government should play in this process. At one extreme, the "Alt-Right" promotes the libertarian belief that government should be minimized and the rights of individuals to do as they please should be promoted at all costs. This position shows a disregard for the value of government and is well illustrated by the campaign promises of Donald Trump to "drain the swamp" in reference to what was perceived as a bloated Washington bureaucracy. The other extreme is a socialist state in which most activities are controlled by the government. In between there are many varieties of governance, including a Scandinavian social democratic model in which the state is quite interventionist, as well as societies in which the state's role is minimized. This book continually poses the question of whether governance is for health and well-being, or to promote the conditions to maximize private profit. It is written on the premise that public sectors are potentially powerful agents for health and well-being and that capitalist economic systems are designed to maximize profit, and thus government regulation and controls are required to temper the quest for profits and to ensure that the health and well-being of people and the planet are protected. Often it is only when regulatory processes are not in place that people are able to appreciate their value. Thus in the aftermath of the Grenfell Fire Disaster in north London in June 2017 the importance of the regulation of fire-resistant building materials was recognized and the dangers of privatizing functions that previously had been the responsibility of government were widely discussed.

The position adopted in this book is that while individuals have agency, their ability to take actions is very often constrained by visible and invisible economic, social, and environmental forces, as explained by the iceberg metaphor in the previous chapter.

Individuals or Society?

> The broad dialectical challenge in social theory is (or should be) addressing the structure-agency problem (also known as the micro-macro problem) that is, unpacking the interactions and interconnections between individual choices and larger institutional forces. (Szreter and Woolcock, 2004: 700)

A constant issue in social theory and policy is unpacking the role of structure and agency in bringing about change. How much is down to individual choice? How much is about changing the structures in which people live? Where does the responsibility of the individual end and that of society begin? In the 1970s the health-promotion movement advocated behavioral approaches to creating health that placed responsibility on individuals, regardless of the social and economic conditions they lived in. These approaches involved providing people with information about the health effects of unhealthy behaviors, such as eating an unhealthy diet or not exercising, on the assumption that it was only their knowledge that was lacking. Large-scale behavioral programs were launched that were designed to persuade people to adopt healthier lifestyles in order to reduce their risk of disease. Evaluations of these programs showed that they met with very limited and often no discernible success (Elder et al., 1993; Mittlemark et al., 1993). When community-wide programs achieved some success, they also included policy change, as in the Finnish North Karelia experiment, which included work with food producers and distributors to encourage the provision of low-fat products, the provision of bicycle lanes, bike racks, jogging tracks, and healthy food choices in restaurants and workplace cafeterias (Puska et al., 2009).

An increasing critique of the individualized behavioral approach led to the adoption of the Ottawa Charter for Health Promotion by the World Health Organization (WHO) in 1986. This charter stressed the importance of healthy public policy and creating supportive environments to promoting health, thus adhering to a structural approach. Individuals were seen to be able to help their own health by being active advocates for healthy public policies and by participating in their communities. The WHO Healthy Cities movement, which encouraged local governments to implement healthy public policies, demonstrates a practical application of the Ottawa Charter (see more details in Chapter 9).

Since the 1980s, the impact of institutions and structures on health has been increasingly recognized. The People's Health Movement published a People's Health Charter in 2000, which states that good health results from supportive social, economic, and political environments. In 2005 the WHO established the Commission on the Social Determinants of Health, which examined the evidence on the determinants of health and concluded that they are overwhelmingly structural. Poor health and health inequities resulted from people not having access to supportive daily living conditions and from an inequitable distribution of power, money, and resources. The Commission advocated a range of policies that evidence indicated would improve health equity (CSDH, 2008). The WHO further underlined the importance of policy to promote health when it developed (with the European Union under the leadership of the Finnish government) the Health in All Policies (HiAP) approach (Leppo, Ollila, et al., 2013). HiAP argues that all sectors of government have a role to play in promoting health and well-being and should be actively engaged in doing so.

Thus public health experts are clear that policy is key to promoting health, especially policies that are coherent and are coordinated across different sectors. The need for such approaches is shown by the example of intimate partners' violence in Box 2.1, which highlights both the limitations

---

BOX 2.1

Cross-Sectoral Policies Most Effective in Addressing Intimate Partner Violence

Globally many people, overwhelmingly women, are the victims of intimate partner violence. WHO (2014) collated 48 population surveys and found that between 10% and 69% of women reported being physically assaulted by an intimate male partner at some point in their lives. This violence has a very significant health and social impact. An individualistic approach to preventing intimate partner violence might involve producing pamphlets to inform men that violence toward women is unacceptable. It might also involve groups for men who have been violent to support them in changing their behavior. However, evidence (Buthart and Mikton, 2014) indicates that approaches that are more systematic are effective. Violence is likely to be lower in countries with strict gun control and in which police are more proactive in responding to reports of violence and prosecuting when necessary. Law reform can help ensure the prosecution of perpetrators. Attitudes toward women are also crucial, and empowerment of women (through the provision of educational and employment opportunities especially) means they are more likely to be able to leave a violent relationship. The availability of social security payments and women's shelters also will make it easier for women to leave. WHO (2014) recommends the promotion of gender equity and changing the social and cultural norms that support violence as vital. Thus preventing intimate partner violence requires policy in many sectors: police, law, schools, workplaces, social security and welfare systems, media, and civil society.

---

of an individual approach and the value of cross-sectoral policies, which can change the basic structures that gave rise to violence.

The absolute centrality of policy to governing for health and well-being means understanding how policy works. This includes how health comes to be on policy agendas, and how policy is implemented and evaluated. To these processes we now turn.

Understanding Policy Processes

Policy processes are now well recognized as being complex, reflecting history as well as the work of lobby groups, the roles of policy entrepreneurs, and the machinations of the political system. While a completed policy document may seem to have resulted from a rational linear process, the reality is more chaotic and uncertain, and reflects ideology and advocacy from actors in dense policy networks as much as evidence (Pressman and Wildavsky, 1984). Policy results from the work of policy networks, which consist of policy entrepreneurs inside and outside government, who often work for years to bring about policy change (see Figure 2.1). Their advocacy and lobbying usually come to fruition when a political window of opportunity (Kingdon, 2011) opens, which leads to the adoption of new policy. This process is usually messy and unpredictable.

Policy processes differ in different contexts by level of government and country. Yet the cycle of formulation, implementation, and evaluation is common (Hill and Varone, 2016).

Formulation: Understanding how policies enter political agenda requires an understanding of local politics, how windows of opportunity to introduce policies can be exploited, the impact of key public health advocates, how politicians can be influenced to adopt healthy public policy, and the ways in which power influences these processes (Kingdon, 2011; de Leeuw et al., 2014). Advocacy coalitions are important in shaping policy choices (Jenkins-Smith et al., 2014), thus highlighting the importance of

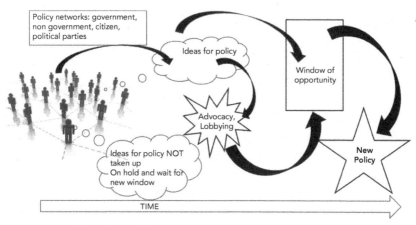

FIGURE 2.1. Policy formulation processes.
Source: Baum

advocacy for health and well-being to counter policy advocacy that favors business interests.

Implementation: While policies for health and well-being may be introduced, this does not guarantee they will be implemented as intended. Policy problems are identified and responses are crafted in policy worlds that have a distinctive constellation of actors (people and networks involved), ideas (the content of policy), and institutions (structures, rules, and mandates) (Howlett et al., 2009). Understanding the dynamic between these three crucial factors is vital for implementation that reflects the intent of policy. It is not uncommon for policy to be adopted but then not implemented in a manner that reflects its original intentions. Thus in the 1980s in the United Kingdom, the attempt to introduce a "poll tax" instead of property taxation met with considerable public resistance, which led to policy failure (Hill and Varone, 2016).

Evaluation: Governing for health will require more attention to assessing the health impacts of public policy. In recent years such evaluation has been increasingly common, including of equity impacts. For example, in the United Kingdom an evaluation of the Blair Labour Government's policies designed to reduce health inequities were assessed and were found not to have achieved their target of a 10% reduction in health inequities (Mackenbach, 2011). However, Bambra (2012) found that the strategies were at least partially successful. Another example of a reporting model is that required for the Australian Close the Gap strategy (designed to reduce the gap in life expectancy between Indigenous and non-Indigenous Australians). The policy outcomes are evaluated, and the Prime Minister reports the results of the evaluation to Parliament annually (Commonwealth of Australia Department of Prime Minster and Cabinet, 2018).

Running through all policy process are power dynamics. Some policy players are much more influential than others. Business councils and other corporate lobby groups generally exert much more influence through their lobbying than environmental or civil society groups. Political power and ideology are generally as, if not more, powerful than evidence in framing policy. Political theory indicates that understanding policy processes requires unpacking the deep-seated presuppositions and assumptions behind policy, determining what they miss as much as what they include, and identifying whose interests are served or neglected as a result (Bacchi, 2009). Thus policies designed to reduce obesity may emphasize the need to change individual choice about food, rather than addressing the increased supply of high-fat and high-sugar foods.

Equally important to understanding the policy process is appreciating the meta-policy messages that public health evidence indicates will best support governance for health.

Meta-Policy Messages for Governance for Health

The key meta-policy messages that need to come from policies designed to support governance for health is that in the twenty-first century achieving good human and planetary health relies on attention to the social, environmental, and economic determinants of health and the balance between them (Figure 2.2). This conception stresses the importance of conviviality, equity, viability, and sustainability.

FIGURE 2.2. The Mandala of health.
Source: Trevor Hancock (1993: 42).

Yet clearly, the elements in this model are in tension. Thus developing the economy, certainly under a neoliberal model (outlined in Chapter 1), nearly always results in further stress on the natural environment, making it less sustainable. The massive inequities in and between countries mean that redistributive processes to achieve equity are likely to be met with opposition. Raworth (2017) has addressed these tensions in her doughnut model of economics. Her model (Figure 2.3) is designed to create a future in which every person's needs are met in a way that safeguards the living world on which we all depend.

Raworth's conception of the doughnut highlights the "sweet spot" between the thick black circles. The requirements for a healthy life and

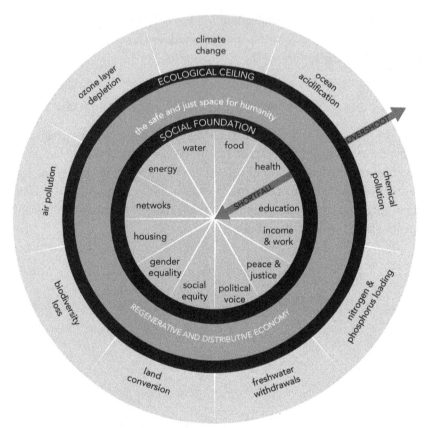

FIGURE 2.3. Doughnut model of economics.
Source: Raworth (2017: 44).

well-being are displayed in the inner ring, and Raworth argues that there is shortfall in many of these for most people in the world. Meeting these requirements must be done in a way that recognizes the ecological ceiling. Beyond this ceiling is an overshoot of pressures on Earth's life-supporting systems through factors including climate change, chemical pollution, air pollution, and loss of biodiversity. Thus the aim of governing for health is to ensure that life is being lived in a safe and just space for humanity. According to this conception, all policies need to concern themselves with life's essentials (including food, housing, energy, education, income and work, peace and justice) in an equitable way, and to do this while avoiding the overshoot on the ecological foundations of life. Thus, environmental policies are fundamental to health and well-being because these are not possible without a healthy planet and, as the singer Steve Forbert reminds us, "Good Planets are Hard to Find." Governing for health, then, must be centrally concerned with living below the ecological ceiling.

In relation to the social foundations displayed in the Raworth model, the Commission on the Social Determinants of Health commissioned work to determine the ways in which the Nordic welfare states (Denmark, Finland, Norway, Sweden) had achieved good health outcomes, as measured by infant mortality and life expectancy (Lunberg et al., 2008a; Bambra, 2009). The ensuing review of the evidence suggested that the following were important characteristics of policy systems designed to promote health (Lundberg et al., 2008b):

- Universal social policies rather than reliance on targeted, means-tested selective policies
- Reducing poverty through welfare state redistribution policies
- Relatively narrow income inequalities
- Emphasis on equality of opportunity and outcomes according to class, gender, and for socially excluded groups
- A broad scope of public services, with provision of services mainly by the public sector locally
- Social spending and social protection are important
- No single policy solution, but an accumulation of policies across the life course, each having a specific effect.

The analysis of the Nordic welfare states indicates that an inclusive society is an important element of a healthy society. Policies can encourage social inclusion and social solidarity.

Successful societies are inclusive of all citizens—a point that is emphasized in the United Nation's Sustainable Development Goals. Inclusion is an important aspect of well-being, and the extent to which it is realized reflects policies and structures within a society. Social exclusion refers to the systematic denial of the resources and recognition that are required for full participation in society for certain social groups. Social exclusion has been conceptualized as resulting from dynamic, multidimensional processes driven by unequal power relationships in the society (Social Exclusion Knowledge Network, 2008). These processes reflect four dimensions—cultural, economic, political, and social—operating at the individual, group, household, community, country, and global levels. They also result in a continuum of inclusion/exclusion and contribute to unequal access to resources, capabilities, and rights required for human development, valued recognition, involvement and engagement, decision-making, material well-being, and the ability to resist the hazards of environmental change. Processes of social exclusion operate differently and have different impacts on groups and/or societies, depending on context. Examples of socially excluded groups are low-caste groups in India, Indigenous populations in many countries, Romany people in Europe, and people living in informal settlements in many cities around the world. Policies are required to reduce this exclusion and, in Raworth's terms, overcome the shortfall in the social foundation of health and well-being through a regenerative and redistributive economy.

The final essential message about the types of policies required in order to govern for health is that they require rethinking economics and its relation to other policies (of which more is said in Chapter 5). We noted in the previous chapter that neoliberalism dominates public policy globally. Its dictums drive international trade agreements and the institutions that maintain them, like the World Bank and the International Monetary Fund, as well as national policies. Yet its mantra of trickle-down solutions to inequities and focus on growth is not compatible with the idea of developing a safe and just space for humanity that recognizes the ecological ceiling (Figure 2.3). Thus this book challenges the currently dominant neoliberal paradigm as not encouraging health for people or the environment.

Conclusion

Policy is the main instrument that governments can use in order to govern for health. The adoption of healthy policies reflects a political will to make health and well-being central to a government's agenda. Such political will generally results from democratic advocacy through civil society such as trade unions, welfare advocacy groups, public health associations, and the like in favor of policies that promote health. The following chapter considers the political dimensions of governing for health.

3

Political Dimensions of Governing for Health

LEADERSHIP, VISION, AND A MANIFESTO

The importance of mobilising political commitment for health is clear to all of us . . . political will is the key ingredient for change. It is not the only ingredient, but without it, change is much harder to achieve. For a paradigm shift, we need political intervention.

—DR. TEDROS ADHANOM GHEBREYESUS, *Director General, WHO (2017: 5)*

Introduction

Politicians are central to governing for health, and this chapter is directed at persuading them to do so. It includes a well-being manifesto and provides evidence to support the value of adopting this manifesto for individual, population, and planetary well-being. Further evidence is provided in terms of how more equitable societies are also more successful, and how pursuing equity can create political capital. The power of the various lobby groups the politicians will encounter and the need to privilege public interests above private profit when assessing the messages from this lobbying are considered. Concomitant to this is the importance of listening to public interest advocates. Civil society advocacy is vital to winning a constituency for a well-being manifesto. The increasing need for global political governance is made in the face of waning power for nation-states and increasing power for transnational corporations.

Good Governance for Health Requires a Vision for a Healthy Society

> During the last generation, economic growth ceased to improve health, happiness, and the quality of life in rich countries. Now, more than ever, we need an inspiring vision of a future capable of creating more equal societies that increase sustainable wellbeing for all of us and for the planet.
>
> —Pickett and Wilkinson (2017: n.p)

Strong political leadership is vital to good governance for health. Without such leadership, the policy directions set out in this book are not going to happen. Political commitment, leadership, and vision set the frame within which public servants are able to enact policies that will be good for health. Illustrating this, an analysis of public policy responses to the 2008 global financial crisis in Europe shows how some political decisions concerning the adoption of an austerity agenda have led to increased rates of disease and death and greater inequities (Stuckler and Basu, 2013). The same comparative analysis also demonstrates that different political responses have resulted in variation in health effects between countries, highlighting the inherently political nature of health. This chapter sets out to persuade politicians that a manifesto to govern for health and equity could win elections and thus enable them to create a positive legacy. A well-being manifesto for the mid-twenty-first century is provided in Box 3.1.

I could hear the objections echoing in my ears as I wrote this manifesto: it is too idealistic; it's unrealistic; what about taking care of the economy first, as it is basic to everything else; that manifesto might sound nice, but I don't think I could sell it to the public; and how would we fund it? There were so many of these objections echoing that I nearly just deleted the manifesto when I had finished it. But then I thought, "No! What the world needs now is a positive vision, and public health is a good base from which to give it." I tested the manifesto by writing about it in a blog site, Croakey.org (Baum, 2017), and received favorable feedback and helpful suggestions for revising it, which are reflected in the version included here.

BOX 3.1

A Well-Being Manifesto for the Mid-Twenty-First Century, 2020–2050

If our party is elected in 2020, we will introduce policies to work for the well-being of society, and we promise to govern for health, well-being, and equity. In order to do this, we will institute the following major policies.

ECONOMIC

We will:

Measure what we treasure and no longer rely on GDP as the measure of our progress; instead, we will introduce a well-researched measure of well-being appropriate to our country and society.

Institute measures to reduce economic inequity, including:

More progressive income tax

Taxes on wealth and inheritance

Combating tax evasion by businesses, especially transnational corporations (TNCs)

Regulate to ensure that TNCs are directly responsible for costs of occupational health and safety, environmental degradation, and unsafe and unhealthy products

Reward small- and medium-sized businesses that show commitment to the local communities in which they operate

Tax high-sugar and high-fat foods

Nationalize or privatize assets and resources based on demonstrable long-term public benefit

Ensure trade agreements that support well-being and that do not restrict the ability of governments to regulate for health

TRANSPARENCY, DEMOCRATIC PROCESSES, AND INCLUSIVITY

We will institute:

Democratic and meaningful participation of citizens in political processes

Meaningful participation of groups with limited economic and social power in policy development

(Continued)

BOX 3.1 *(Continued)*

Restriction on lobbying by powerful interest groups by creating a transparent register of lobbyists and capping donations to all political parties

Engagement with and support for public interest civil society

Media diversity and facilitation of independent journalism

Cultural diversity and safety

LIFELONG LEARNING

We will:

Make all public education free

Reduce subsidies to private education

Dramatically increase the investment in public early childhood education and affordable quality childcare

Support lifelong learning as crucial investment

EMPLOYMENT

We will:

Create public-sectors jobs to engage people at all stages of the life cycle and focus on job creation

Increase income support to the unemployed to a livable level

Legislate and support training for gender equity in all workplaces

Recognize the social and economic value of unpaid work

HEALTH CARE

We will:

Ensure universal access to high-quality and appropriate publicly funded health care and progressively make community-controlled primary health care the backbone of a system that focuses on prevention and promotion as well as cure and rehabilitation

Invest in the evaluation of new and existing medical technologies to ensure they have more benefits than harms and are cost-effective

Eliminate subsidies to private health insurance and invest funds in a public health system

HOUSING, URBAN AND RURAL ENVIRONMENTS

We will:

Provide safe and secure housing for all citizens

BOX 3.1 *(Continued)*

Create healthy urban environments that are safe, are friendly to pedestrians and cyclists, and that encourage social interaction
Invest in rural towns to increase their attractiveness as places to live

ECOLOGICAL HEALTH

We will:

Institute measures that are designed to dramatically reduce the nation's carbon output and that favor renewable energy
Maintain and restore our rivers, lakes, and seas
Protect our lands from excessive exploitation by mining and agriculture
Protect and treasure our biodiversity

Is There Evidence for This Manifesto?

Yes, actually there is good evidence, much of which is summarized in the other chapters in this book and in numerous reports from the United Nations and national governments, including the 2008 WHO Commission on the Social Determinants of Health and the material supporting the Sustainable Development Goals. Here are some "killer facts" to support the well-being manifesto.

The Wealthiest Countries Are Not the Healthiest

Some countries have managed to achieve good health at low cost, showing that it isn't necessarily how wealthy a country is that determines health, but rather how the country uses its resources. Amazingly, Costa Rica and Cuba both achieve longer life expectancy than the United States, have only a fraction of their national income, and spend about 10% of the amount the United States spends on health care (Baum, 2016: 50). These high-performing countries in terms of health have been the subject of concerted study twice (Halstead et al., 1985; Balabanova et al., 2011) and the conclusions are that investments in health, with a focus on primary health care and equitable access to health services, education (especially for women), indigenous agriculture, and sustainable food supplies, are vital. Strong political commitment and will, supported by widespread democratic participation, were also evident, along with active advocacy from civil society movements.

Unequal Societies Are Less Healthy Overall, Which Affects Everyone, Not Just the Most Disadvantaged

There is accumulating evidence that societies in which there are more income inequalities between people also have poorer physical and mental health, more illicit drug use, higher rates of obesity, more violence, less cohesiveness and trust, and reduced educational attainment and social mobility (Figure 3.1) (Pickett and Wilkinson, 2015).

We Are More Unequal Than in the Past

Within and between countries, patterns of economic inequity have varied over the last two centuries, and reached a peak in the pre–World War II period. After the war they steadily declined until the 1970s, and from there, coinciding with the era of neoliberalism, they have increased, as shown

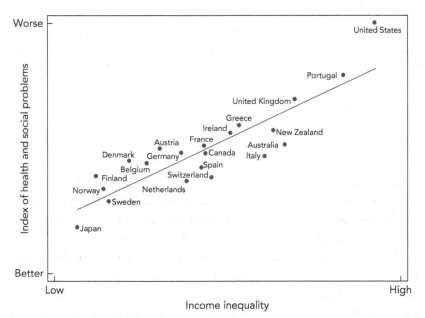

FIGURE 3.1. Index of health and social problems in relation to income inequality in rich countries.

Note: Income inequality is measured by the ratio of incomes among the richest compared with the poorest 20% in each country. The index combines data on life expectancy, mental illness, obesity, infant mortality, teenage births, homicides, imprisonment, educational attainment, distrust, and social mobility. Raw scores for each variable were converted to z-scores and each country given its average z-score.

Source: Wilkinson and Pickett (2009: 174).

in Chapter 1. Political decisions of the immediate postwar period were responsible for the decline in inequity in rich countries. Social welfare and progressive taxation regimes meant that the profit-seeking tendencies of capitalism were tamed. If this has happened before, it can happen again—given the right political decisions. Chapter 5 on fiscal governance for health and well-being sets out the economic arguments for greater equity. Equity between nations has also declined since the nineteenth-century industrial revolution. Since then, massive gaps have opened up (Wade, 2017). While there has been a growth of middle classes in middle-income countries, especially India and China (Milanovic, 2016), if an absolute Gini coefficient is used, then global income inequity has increased from 0.57 in 1988 to 0.72 in 2005 (Anand and Segal, 2015). The gross domestic product (GDP) of rich countries has increased relative to that of low- and middle-income nations. Hickel (2016) reports that in real terms, the gap between the GDP per capita of the United States and other regions has grown. This difference is calculated as 206% compared to Latin America, and 207% for sub-Saharan Africa, and 196% for South Asia. Wealth is also more concentrated among rich individuals, as noted in Chapter 1, including the astounding statistic that the forty-two richest men in the world own as much wealth as the poorest 3.7 billion people. Political decisions created these massive gaps and could, in the future, reduce them.

Environments Shape Behaviors

Crucial evidence has stacked up that people's behaviors change most when the environments they live in are supportive of health and well-being. Thus people who live in walkable suburbs are more likely to walk; banning smoking in public places and introducing plain paper packaging is far more effective in reducing smoking than education and pamphlets about smoking; making healthy food cheaper encourages healthy eating more than health education; encouraging strong cultural roots in Aboriginal communities reduces suicide; supportive workplaces reduce stress. A well-being agenda would focus not on blaming people for their poor health, but on using governance processes to develop environments in which health and well-being can flourish.

Despite these "killer facts," as politicians know, even though academics often put a good deal of weight on evidence, in real-world politics it is only one consideration. An Australian health minister who held office in the 1990s put it like this:

Evidence is a lovely idea but it's got to actually fit with the direction or the trendy issues of the time or the direction of the government at the time. Evidence doesn't dictate health policy, never has and possibly never will. It backs up policy directions. (quoted in Baum et al., 2013: 141)

Given that evidence is then only one factor in the maelstrom of political decision-making, the following section considers the ideologies and political interests that are needed to support a wellness manifesto.

Enacting the Wellness Manifesto

The wellness manifesto is unashamedly idealistic. Inevitably, idealism meets the *real politik* of the political world, which is complex, interactive, uncertain, and, most centrally, driven by power. Enacting a wellness manifesto will require political circumstances that overcome significant obstacles and that are able to muster and maintain long-term popular support for the agenda. The most crucial of these circumstances are examined in the following.

Public Interest Political Ideology

Responses to the manifesto will depend on whether the ideologies of politicians and their political parties stress personal responsibility or the impact of the distribution of social and economic advantage (Baum et al., 2013). Commentators have noted that since the era of Reagan and Thatcher the values of neoliberalism have dominated political discourse and have come to be seen as the "natural" way of doing government business (Harvey, 2007; Davis, 2014). Neoliberalism favors privatization of government assets, reduction of public services, deregulation of private businesses, and a belief that efficient markets will lead to trickle-down benefits for all. These beliefs have created a very favorable environment for the growth of TNCs, many of which are larger and more powerful than nation-states. However, increasingly, the neoliberal prescription is being questioned. Many so-called free markets are based on considerable government subsidies. The evidence of increasing inequities challenges the trickle-down theory, as the idea that it would eventually reduce inequities has proven false—so much so that the global growth of inequity is becoming a hot political topic. Leading politicians, such as Jeremy Corbyn (Labour opposition leader) in the

United Kingdom, Bernie Sanders (Senator and former Democratic presidential nominee contender) in the United States, and Bill Shorten (Labor Opposition leader) in Australia, are pointing to the growth in inequities and saying they must be reduced. As we saw earlier, evidence on the society-wide impact of inequities indicates that less equal societies have worse outcomes on a range of measures (Wilkinson and Pickett, 2009). There is also evidence that life expectancies are either stagnating or declining in countries with rising levels of inequity (Marmot, 2018).

Understanding Power as Central

Politics is a continual struggle for power among competing interests (Kickbusch, 2015). Any political party wanting to implement a wellness agenda will face concerted opposition from vested interests. The WHO Commission on the Social Determinants of Health noted in its final report that "the distribution of money, power and resources at global, national and local levels" (CSDH, 2008: 110) were vital considerations in bringing about increased health equity. The immediate past director general of WHO noted on several occasions during her tenure that corporate vested interests impeded health. In 2016 she spoke of how the tobacco industry had fought plain packaging legislation in Australia and commented that this example shows that "[c]hanging the environment in which people make their lifestyle choices requires extraordinary government commitment, courage, and persistence, even when we have all the facts on our side" (Chan, 2016c: n.p). The fossil fuel industry exerts similar powerful influences on policy agenda and works to undermine the acceptance of evidence on climate change (McMichael, 2017). The power struggles inherent in politics are the reasons why the wellness manifesto stresses the need to tame the lobbying power of vested interests and to restrict political donations. In many countries at the moment, no such safeguards exist and political players are prey to lobbyists on behalf of powerful, usually corporate interests, which, as Chan points out, are usually antagonistic to health and well-being.

Medical power, including the interests of the transnational biomedical industry, is highly influential in the health sector. Such is its impact that it often undermines the health sector's ability to exert stewardship for health equity and action on the social determinants of health (see Chapter 4). Powerful medical lobby groups can work against a wellness agenda. An interview study of 21 Australian health ministers (Baum et al., 2014) demonstrated that the provision of hospital services was the top issue for health ministers. Even if they were very committed to implementing measures on the social determinants of health, they often ended up spending their tenure as minister, responding to perceived crises in hospitals concerning waiting lists, meeting demands for more medical technologies, and the other needs of the acute care system. This left them little policy space in which to plan preventive and promotive action on social determinants. A government will need great determination to overcome pressure from organized medicine and biomedical industries. In the face of this power, exerting stewardship for health will require visionary and committed leadership.

Visionary Leadership for the Manifesto from the Top

The centrality of the wellness agenda to all government activity means that the head of government has to provide leadership for it, and the central agency of government must direct it. Lessons from the Health in All Policies strategies have shown that such political leadership is vital (Delany et al., 2015). The manifesto should be developed as a government-wide vision and strategy, and should include adopting indicators to measure wellness (see Chapter 5, which presents some such indicators). Inspirational leadership should be able to garner support for the well-being manifesto. Toughness will be required to resist pressure to succumb to the current political status quo, which emphasizes the pursuit of economic goals, often to the exclusion of broader social, health, and environmental goals.

Overcoming Short-Termism

In relation to sustainable development, Roggema (2012) (paraphrased in Matan and Newman, 2013: 3) noted that the required visionary long-term leadership is often not present because politicians are inherently reluctant to commit to policies that have no simple solution, no clear end point, that are likely to cost a lot with few short term benefits and that (most significantly) will not show clear results until well after the proponent's political career has ended. The same is true for well-being. A political will has to be created in which the politician and party are convinced that well-being will be an attractive option to electors. They also will need to be prepared to argue for a long-term perspective. Part of this will is likely to be the desire to leave a legacy that ensures a politician's reputation as a reformer who improved society.

Citizens and Civil Society Partnerships

Listen to civil society. Civil society organizations are society's con-
science. They are best placed to hold governments and businesses,
like the tobacco, food, and alcohol industries, accountable. They are
the ones who can give the people who suffer the most a face and
a voice.

—Dr. Margaret Chan May (DG WHO
World Health Assembly, 2017: n.p)

Major social changes result from pressure from organized public interest
civil society movements (see Chapter 10). The well-being agenda will be
supported by environmental groups, public health and health-promotion
associations, welfare lobby groups, and online activist groups such as
AVAAZ and GetUP, to name a few. These groups do not have the economic power of the corporate world, but they can muster considerable
popular support and thus leverage "people power". Politicians are often
far more receptive to lobbying and advocacy from corporate interests than
they are to that from civil society groups, especially when political systems allow generous donations to political parties. However, democratic
governments should welcome dissenting voices from public-interest civil
society. A worrying trend (examples of which are provided in Chapter 10)
is for governments to crack down on civil society, either through direct
suppression or more indirectly, such as by making advocacy forbidden
under funding agreements (Maddison and Carson, 2017). A government
committed to well-being should welcome the public interest voices of civil
society.

Social media will be important in garnering support for the well-being
manifesto by increasing the awareness that health is improved when daily
living conditions at home, at work, and in the community nurture health.
This awareness, powered by civil society, will help create the essential political will. The big political challenge is to turn this general awareness into
a loud citizen voice for a well-being agenda. Bringing this voice out into
the open will require leadership that ignites people's hearts and minds. It
will also require overcoming the false consciousness that is evoked by the
advertising industry (such as shopping as the route to well-being) and the
entire economic fiction that portrays neoliberalism as good for everyone's
health and well-being. Passionate advocacy to citizens, using all the power
of progressive civil society, is required to turn around the taken-for-granted

neoliberal agenda. To harness the citizen voice for well-being, the public service will have to develop an organizational culture and set of practices that actively encourage and support citizen and civil society involvement in the processes of governance. Lees-Marshment (2015: 5) notes that "inferior forms of public input make political leadership harder." She goes on to say that much public input is not well done, and when this is the case it can be captured by interest groups. However, if it is well done, then it has many benefits for political leaders (see Figure 3.2). Lees-Marshment interviewed former politicians and demonstrated how public input to policy can help politicians exercise political leadership.

Empowerment itself is good for health, so the very process of encouraging citizen participation will in and of itself be promoting health (Laverack, 2004).

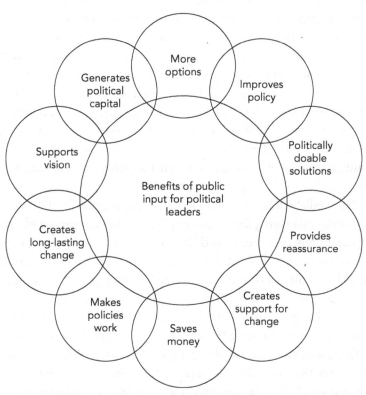

FIGURE 3.2. Benefits of public input for political leaders.
Source: Lees-Marshment (2015: 231).

Political Dimensions of Global Health Governance

In our increasingly globalized world, the power of national and subnational governments is decreasing, and mechanisms of global governance are powerful in setting the political agenda. The Lancet–University of Oslo Commission on Global Governance for Health (Ottersen et al., 2014) has stressed that global governance structures favor the interests of powerful countries and corporations more than the public interest and equity. This situation needs to be redressed. The Global Health Watch 5 (an Alternative World Health Report) (2017) notes that global governance is characterized by "big-power bullying" and acknowledges that there is a historic competition between the nation-state and the transnational corporation as the principal agent of governance. The Lancet–University of Oslo Commission (Ottersen et al., 2014) also concluded that the political dimensions of health and power disparities were vital to understanding global governance frameworks. They identified five dysfunctions in the global system: lack of democracy, weak accountability and transparency, entrenchment of existing power and institutional resistance to change, inadequate policy attention to health considerations, and the absence of institutional mechanisms to promote health concerns. The WHO Commission on the Social Determinants of Health also recognized that global governance did not currently favor health equity. The Sustainable Development Goals (SDGs) also acknowledge that the system of global governance requires some reform, but do not challenge its basic architecture. Enacting a wellness manifesto will require effective global governance. Thus it is vital that nation-states exercise their power to regulate and control the behavior of massive TNCs and join together to create a global governance system. Public interest governance is vital, as a world dominated by corporate interests will be about profit seeking, not well-being.

Many critics have pointed out that many free trade agreements can undermine health and well-being (Friel, Gleeson, et al., 2013; Thow, Snowdon, et al., 2015). Health and well-being need to be central considerations in multilateral and bilateral trade agreements. The United Nations system is central to public interest global governance, but it is increasingly under threat. Nation-states are reducing their commitment to its agencies (Global Health Watch 5, 2017) and much funding to WHO now comes from unaccountable foundations such as the Gates Foundation. A further threat is the increasing influence of corporate interests over UN agencies. Thus under the cover of front groups, food TNCs are able to join crucial committees of WHO and the Food and Agriculture Organization (FAO) (Freudenberg, 2014). Political leadership is required within the UN system and from national governments to ensure the future of the United Nations as a nonpartisan global leader for a well-being agenda. The SDGs went some way toward providing this, but more is needed so that the basic architecture of our global governance is designed to promote health, rather than support private profit making.

Conclusion

Our societies are desperately in need of visionary, progressive leadership that can challenge the prevailing focus on economic goals to the detriment of our collective well-being. Governing for health and well-being will require political courage and commitment. Challenging a ruling regime is not for the faint-hearted, as Nelson Mandela recognized when he noted that poverty and inequity are "not a preordained result of the forces of nature or the product of a curse of the deities. But the consequences of decisions which men and women take or refuse to take" (Nelson Mandela, quoted in Heywood and Altman, 2000: 173). Political leaders have the choice to make decisions for the collective good and to govern for health. They will need support from active citizens and expression of a popular will in order to enact the necessary policies. Their first task is to show moral leadership and the determination to create a healthy, equitable, and sustainable future for us all.

4

Health Sectors as Actors and Advocates for Health and Health Equity

Runaway commodification of health and commercialization of health care are linked to increasing medicalization of human and societal conditions, and the stark and growing divide of over- and under-consumption of health-care services between the rich and the poor worldwide.

—COMMISSION ON THE SOCIAL DETERMINANTS OF HEALTH (2008: 95)

Introduction

Many assume that the health sector is the central government agency for health. Yet very often, health sectors are actually "illness care" sectors that give little concern to the production or maintenance of health. This chapter argues that this state of affairs needs to change so that health sectors do become stewards of the health of the population they serve. Achieving such health sectors will require strong and determined leadership that is able to ensure that curative functions are effective, while also ensuring that disease prevention and health promotion flourish. This is vital to governing for health.

This chapter presents a vision for health sectors that would enable them to contribute to improved health in an equitable manner. It then examines the ways in which biomedical individualism and the growing pressures for privatized service provision impede the realization of this vision. The importance of comprehensive primary health care and universal coverage based on publicly funded systems is then examined. I give particular attention to community strategies, including community ownership of health services, that strengthen communities and build bridges between disadvantaged communities and services that these communities often find hard to reach. The chapter concludes with a consideration of the importance of health sectors exerting stewardship for health by ensuring that population health data are available, health impact assessments are conducted, and government-wide approaches such as Health in All Policies are nurtured. First, I present a vision of how a health sector would look if it were governing for health.

Vision for the Health Sector

Reorientation of health sectors so that they have more focus on prevention, health promotion, and social determinants of health will require a new vision. In the past, visionary perspectives have come from WHO, particularly through the 1978 Alma Ata Declaration on Primary Health Care, which established the goal of achieving Health for All by the Year 2000. This declaration envisioned the goal of health for all as an objective that could be achieved by making primary health care the basis of health systems. This would mean positioning community participation as central, making intersectoral action on social determinants core business, focusing not just on cure but also on rehabilitation, prevention, and promotion, using appropriate technology, undertaking local comprehensive planning, and reorienting the economic system to focus on people's needs. This vision has never been achieved in full, but it continues to inspire many (such as the global People's Health Movement, www. phmovement.org), and has subsequently been endorsed by the WHO Ottawa Charter for Health Promotion (1986) and the Commission on the Social Determinants of Health (2008). Drawing on these documents, Box 4.1 presents the leadership role required within the health system and then describes the stewardship role that health systems can play beyond their own domain.

Taming Medicine and the Profit Motive

Achieving a new vision for the health sector will require strong political and bureaucratic leadership that is prepared to challenge both the biomedical individualism of most health systems and the growing pressures for privatized service provision. We now turn to these issues.

BOX 4.1

Characteristics of a Health Sector Governing for Health and Equity

LEADERSHIP FOR HEALTH-PROMOTING HEALTH SECTORS

- Publicly funded, universal, accessible primary health care and hospital care that is free at the point of use are provided.
- Comprehensive primary health care is established as the basis of the system.
- Emphasis is placed on right care—addressing underuse and overuse.
- Decision-making processes involve local communities.
- Planning, including allocation of resources, is based on the needs of populations in terms of disease burdens and social determinants of health.
- Policies are developed that are explicit about closing health equity gaps and that stress the importance of prevention, health promotion, and action on social determinants of health.
- Funding for prevention, health promotion, and action on the social determinants of health is progressively increased as a proportion of the overall health budget until it reaches at least 5% of the budget.
- Leaders are well-equipped and prepared to advocate for the importance of equity-focused health systems.

STEWARDSHIP: ENCOURAGING ACTION IN OTHER SECTORS TO PROMOTE HEALTH AND HEALTH EQUITY

- Health sectors are a catalyst for a Health in All Policies approach or similar intersectoral programs of action.
- A health equity surveillance system is developed.
- Health impact assessments with a focus on equity are conducted on major developments.
- Reform of health professional (including medical) education includes more emphasis on social determinants, understanding of population health theory, and skills development and exposure to inter-professional collaboration.
- Professionals in all sectors (including urban and transport planning, education, environment, agriculture, trade and industry) are trained

(Continued)

BOX 4.1 *(Continued)*

and educated on the importance of social determinants to health and well-being.

- National health and medical research bodies are encouraged to direct funding to public research on determinants of good population health and health equity and on interventions in all sectors to support population health equity.

Adapted from Baum, Bégin, et al (2009).

Medicine in Its Place

A health sector that is governing for health needs to put medicine in its place. Medicine has made vital contributions to improving population health, and is important for responding to illness. Estimates suggest that between 20% and 25% of improvement in population health can be attributed to medical intervention, and between 50% and 75% to social determinants (Bunker et al., 1994; Standing Senate Committee on Social Affairs, Science, and Technology, 2001).

There is also evidence that while biomedicine is making breakthroughs, it is delivering diminishing marginal population health returns (Bowen and Casadevall, 2015). In addition, awareness of "disease mongering," defined as "a process that turns healthy people into patients, causes iatrogenic harm, and wastes precious resources," is the latest face of over-medicalization (Moynihan, Doran, and Henry, 2008). Medical science also focuses on the diseases of rich countries rather than those of poor countries, even though the disease burden is greatest in low-income countries. Yet biomedical individualism is at the heart of health policy in rich and poor countries. Overwhelmingly, health sector budgets are spent on hospital services. The percentage spent on the preventive and promotive functions of public health is very small, varying from the highest OECD country, Canada, which spends 6%, followed by the United States at 3%, and the lowest at 0.7% in Latvia (Jackson and Shiell, 2017: 18).

Why is so little spent on preventing illness, compared to the funds spent on treating it? Tesh (1988) points to the "hidden arguments" in health policy, which often mean that the impact of political ideologies remain hidden, even though they are driving policy. Medical dominance and its inherent individualism have been noted since the nineteenth century, most famously by Virchow (2006), and more recently by Doyal (1979), Sanders and Carver (1985), and Navarro and Shi (2001), in relation to low- and middle-income countries. This dominance means that health sector policy actors very easily revert to the acceptance of medicine as the main game of health. A study of Australian health ministers demonstrated the strong pressure on politicians to reinforce the medical model and consequently not give their attention to prevention, promotion, and social determinants (Baum et al., 2013). Medical associations are powerful advocates and almost always advocate primarily for more hospital and medical services. There is also a strong public demand for curative services, as medical advocates have been very effective in promoting their benefits, rather than the reality that population-wide preventive and promotive measures are the most effective for improving population health. This presents a real dilemma for policy actors because if they want to govern for health, they must resist the powerful professional advocacy for more curative services.

A new movement within medicine has emerged recently—*Right Care. The Lancet* is championing this and has published a series of articles on it. This series examined the areas and extent of the overuse and underuse of health and medical services around the world. It defines overuse as "the provision of medical services that are more likely to cause harm than good" and underuse as "the failure to use effective and affordable medical interventions" (Kleinert and Horton, 2017). Application of this approach promises to improve population health, as it will increase care to those who are underserved and avoid harm to those who are receiving care from which they are not likely to benefit.

Public or Private Provision?

Commodification of social resources through the growing market economy under neoliberalism has resulted in a large and growing private health-care sector globally. For example, Sengupta et al. (2017) describe the massive growth in privatized health care in South Asia and note that this trend has been very regressive. They also observe that the trend is encouraged by some public policies. Examples are the opening up of the national market through an increase in foreign direct investment, made possible through trade deals, medical tourism, and failure to invest in strong public services. They present the growth of privatization as a barrier to achieving the Sustainable Development Goal (SDG) 3.8 of universal access to health care. There is a growing civil society protest against the privatization of health services and the introduction of for-profit services (Figure 4.1).

Health systems are grossly underfunded in most low- and middle-income countries, in part as a result of domestic policies, but also largely because of power imbalances at the global level and the generation of neoliberal policies from the World Bank and the International Monetary Fund (Global Health Watch 4, 2014: 161). In rich countries, austerity politics has seen once strong public systems come under threat from private interests. The UK National Health Service is a prime example, and Pollock and Roderick (2017) note that it has been opened up to private markets and has been starved of public funds. Privatized health sectors are geared toward profit and thus stress maximizing the number of patients treated in hospitals and fee-for-service out-of-hospital care, rather than working to achieve improved population health outcomes. A review of the evidence on the impact of marketization on equity (Bambra et al., 2014: 458) concluded that "private insurance and out-of-pocket payments as well as the marketization and privatization of services have either negative or inconclusive equity effects." Among rich countries, the more privatized their health

FIGURE 4.1. Protests in Manila to mark World Health Day, 5th of April 2018, against the privatization of health services.

Source: Courtesy of Delen de La Paz, People's Health Movement Philippines.

systems are, the larger the percentage of their GDP is spent on health. Thus the US highly privatized system incurs 17.9% of GDP, compared to the OECD average of 9%. Most low- and middle-income countries spend much less—India 4.5% and China 5.5 (OECD, 2017a).

A Health Sector Focused on Universal Health Coverage and Primary Health Care

> Achieve universal health coverage, including financial risk protection, access to quality essential healthcare services, and access to safe, effective, quality, and affordable essential medicines and vaccines for all.
> —SDG Goal 3.8

Globally many people do not have access to optimum health care. The starkest contrast is between high- and low-income countries. The health divide is massive, from Japan's life expectancy of 83.8 years to a life expectancy as low as 51 years in Sierra Leone and the Central African Republic (World Bank, 2016). Yet health services are most available in the high-income countries, perfectly illustrating the inverse care law pointed to by Tudor-Hart (1971), whereby the availability of care is greatest for those least in need. Thus, access to health care is an important social determinant of health. WHO (2018a n.p) defines universal health coverage (UHC) as meaning "that all individuals and communities receive the health services·they need without suffering financial hardship. It includes the full spectrum of essential, quality health services, from health promotion to prevention, treatment, rehabilitation, and palliative care." This definition of UHC embodies three related objectives:

1. Equity in access to health services—everyone who needs services should get them, not only those who can pay for them;
2. The quality of health services should be good enough to improve the health of those receiving services; and
3. People should be protected against financial risk, ensuring that the cost of using services does not put people at risk of financial harm.

Almost all OECD countries (with the exception of the United States) and an increasing number of low- and middle-income countries have adopted the goal of universal health coverage. There are clear policy messages about how UHC can be achieved in such a way that all citizens and residents receive appropriate care. Health systems need to establish the achievement of health-care access equity as an aim. Health systems should be free at the point of care so that people do not suffer financial stress or even ruin because of out-of-pocket expenses. This is an issue in countries at all levels of development where out-of-pocket expenses are prevalent. The often catastrophic costs of unsubsidized care and the prospect of not being able to access care when needed support the case for pooling the risks to individual citizens. Pooling risks allows health care to be free at the point of use and to be paid for through contributions collected from citizens from taxation or insurance. Thus national health policy should be directed at establishing effective, equitable, and efficient public health sectors. Careful planning is required to achieve such systems, allocating resources according to need and accounting for the heavier disease burden experienced by either some segments of the population or some areas. Internationally, efforts should be intensified to ensure that all citizens and other residents including refugees have access to effective health care.

Primary Health Care at the Heart of Effective Health Systems

Universal health coverage is one important step toward equity in health service provision. Stigler et al. (2016) note that while financing and human resources are important, an overall framework to shape health systems is vital. They argue that primary health care provides such a framework, as it builds the backbone of an effective health-care system, and can improve health, reduce growth in costs, and lower inequality. The pillars of primary health care were established by the 1978 WHO Alma Ata Declaration on Primary Health Care. The elements of this Declaration were spelled out in the vision noted earlier. The Pan American Health Organization (2009) also stressed the importance of primary health care as the basis of a health system, as shown in Figure 4.2. The director general of WHO (Ghebreyesus, 2018) also continues to endorse primary health care, as shown by a recommitment to the 1978 Alma Ata Declaration on the fortieth anniversary of its adoption.

A primary health care–based system stresses equity and solidarity and places these values at the center of the system. It also stresses the importance of community participation and ensuring that there are mechanisms in place to encourage this. Beyond this, the system needs to provide services and initiatives that provide for effective and high-quality cure, rehabilitation, prevention, and promotion.

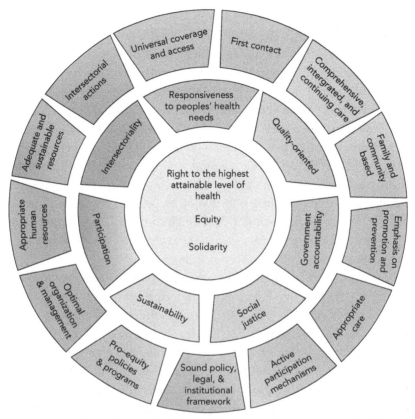

FIGURE 4.2. Core values, principles, and elements in a primary health care–based health system.

Source: Pan American Health Organization (2009).

Curative and Rehabilitative Services

Everyone needs curative services when they are sick and then often also need rehabilitation services to regain function. Special efforts are required to ensure that these services are made available, accessible, and acceptable to all sections of a population. These efforts are supported by policies conceived around demographic groups (old, young, men, women, transgender), for Indigenous people (given their poor health status worldwide; see Anderson et al., 2016), particular ethnic groups including Romany in Europe, refugees and asylum seekers, or according to priority diseases for the country, such as HIV/AIDS, diabetes, or cancer. Devising such policies provides impetus to services to adopt practices that will result in improved service access and acceptability to groups that are at risk of marginalization.

Preventive and Promotive Strategies

These strategies within the health sector need to ensure that the system has as much orientation to prevention and health promotion as possible, with equity in the foreground. A health-promotion strategy focused on behavior change is likely to only benefit those in a position to make healthy lifestyle changes (Baum and Fisher, 2014). Prevention and promotion need to be built into care. Patients should be made aware of how their lifestyle has an impact on their health, but should not be blamed for these lifestyles as they generally reflect people's living circumstances. Health-promotion information needs to be tailored in order to be effective. There is plenty of evidence that only providing information to people is unlikely to lead to behavior change (Baum, 2016). Delivering information in innovative ways (e.g., through TV soap operas, social media) can help, as can tailoring it to specific groups, like young people or Indigenous people.

Program strategies based on more than individual appointments are particularly effective for people who face multiple adverse issues in their lives. For such people, a short appointment with a health professional is often unsatisfactory. Reasons for this include language, culture, fear of highly educated professionals, and the fact that adverse social determinants make it very difficult to follow through on either treatment plans or referrals. Using groups and community development strategies can help overcome some of these barriers. Publicly funded community health programs and services have been the most effective at using these strategies (Lefkowitz, 2007; Baum, 2016, Chapter 21, "Community Development in Health"; Canadian Association of Community Health Centre, 2018). They are often overlooked as a health strategy, partly because they do not fit the dominant biomedical individualist model. Funding under the medical model is primarily directed at individual encounters with health professionals. Examples of the issues for which groups can be helpful include self-management of chronic disease; supporting people leaving violent relationships; living with mental health issues such as depression, anxiety, and low self-esteem; and gaining confidence with parenting. In Nepal, groups for women were shown to be effective in improving birth outcomes (Manandhar et al., 2004). In Latin America, inspired by Paulo Freire (1972), groups and community development have formed the basis of consciousness-raising about the political and social causes of illness.

Community Participation and Community Control of Services

The Alma Ata Declaration enshrined community participation as crucial to an effective health system. Meaningful community participation will contribute to effective and accessible services, in itself is good for health, and contributes to an empowered community. A systematic review of the literature on the influence of national political context on health equity found community empowerment consistently associated with improvements in health equity (Beckfield and Krieger, 2009). Evidence has accumulated to show that control of life is vital to good health for individuals (Marmot, 2004) and that being involved in planning and managing services gives individuals a greater sense of control over their lives. Not having control creates stress and contributes to chronic conditions through various biological pathways. A study in Canada showed that when First Nations communities had control over multiple aspects of their life (including education and community decision-making), suicide rates in those communities were lower (Chandler and Lalonde, 2008). Community control is also an important way of decolonizing services. This is important because colonization continues for Indigenous peoples worldwide as their culture, sovereignty, and self-determination continue to be eroded through stigmatization, racism, discrimination, and policies enacted on, rather than developed with them (Sherwood, 2013). The history of colonialism means that community-controlled health services are most successful if their funding bodies develop respectful means of accountability and oversight (Dwyer et al., 2009; Freeman et al., 2017a). Including Aboriginal organizations in regional planning for health services increased use of these services (Kelaher et al., 2014a). In the United Kingdom, where the NHS is being effectively privatized despite government pronouncements that this is not happening, attention is turning to initiatives that give control to local people to work to improve their own health and have more control over services. One example is Health as a Social Movement, which has been working with six communities in the United Kingdom to increase their control over health through connecting people and encouraging them to work together so that they gain more control over their lives and health (New Economic Foundation, 2018). The pathways by which community participation in health can lead to improved equity in access are shown in Figure 4.3.

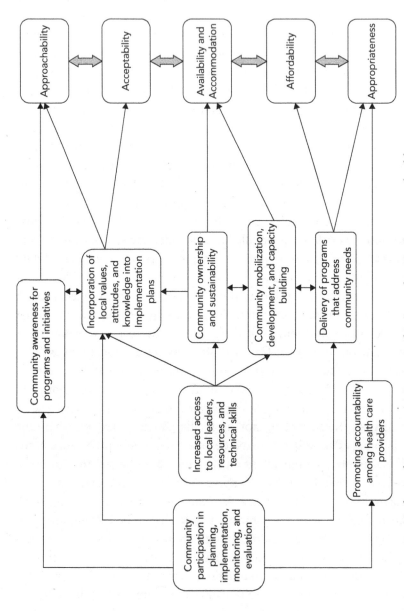

FIGURE 4.3. Pathways between participation and improved equity in access to health care.

Source: Kelaher et al. (2014b).

Workforce for Health

Reorientation of a health system to focus on health and health equity will require a workforce that is equipped to make the change. Crucially, strong political and bureaucratic leadership is required that understands the importance of primary health care, is committed to the aim of universal coverage, and is prepared to work effectively with other sectors. The leaders will also have to resist biomedical dominance and the growing pressure to privatize health services, as noted earlier. Ministers of Health come under great pressure to medicalize systems and focus on hospital care to the exclusion of the other aspects of health systems (Baum et al., 2013). Consequently, they require considerable fortitude, depth of understanding, and commitment to the vision for the health sector described in the preceding.

The Alma Ata Declaration stressed the importance of a multidisciplinary health workforce in which each member of the team makes a unique contribution according to his or her skills. Doctors, nurses, and allied health professionals such as physiotherapists, occupational therapists, social workers, and psychologists are all vital team members. Community health workers also have been shown to be effective, especially in low- and middle-income countries such as Brazil, Ecuador, Thailand, Iran, and Sri Lanka (Perry et al., 2014).

Health professionals are trained primarily to treat illness. Little curriculum time is devoted to disease prevention or health promotion. Changing the health system requires changing training to stress the importance of primary health care and health promotion. The growth of a network of socially accountable medical schools in high-, middle-, and low-income countries has been an important international development to make training more aligned to an equitable health system (Murray et al., 2012). Social accountability stresses the need to be responsive to local communities and to address health inequalities, rather than medical schools' more traditional concerns with prestige, research competitiveness, and training doctors for narrow, specialized careers in urban areas. Research on primary health care found that when health professionals are committed to a comprehensive form of primary health care, they will experience dilemmas in their practice and risk burnout when the broader health system does not support their work (Freeman et al., 2017b).

Once health professionals have a detailed understanding of health promotion and primary health care, they are well positioned to become advocates. Doctors can be particularly effective in advocating for good health governance as they are usually well trusted and respected by the community. As examples, an Australian oncologist has started an international movement to encourage superannuation (pension) funds to disinvest in tobacco companies (Gulland, 2016), and Sir Michael Marmot has taken positions as president of the *British Medical Association* and the *World Medical Association* expressly in order to advocate for action on the social determinants of health equity (Marmot, 2015).

A final equity issue for the health workforce is its maldistribution. For example, in Sierra Leone there are 0.024 physicians per 1,000 persons, while in the United States the figure is 2.5 per 1,000 (WHO Global Health Observatory, 2018). Similar patterns are evident within countries, where more affluent areas with better health have the best provision of doctors, while poorer areas have the worst health status, dubbed "the inverse care law" (Tudor Hart, 1971). Urban areas have better supplies of health professionals than rural. The low number of health professionals in low- and middle-income countries partly reflects the drain of professionals from these countries to rich countries. In recognition of this issue, WHO has adopted a Global Code of Practice on the International Recruitment of Health Personnel (WHO, 2010). While this Code provides guidance on ethical recruitment, the rights of health workers, and strengthening of health systems, it is silent on the issue of financial compensation. The Global Health Watch 4 (2014) argues that reparations should be paid by the receiving countries (to recognize the resources the donor countries have invested in training the doctors). Norway and Ireland are two high-income countries that have used the WHO Code to adopt a health workforce strategy that aims to reduce the global and regional brain drain by building their own health workforce and ensuring that they train enough for local needs.

Exerting Stewardship for Health

Directly affecting the impact of most social determinants of health is outside the remit of the health sector. However, the sector does have a crucial role to play in monitoring the impact of social determinants on health and in catalyzing action in other sectors to promote and protect health.

Monitoring the Impact: Describing Health Inequities and Assessing Impacts

An equity-oriented health sector should collect and analyze data about the social determinants of health and comparative health status, and assess health impacts.

Collecting and Analyzing Equity Data

The Commission on the Social Determinants of Health (CSDH, 2008: 180) recommended that "national governments establish a national health equity surveillance systems with a routine collection of data on social determinants of health and health inequity." This would require analysis of data, stratified by social groups, and bringing together existing databases. The range of data is indicated in Box 4.2.

WHO has continued the work of the CSDH and has developed a framework (WHO, 2018b) and a set of indicators for the global monitoring of action on the social determinants of health and universal health coverage.

It is important for the health sector to make health equity data accessible. This can be done by funding public health observatories, such as the one in Scotland (http://www.scotpho.org.uk/; accessed May 10, 2017). This website contains interactive tools to examine local data and make comparisons, and enables comparisons between Scotland and the rest of Europe. Analyses are available for a range of diseases. For example, the page on suicide (http://www. scotpho.org.uk/health-wellbeing-and-disease/suicide/key-points, accessed May 10, 2017) reports the trend, the breakdown by region, gender, and social class, and provides a comparison with the rest of the United Kingdom. As well as collecting such data, it is important to use the data to inform the development of policies and services. The Scottish website is very policy relevant, providing data calculations of the projected financial savings to the health system and health benefits to the population of a range of policy interventions, including introduction of a living wage and a rise in council taxes.

Data collection on equity may frequently be subject to political pressure if the data do not paint a positive picture. This was shown very clearly in the United Kingdom in 1980 when the Black Report on health inequities was published, only to have its recommendations ignored by the in-coming Thatcher government. In December 2017 it was reported that US Centers for Disease Control staff had been forbidden to use the term "health equity" in presentations (ABC, 2017). Such bans are a response to the power of health equity data to highlight injustice and support the case for policies that would support governing for health.

BOX 4.2

Comprehensive National Health Equity Surveillance System

HEALTH INEQUITIES

Health outcomes (mortality, and illness and disability) stratified by sex, gender, socioeconomic stratifiers (education, income, wealth, occupational class), ethnicity/race/indigeneity, urban/rural

Summary measures of relative health inequity (e.g., rate ratio)

DAILY LIVING CONDITIONS AS DETERMINANTS OF HEALTH

Health behaviors (smoking, alcohol, physical activity, diet and nutrition)

Physical environment (water and sanitation, housing conditions, transportation, quality of urban infrastructure, air quality)

Social environment (social exclusion, discrimination, crime; density of fast food outlets)

Working conditions (hours worked, union coverage, occupational injury)

Health care (coverage, access)

Social protection (coverage, generosity)

STRUCTURAL DRIVERS OF HEALTH INEQUITIES

Gender (norms and values, economic participation, sexual and reproductive rights realized)

Economic (income and wealth distribution)

Education (school and higher education participation rates)

Sociopolitical context (civil rights, employment conditions, public spending priorities, macro-economic conditions)

All data should be stratified whenever possible.
Source: Adapted from CSDH (2008: 182).

Health Impact Assessment

The CSDH and WHO (2011) have called for the implications for health and the distribution of health impacts to be routinely considered in policymaking and practice, through collaborative action by the health sector and non–health sector actors. Health Impact Assessment (HIA) is one of the few methods available to policymakers to assess the social and environmental determinants of health prior to projects being implemented. It is designed to maximize future health benefits and minimize risks to health (Haigh et al., 2013). HIA uses a process of screening, scoping, identification and assessment, decision-making and recommendations, and evaluation. HIAs have been used for a variety of purposes. Harris-Roxas and Harris (2011) define four types: mandated, decision support, advocacy, and community led. They also note that HIAs can be equity-focused. Examples of each are given in Box 4.3.

HIAs can both stress technical issues (such as measuring the likely impact of developments on air and water quality) and consider social and emotional health issues (such as the impact of an urban development on social interaction or mental health). The role of health sectors is to contribute to mandated HIAs with technical knowledge, to conduct HIAs which can inform decision-making within government, and to be responsive to HIAs conducted by advocacy and community groups. Legitimation of HIAs is important because while the method is not perfect, it is an

---

BOX 4.3

Type of Health Impact Assessment (HIA)

Mandated: most often conducted on major project proposals under environmental protection legislative requirements by the project proponents. Examples are HIAs of major infrastructure projects, such as those to build roads, airports, or pipelines.

Decision Support: conducted by governments with a view to improving proposals for initiatives such as regional development or recovery from a disaster, or planning for new health services.

Advocacy: conducted by advocates to influence a proposal. Examples are assessment of new government policy or of corporate activity such as of a fast food company (Anaf et al., 2017).

Community-Led: conducted by potentially affected communities to use as a lobbying tool. Examples are health and environmental impacts of river pollution.

Equity-Focused Health Impact Assessments (EFHIAs): recommended in each of the preceding areas to add a consideration of the differential impact of initiatives.

Source: Adapted from Harris-Roxas and Harris (2011).

important means of exerting the precautionary principle whereby, if there are possible serious risks and threats to health, the lack of scientific knowledge should not be a reason to postpone preventive action.

Catalyzing Action in All Sectors in Order to Promote Health

There are many ways in which the health sector can catalyze action in other sectors. Table 4.1 provides examples of mechanisms that encourage intersectoral collaboration for health and equity.

Health in All Policies

A cross-sectoral mandate is vital to effective health promotion. The Alma Ata Declaration (WHO, 1978) urged "intersectoral action for health." The Ottawa Charter argued for "Healthy Public Policy" (WHO, 1986), which Milio (1986) defined as multisectoral in scope, and participatory in strategy. More recently, Health in All Policies (HiAP) has extended intersectoral action by facilitating other sectors to routinely consider and account for the health impact of their policies, plans, and implementation. HiAP was promoted by WHO as one means to bring about follow-up action from the CSDH, and has produced training manuals and resources to support HiAP's implementation (WHO, 2015b). Box 4.4 provides examples of HiAP from South Australia and California.

Conclusion

Governing for health requires the health sector to move beyond the biomedical individualism that governs so much of its activities to a position where it is able to show leadership for health within its own sector and exert stewardship for health across society. Being able to do this will require strong, determined, and well-informed political and bureaucratic leadership that can challenge the power behind the current model within health sectors and thereby establish new service models that are concerned with the continuum of care, rehabilitation, prevention, and health promotion in equal measure. Evidence indicates that health systems should be based on a comprehensive model of primary health care. Publicly funded services that are free at the point of use will be required to support this model. Leaders will also need to foster work with other sectors to encourage them to consider their health impact and to seek policies that, while meeting the sectors' core objectives, also promote health and well-being.

Table 4.1 Examples of Mandates and Structures That Encourage Collaborative Work for Health and Equity across Sectors

Mechanism	Description	Example
Mandates		
Laws, regulations	Legal frameworks designed to foster collaboration across sectors to promote health-supporting policies	Article 152 Treaty of Amsterdam, which allows the European Union to take public health action
		WHO Framework Convention on Tobacco Control ratified by 18 nations
		UN Convention on the Rights of the Child
		Public Health Laws, which encourage cross-sector action (e.g., Norway, Quebec, and South Australia)
		Health Care Act in Finland, which requires consideration of health impacts in municipal policymaking
Agreement protocols	Formal or informal agreements of collaboration between government, universities, civil society	US Presidential Memorandum establishing taskforce on Childhood Obesity (under President Barack Obama)
Political commitments	Political agreements to support action for health equity	Supportive statements in manifesto of political parties
		Bipartisan political support
Structures		
Inter-ministerial committees	Composed of representatives from various governmental sectors, most often horizontal (i.e., similar administrative levels—national, subnational, district) but also vertical. Can include nongovernmental organizations (NGOs), private sector and political parties, and/or can be permanent, time limited, with generic tasks, or ad hoc centered around a specific task	Advisory Board for Public Health (Finland).
		Intersectoral Commission of Employment (Peru)
		Intersectoral Commission for the Control of Production and Use of Pesticides, Fertilizers and Toxic Substances (Mexico)
		Health in All Policies Task Force (California)

(Continued)

Table 4.1   Continued

Mechanism	Description	Example
Merged or coordinating ministries	Ministries with a mandate that includes several sectors or that are responsible for intersectoral coordination	Ministry of Social Affairs and Health (Finland) Ministry of Health and Family Welfare (India) Department of Social Development (South Africa
Expert committees/ forums	Comprising experts from public-sector structures, academic institutions, NGOs, think tanks, community, or private sector; may be ad hoc or permanent, and may focus on a general area or be specific	UK National Institute for Health for Health and Care Excellence, Public Health Advisory Committees Thailand National Health Assembly
Support units	Unit within ministry of health or other ministries with a mandate to foster intersectoral collaboration	Health in All Policies Unit (South Australia, Australia)
Networks	Flexible coordination mechanism composed of institutional partners	Canterbury Health in All Policies Partnership (Canterbury, New Zealand). Regional Roundtables in south of Adelaide for action on (1) drug and alcohol; (2) early child development
Community coalitions	Local organizations that promote collaboration among different sectors	County Health Council coordinating ebola response efforts in Margibi and Lofa (Liberia)
Public health institutes and observatories	Public health institutes with capacity to monitor public health and its determinants, and to analyze policies and their potential health implications across sectors	See International Association of National Public Health Institutes (IANPHI) for a comprehensive list: http://www.ianphi.org/ See also http://www.scotpho.org.uk/

Source: Adapted from Ollila et al. (2013): 11–13; WHO (2013a): 8–9.

BOX 4.4

Health in All Policies (HiAP) in Action: South Australia and California

South Australia (SA) adopted the HiAP approach in 2007 and initially relied on Health Lens Analysis to examine the potential for all government sectors to promote health while also achieving their core sectoral aims. Over time, SA HiAP has evolved and has been supported by a new Public Health Act, which created the mechanism of Public Health Partner Authorities. These are based on an agreement between health and agencies in other sectors and specify the health-promoting actions that can be taken by these agencies. SA HiAP has been involved in projects associated with urban planning and reducing carbon footprints of new developments and infill developments replacing existing housing stock with apartments and houses with smaller footprint, healthy parks (see Chapter 8), literacy programs, active transport options, and increasing the percentage of the population with healthy weight. HiAP stresses the crucial importance of understanding and then working with other sectors to achieve their core goals (Baum et al., 2017) while also encouraging them to adopt policies and strategies that promote health.

More details of HiAP in SA are available at http://www.sahealth.sa.gov.au/wps/wcm/connect/public+content/sa+health+internet/health+reform/health+in+all+policies/south+australias+hiap+approach

In California, the HiAP Task Force is housed under the Strategic Growth Council (SGC), and brings together 22 state agencies, departments, and offices, with a common goal of working together to support a healthier and more sustainable California. The Task Force uses the following filters to decide whether to support initiatives, by asking if they

1. Promote health, equity, and sustainability
2. Support intersectoral collaboration
3. Benefit multiple partners
4. Engage stakeholders
5. Create structural or procedural change.

The California initiative has produced an excellent resource to guide other state and local governments that wish to adopt an HiAP approach (http://www.phi.org/uploads/files/Health_in_All_Policies_Guide_for_State_and_Local_Governments.pdf, accessed April 28, 2017)

Source: https://www.cdph.ca.gov/programs/Pages/HealthinAllPolicies.aspx

5

Fiscal Policy

CENTRAL TO GOVERNING FOR HEALTH

Economics is a political argument. It is not—and can never be—a science; there are no objective truths in economics. . . . Therefore, when faced with an economic argument, you must ask the age-old question, "Cui bono?" (Who benefits?).

—HA-JOON CHANG (2014: 327), *Professor of Economics, Cambridge University*

Introduction

Fiscal policy is central to governing for health. It determines what resources are available, largely from taxation, to invest in health and well-being. It also determines how equitably and effectively national resources are used. The decisions made by treasurers, finance ministers, and chancellors of the exchequers are vital to health, yet this is rarely recognized, and the economic sphere is treated as if it were somehow separate from the rest of society.

This chapter argues that in order to govern for health, this view has to change, with economic decisions made to serve the health and well-being of society. In making this argument, the chapter starts with a consideration of the health-damaging effects of neoliberalism and then asserts and examines five action points that would lead to fiscal policies that support health and well-being.

Neoliberalism Governing Fiscal Policies and Driving Inequities

Currently, fiscal policies in most countries and international agencies are neoliberal and focused on economic growth, largely to the exclusion of other considerations. Their aim is to create a global economy freed from as many restrictions as possible, and which encourages economic growth through free trade and market economies. Yet economic growth and the resultant wealth production rely on the exploitation of non-renewable resources, especially fossil fuels. By 2011 humans were annually using 135% of the resources that can be sustainably generated in one year (Ecological Footprint, 2012). Yet neoliberal economics does not account for the impact of resource extraction and use on the environment. Unquestioned growth and wealth production are only desirable in an economic system that does not count these external costs. Korten (2016: n.p) calls the obsession with economic growth the "Great Growth Con," which ignores the fact that "humans are part of an interconnected web of life—dependent for our well-being upon one another and the living Earth." The justification for these neoliberal policies is that they will result in more wealth, and this will trickle down to have a society-wide benefit. Yet as the evidence accumulates, this argument looks weaker and weaker. Instead, since the introduction of neoliberal policies in the early 1980s under Margaret Thatcher in the United Kingdom and Ronald Reagan in the United States, inequities have grown massively. Welfare states have been undermined, and global corporations have gained more and more power and influence. Nation building and protection of vulnerable members of society and the environment have been sacrificed. Credit Suisse has calculated that the wealth of just 42 people in the year September 2016-August 2017 equals that of the 3.7 billion in the poorest half of the world's population. This staggering figure is part of a trend by which inequities are rapidly increasing and which fiscal policies around the world are encouraging. These economic inequities underpin health inequities. Luckily, reducing health inequities appears to have fiscal benefits, too. As noted in Chapter 3, Wilkinson and Pickett have shown that in OECD countries, more equal countries or regions do better on many measures of health and well-being, suggesting that economic inequalities are not good for health and well-being (see Figure 3.1). Chang (2014) notes that apart from ethical arguments in favor of reduced inequities, there are an increasing number of economic reasons. These include the following:

- High inequality reduces social cohesion, thus increasing political instability.
- Political instability makes the future less certain and thus reduces returns on investment.
- Reduced returns on investment reduce economic growth.
- High inequality creates barriers to social mobility, thus wasting a society's talent.

A study conducted for WHO in Europe (Suhrcke and Cookson, 2016) noted that the health that is lost as a result of the health gradient is both a lost capital good (which leads to less labor productivity) and also a lost consumption good, as people value good health. The study developed scenarios of reduced health inequities for 11 European countries and then estimated the hypothetical life-years saved. These were given a monetary value, which enabled an estimate of the economic benefit of reducing health inequities. The results of the analysis indicated that for even the least ambitious scenario (where death rates for the least wealthy quintile were reduced to those of the second poorest), monetized benefits ranged from €0.643 billion in Denmark (0.3% of GDP) to 60.026 billion in Italy (4.3% of GDP). These figures suggest that sound fiscal management includes policies to reduce health inequities. Thus this chapter calls on those responsible for fiscal management to broaden their vision beyond the current neoliberal paradigm and to adopt measures that take a society-wide rather than an economy-wide perspective. By doing this, fiscal policy players can make a huge contribution to improving the welfare of their entire populations.

A Vision for Healthy Fiscal Policy

How would fiscal management for health and well-being differ from the current focus on neoliberal economics? I propose five action points based on key texts from economists who have questioned the dominant neoliberal paradigm. Readers who want to explore these ideas in more detail are referred to Chang (2014), Korten (1995), Stretton (1999), Quiggin (2010), Fioramonti (2017), and Raworth (2017). The five actions points are as follows:

- *Measure what is treasured*: indicators of real economic progress are adopted, the assumption of economic growth is challenged, and the needs of people and the environment are counted, resulting in new indicators of economic and social progress.
- *More regulation of finance and transnational corporations*: regulation of transnational corporations and financial markets to ensure that their activities create more societal benefits than costs and focus on health as well as wealth.
- *Development of local economic activity*: local industries and alternative models of economic organization are developed and supported.

- *Public ownership of essential assets*: the mass privatization of essential services is reconsidered and the benefits of public ownership asserted.
- *Reducing economic inequities becomes an explicit goal of fiscal policy*: fiscal policies such as progressive taxation are used as a mechanism to redistribute income and wealth and to fund health, education, welfare, and social security systems within countries, which are implemented and viewed as an investment in health and well-being.

The evidence for these five actions points are considered in more detail in the following.

Measure What We Treasure

An important task for fiscal policy actors is to appreciate the limitations of relying on a single economic measure of national progress. Of course the economic system contributes to national well-being, but so do other aspects of our society, and measuring these is important.

Problems with Gross National Product

Most countries measure how well they are traveling with a single indicator, the gross national product (GNP). As a result, many other areas of importance are excluded from the national accounting, including the environment, social and emotional well-being of the population, and how equitably resources are distributed. There have been many criticisms of the GNP as a measure of the health of an economy, let alone more general well-being. GNP measures the annual national revenue of firms and industries, production being valued at the price people pay for it. An increase in the GNP is seen as "economic growth" (Stretton, 1999). This is not necessarily good for health. Consider these examples:

- An increase in road accidents means a greater need for crash repairers, so production is up.
- If more baby formula is manufactured so that fewer babies are breastfed, then this contributes to economic growth.
- After a cyclone there is need for reconstruction, which is good for economic growth.
- If a coal mine is developed and pollutes the environment, it contributes to growth, but if the area of the mine is not developed and left to nature, it is accorded no economic value.

- If more people become addicted to minor tranquilizers, the pharma-ceutical industry will increase production and contribute to economic growth.
- If a fast food chain sells more high-fat and high-sugar products and contributes to the obesity epidemic, this adds to GNP, and no account of the cost of disease associated with obesity is measured.

Not only does the GNP value many things that detract from health, it also undervalues activities that are not part of the formal system of production. In her groundbreaking analysis, Waring (1988) shows that conventional economics does not count much of the work done by women, for instance. Housework, child care done in the home, emotional caring, and unpaid caring for sick people all remain uncounted by GNP (Pocock et al., 2012). Similarly, the resources of nature, which form the basis of all economic activity, are accorded no value at all, despite the fact that a healthy and sustainable ecosystem is essential to the survival of the official market economy.

Externalities

Conventional economic measures do not factor in "externalities," which occur when economic activity affects people or the environment external to that activity (Daly and Cobb, 1990; Jacobs, 1991; Hamilton and Denniss, 2005; Fioramonti, 2017; Raworth, 2017). As an example, Brown (2011: 8) notes that if the full costs of producing petroleum is considered (climate change, treatment of respiratory illness, oil spills, and the US military pres-ence in the Middle East to ensure access to oil), then the cost increases three-fold. Quiggin (2010) notes that the notion of externalities was introduced in the 1920s by Pigou to enable economics to incorporate negative impacts on the environment. Yet measurement systems that discourage manufacturers and others from externalizing their environmental costs still have not been adopted. Chang (2010) argues that companies will "over-produce" pollution because if there is no government regulation, they don't have to pay for the cost of dealing with it. Green economics argues for a system of decision-making that counts externalities and does not have growth as its overriding aim. Examples of the type of measures required are carbon taxes to limit the externality of carbon emissions and a sugar tax to compensate for the health impacts of high-sugar food and drinks, which are fueling a global chronic disease epidemic whose costs are incurred by national health sys-tems, rather than the corporations selling the food and drinks.

Alternative Measures of Progress

> If more of us valued food and cheer and song above hoarded gold it
> would be a merrier world.
> —Bilbo Baggins (J. R. R. Tolkien, *The Hobbit*, 1996: 266)

Meaningful assessments of progress would consider ecological limits, social progress, and the distribution of wealth (Kubiszewski et al., 2013; Fioramonti, 2017). Many attempts have been made to develop new ways of assessing progress. Herman Daly proposed the idea of a "steady state economy" to encourage an economy that lived within ecological limits. Progress toward such an economy could be measured by an Index of Sustainable Economic Welfare (Daly and Cobb, 1990). In the United Kingdom, the New Economics Foundation (NEF) reports annually on the "Happy Planet Index" (HPI) (see Box 5.1). In 2016, no G8 economy was in the top 30 countries of the HPI. Costa Rica topped the HPI list, achieving a higher life expectancy than the United States on about one-tenth of GNP (Jeffrey, 2016). The Kingdom of Bhutan has also developed the concept of "Gross National Happiness" (Givel, 2015) as a set of guiding principles, rooted in Buddhism, to navigate development in a globalized world. The principles value social, cultural, and environmental factors above economic development. A UK report (Centreforum Commission, 2014: 7) has called for the "pursuit of happiness" to be established "as a clear and measureable goal of government." A Genuine Progress Indicator has also been developed (see Box 5.1). Kubiszewski et al. (2013) note that it is not perfect, but it is a far better approximation of economic welfare than GDP. In 2010 a Universal Declaration of the Rights of Mother Earth was adopted in Cochabamba, Bolivia. The Declaration sees Mother Earth as "an indivisible, living community of interrelated and interdependent beings with a common destiny" that "is the source of life, nourishment and learning and provides everything we need to live well." It observes that the capitalist economic system has "caused great destruction, degradation and disruption of Mother Earth, putting life as we know it today at risk through phenomena such as climate change" (Global Alliance for the Rights of Nature, 2010: 1).

Fiscal policy actors have a stewardship responsibility to make more holistic assessments of well-being and human progress. Society-wide discussions are required to increase the acceptability of alternative and

BOX 5.1

Indicators That Capture Real Economic
and Social Progress

The Happy Planet Index ranks the nations of the world according to their performance on three criteria that are designed to summarize national performance in delivering long and happy human lives without overstretching natural resources. Average life expectancy, life satisfaction, and inequality in outcomes are weighed against the impact of the ecological footprint, as expressed in a simplified way by the formula:

$$HPI = \frac{experienced\ well\text{-}being \times life\ expectancy \times inequality\ of\ outcome}{Ecological\ footprint}$$

Source: http://happyplanetindex.org/about#how (accessed January 2, 2017)

The Genuine Progress Indicator (GPI) measures economic activity and its social and environmental impact. The GPI is designed to measure sustainable economic welfare rather than economic activity alone. To accomplish this, the GPI uses three simple underlying principles for its methodology:

- account for income inequality,
- include non-market benefits that are not included in GDP, and
- identify and deduct bads, such as environmental degradation, human health harms, and loss of leisure time.

The developers of the GPI identified 26 indicators, then populated them with verifiable data. As one example, the pure economic activity stemming from the explosive growth of urban sprawl contributes greatly to the GDP. Yet, along with sprawl come non-economic costs such as increased commuting time, increased traffic congestion, land use conversion, and automobile impacts. In short, just because money is being exchanged within an economy does not necessarily lead to sustainability or prosperity, and the GPI is an attempt to calculate the full impact of economic activity.

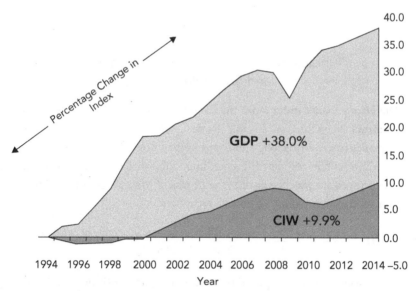

FIGURE 5.1. Trends in the Canadian Index of Well-being (CIW) and GDP (per capita), 1994–2014.

Source: Canadian Index of Well-being (2016: 3).

non-economic measures of progress. Where such measures have been instituted, they indicate that economic progress does not necessarily equate to social and environmental progress. Thus the Canadian Index of Well-being (2016) shows the gap between the GDP and a more holistic measure of progress. While there has been a 38% growth in the GDP since 2008 in Canada, well-being has only increased by 9.9% (Figure 5.1).

Regulate for Health's Sake

Under neoliberalism, the economy of the world has been shaped to benefit the needs of transnational corporations (TNCs) and financial speculators. Under this regime, TNCs have grown in size and influence so that of the world's largest economic entities, 63 are TNCs and 37 are governments (Freudenberg, 2015). TNCs shape our world profoundly and have a massive impact on population health and health equity. TNCs now exercise vast social, economic, and political influence in the global market economy and within individual countries. Their practices and products have potent impacts on population health through production methods, the products themselves, and how they shape social determinants of health or influence regulatory structures. At the same time, financial speculation has increased dramatically and has created an unstable economic system in which profit has been divorced from productive activity (Harvey, 2007; Fioramonti, 2017; Raworth, 2017). Deregulation of rules and restrictions (many of which protected health and equity) on corporations and financial speculators, trade agreements that support transnational rather than local enterprises, and privatization of previously publicly owned assets have seen most recent fiscal policy supporting corporations, rather than people's health and well-being. A very stark example of the need for tightened regulation on fiscal bodies has been forcefully shown by the Australian 2018 Banking Royal Commission, which has unearthed hundreds of examples of misconduct by Australian banks, many of which have seen people lose their life savings or become burdened with debt beyond their budget. The Commission hearings caused outcry among the Australian public. A journalist following the proceedings commented, "What we have seen this past fortnight with the banking royal commission . . . is what happens when so-called free markets operate without, or with no fear of, regulatory control. There is no benevolent invisible hand leading companies to produce optimal outcomes for the economy—merely a hand that drives action towards higher profits at whatever cost" (Jericho, 2018: n.p). It is evidence such as this which means that the social and health impacts of TNCs have been the increasing focus of public health attention. Moodie et al. (2013), Freudenberg (2014), and Kickbusch et al. (2016) detail the many ways in which unregulated corporate activity is posing a risk to health. Korten (see, e.g., 1995, 2015) warns of the dangers of the increasing and unregulated power of corporations and sees this posing a threat to the very foundations of democratic society. The work of these authors indicates that the following forms of regulations would restore balance to the global economic system and protect human and environmental health:

1. *Making a level playing field in terms of political influence.* This will require reforming systems of political campaign finance and making lobbying activity much more open. The aim of this is to greatly reduce the power of TNCs in the political process and thereby restore trust in democratic systems.
2. *End the legal fiction of corporate personhood.* Korten (2015) claims that the legal fiction in the United States that the corporation is a natural person under the law is the means by which corporations have become unaccountable. He says this measure would place strict limits on corporate privileges and facilitate the conduct of business in the public interest.

3. *Establish an international agreement regulating international corporations and finance.* Currently, trade agreements and the World Trade Organization (WTO) maintain an international trading regime that permits TNCs to operate with very few controls on their activities and to appeal to the WTO and national courts if there are restrictions that impede their profit-making. This item would use international agreements to control the TNCs and hold them accountable to the public good.

4. *Eliminate corporate welfare.* TNCs receive considerable direct public subsidies and tax breaks. These funds could be diverted to activities that promote health.

5. *Introduce mechanisms to prevent unproductive financial speculation,* which only serves to make short-term profits for the speculators and which many economists see as having fueled the 2008 global financial crisis (Quiggen, 2010). Chang (2014) says that the financial system has become too complex to control and needs to be made simpler by limiting the proliferation of unnecessarily complicated financial products.

If these measures were instituted, then the resultant fiscal governance for health would contribute greatly to an economy that supported people and environments, rather than continuing the current domination by publicly unaccountable corporations that put profit above health in every decision they make.

Local and Horizontal Economic Activity Encouraged

Changing the model of corporate capitalism means that more attention needs to be given to the shape of economies that are likely to promote health and well-being. Public policy should be proactive in promoting human-scale, stakeholder-owned enterprises to displace the subsidized TNCs. Many individuals and organizations are giving thought to what shape our new economy should be. These ideas come from development agencies (e.g., Oxfam; Hardoon, 2017), academics (Fioramonti, 2017; Raworth, 2017), and as noted earlier, from an increasing number of economists. Korten (2005, 2015), for instance, suggests that the TNCs could be broken down into smaller firms that are linked to their local communities and are controlled by people with a stake in the community. Fioramonti (2017) explores the notion of a "well-being economy" and sets out three features that need to characterize it:

Adaptability: a new economy should operate as a network and replace the current vertical structures with horizontal ones that are able to build resilience and which, by consisting of multiple nodes, will be more easily able to adapt to changing circumstances.

Integrated: whereby local economic activity of consumption and production are set within the broader biosphere and do not exceed earth's natural limits.

Empowering: so that people are not seen as passive "consumers" but rather as controlling agents in local economies.

Small and medium-sized enterprises that have links to local communities conform to this model, whereas the current democratically unaccountable TNCs are a long way from this model. The cooperative model, with roots in the nineteenth century, also has lessons for a healthier economy.

Cooperatives: A History of Prosperity with Equity

The cooperative movement was spearheaded by the writings of Robert Owen, Charles Fourier, and others, and led to the establishment of the first cooperative organizations in Britain and the United States in the 1830s. The key principles for cooperatives are ownership by the users, democratic management, and proportional distribution of benefits. In addition to providing direct benefits to members (owners), cooperatives help build communities by retaining jobs locally and recycling any surpluses through members into local economies. Cooperatives and mutual societies are already prospering in many places across the globe, including the retail, agricultural, banking, insurance, housing, and energy sectors (Zewli and Cropp, 2004). In Western Europe the proportion of the population belonging to cooperatives averages around 30%.

The Mondragon Corporation (2015) is an example of a large successful industrial cooperative and is a federation, based in the Basque country of Spain (Figure 5.2). At the end of 2015, it employed 74,335 people in 257 companies and organizations in four areas of activity: finance, industry, retail, and knowledge. Sales exceeded €11 billion, with total investments of €316 million. While it has been successful in restricting the difference in salaries between workers and executives, it has also been criticized for establishing a two-tier system of owner-workers and non-owner workers. Nonetheless, it has shown that cooperatives can be long lasting and

FIGURE 5.2. Mondragon Corporation, Basque country, Spain.
Source: Flickr\Fagor Automation.

successful. That the Basque region survived the global financial crisis in 2008 better than other areas of Spain has been attributed to Mondragon.

In Britain the Co-operative Group (known as "the Co-op") (Co-operative Group Ltd. 2017a&b) is the largest consumer cooperative in the United Kingdom, with over 70,000 employees, and is owned by more than 4 million active members. It has diverse retail businesses, including food and electrical retail; financial, insurance, legal, and funeral services (Figure 5.3). Members pay £1 and commit to the Co-op's values and principles. They are democratically involved in setting business strategy and social goals and share in any profits. The Co-op focuses on ethical and sustainable products and practices.

Imagine the world if cooperatives had dominated in the last 50 years rather than TNCs. Cooperatives comply much more closely to Fioramonti's (2017) idea of a well-being economy and are likely to have been healthier for people and the environment.

Raworth (2017: 233) also argues that a new approach to business is needed that embeds "benevolent values and regenerative intent at the company's birth." She cites the example of Anita Roddick's Body Shop, which invested its profits in The Body Shop Foundation, and the growing number of structures that are intentionally distributive by design,

FIGURE 5.3. UK Co-operative Supermarket.
Source: Courtesy of shutterstock.com. Co-operative food shop in Leeds, England UK, 9th February 2016.

including cooperatives of the types discussed in the preceding, community interest companies, and benefit corporations. In these the corporate bylaws or articles of association are written to mandate governance that is regenerative and distributive in design. To support such enterprises, Raworth (2017) argues for the need for "finance in service to life," rather than speculation, and argues for states to become transformative partners in creating a regenerative economy.

Essential Services in Public Hands

Governing for health requires governing for the public good. Under neoliberalism, arguments frequently have been made that the privatization or contracting out of public services will result in cheaper and more efficient services. As a consequence of these arguments, the privatization of public services has been a feature of public policy under neoliberalism. This has included the sale of infrastructure, including electricity networks, water, and hospitals, and the outsourcing of services like information technology (IT) support for government agencies. In the 1980s the World Bank mandated privatization as part of its Structural Adjustment Packages (SAPs) for low- and middle-income countries. Despite the recognition that SAPs had adverse impacts, including on health (Stiglitz, 2002), pro-privatization arguments have remained constant. They maintain that privatization will encourage competition and thus lower prices.

Quality will improve because markets are inherently efficient and there will be an increased choice of services for consumers. For the private sector, privatization offers profits in the short term, and for governments a short-term injection of cash from the sale of public assets. By contrast, public health is concerned with long-term improvements in well-being and a decline in disease, and privatization does not appear to deliver on such improvement. Much of the pressure for privatization comes from the private sector, which will benefit from the sale of public assets. Despite their conflict of interest, private sector advocacy groups (for example, business councils) actively lobby in favor of privatization. They have much more power in policy debates than civil society groups that lobby against privatization on public interest grounds (see Figure 5.3).

While many claims were made for the supposed benefits of privatization, there is relatively little evaluation of whether these subsequently have been proven. The evidence that is available suggests that the privatizations of the 1980s did not live up to their promises. Fiscal policy actors need to consider the evidence concerning privatization before assuming its benefits.

The following subsections detail the key health and equity issues that need to be considered when decisions are made about privatizing public assets or functions.

Saving Public Monies

This is important because if privatization did save public monies, then it could be reinvested in areas that would benefit health, well-being, and equity. Quiggin (2010) argues that privatization will yield net fiscal benefits to governments only if the price for which the asset is sold exceeds its value in continued public ownership. He notes that this often is not the case. In addition, privatization requires an increase in regulatory bodies to monitor the private sector, and this is at the cost of the private purse. For outsourced service delivery, designing, procuring, reviewing, and revising outsourced delivery models are costly processes.

More Efficient Service

Neoliberalism claims that markets are more efficient. Quiggin (2010) notes this is often not the case and that some privatizations merely result in private monopolies that are not efficient. Private prisons in the United States have been shown to operate much less efficiently than those publicly run (Lopez, 2016).

Equity and Impact on People Living in Disadvantaged Circumstances

Equity appears to be the big loser from privatization. Private sectors are not good at ensuring equity of access or working for equitable population health gain. Generally the impact of privatization has been more adverse on low- and middle-income countries. There the processes have weakened already fragile institutions and have decreased the control and accountability of governments in systems where governance was weak (Carpenter, 2000). In Chapter 4 on health systems and Chapter 6 on education systems, we see that evidence indicates that private provision is not good for equity. A report from the Australian Centre for Policy Studies found that outsourcing human services risks "poorer outcomes for the most disadvantaged and erodes public sector capability to design and (where necessary) deliver effective services for the most vulnerable" (Farrow et al., 2015: 6). It also noted that public sector officials become removed from the actualities of peoples' lives and become disconnected from the complexities of service delivery and so are less able to make sound policy. Additionally, blurred lines of responsibility mean that no one organization is held responsible for failures. Water privatization has been linked with major social and health costs. These impacts vary between countries, but common effects are evident. For example, when water becomes more expensive and therefore less accessible, women and children, particularly in low and middle income countries, are most likely to bear the burden (Whelan and White, 2005: 142). Hutton (1995) examines the impact of the privatization of housing, transportation, and education in the United Kingdom in the 1980s and finds that it had particularly bad consequences for the poorest part of the population. Ferreira (1997), a former World Bank economist, argues that even when privatization is designed to be egalitarian, it may lead to increases in inequality and possible poverty. An assessment of SAPs and the privatization of the public sector they enforce by Joseph Stiglitz (2002), former chief economist at the World Bank, rated them as failures on both economic and social grounds.

Impact on Social Capital and Solidarity

Privatization extends the market into many areas of life and has the effect of limiting collectivism, which, in turn, diminishes solidarity. The extension of market activity may also impede the creation of bridging social capital by which people are linking by sharing a common public service, which treats all citizens equally. Such social capital is an important element of a healthy society. The pressure on NGOs that are bidding to offer outsourced services to adopt business-like forms of operation tends to erode or undercut their role in creating and maintaining a strong civil society that contributes to social capital (Considine et al., 2014). Competition between NGOs can also lead to fragmentation of services and barriers to access. Owning key infrastructure or assets can be a source of national pride and can reinforce citizenship, as is shown by British support for the National Health Service. A recent project of Public Service International canvassed citizens' views of privatization through a series of public forums in Australia and uncovered widespread discontent with the privatization of both infrastructure and services (Hetherington, 2017). There are also many civil society protests against privatization. Examples include the People's Health Movement in the Philippines, campaigns against the privatization of health services in India and South Africa, and campaigns by many groups in Latin America and Africa against the privatization of water. For example, an "Our Water, Our Right" coalition of civil society groups was formed to challenge the privatization of water in Lagos state, Nigeria (Figure 5.4) (Public Service International, 2017).

Given the relative absence of evaluation of privatized/outsourced services and inconclusive results, governments should be far more cautious about privatizing and outsourcing essential services in the future. What evidence there is suggests that the short-term financial gains are considerably outweighed by the long-term threats to health and equity.

Reducing Economic Inequities as a Goal of Fiscal Policy

Fiscal governance for health needs to be concerned with measures that reduce economic inequities. Crucial aspects of this fiscal governance are progressive taxation, minimum incomes, and universal social security. Each are examined in the following.

Progressive Taxation: Good for Health and Equity

Taxation is vital to a society's sense of solidarity and fairness. It is also one of the ways governments can tame the profit-seeking activities of the private sector, and provide funding for government services such as welfare, education, public health, and environment protection. Reynolds (2011: 175–176) notes that taxation can achieve the following public health purposes:

FIGURE 5.4. Rally in Lagos by the "Our Water, Our Right" Coalition, March 2017.
Source: Used with permission of Sani Baba/Public Service International.

- Provide general revenues for governments
- Contribute to the costs of particular problems associated with the consumption or use of a commodity
- Emphasize that activities which place a stress on "public goods" (e.g., production of carbon) ought to have price signals attached to them (carbon tax)
- Provide revenue for a particular purpose (by hypothecating or dedicating a proportion of the receipts for health promotion); and
- Encourage a change in consumption or behavior, for public health or other purposes (e.g., sugar tax).

Neoliberal governments promote low taxation regimes on the grounds that higher taxes on high personal incomes, corporate income, and wealth are detrimental to growth and employment. Yet Richardson (2016) reviews the data and shows that there is no correlation between low corporate tax rates and economic growth in OECD countries. Further, he shows that countries with lower company tax rates have lower standards of living, measured as purchasing power of GDP per capita. Corporate tax rates were higher in the 1960s and 1970s than in previous periods and have been progressively decreased since neoliberalism dominated public policy. Thus the US Trump administration lowered the corporate tax rate from 35% to 21% in December 2017. In Australia the top marginal tax rate has declined from 75% in the 1950s to 45% (Richardson, 2016). West (2016: n.p) argues that the big four global accounting firms have been instrumental in advocating for low taxation regimes, noting that while they advise "governments on tax reform, they make lavish fees advising their multinational clients how to avoid paying tax." The International Labour Organization (Godar et al., 2014) has argued that the trend to lower taxes can be reversed without damaging economies through measures such as a financial transaction tax and moving to progressive taxes on income and wealth and away from regressive consumption taxes. Surveys in different countries indicate that people are prepared to pay more tax if they believe the money collected is spent on good public services (Ortega et al., 2016). There is also evidence of widespread support for increased taxes on businesses and the introduction of measures to reduce tax avoidance measures (see, e.g., Hetherington, 2016). The extent of tax evasion was made evident by the Panama Papers, published in 2016 (International Consortium of Investigative Journalists, 2017). Zucman (2017) reports that offshore wealth is heavily concentrated in a few hands. About 50% of the wealth held in tax havens belongs to households with more than $50 million in net wealth, a group that private bankers call "ultra-high-net-worth individuals." These are about 0.01% of the population in OECD countries. There is also extensive evidence of the ways in which corporations structure themselves to avoid paying tax in many of the countries in which they operate (Braithwaite and Drahos, 2000). Tax Justice (2017) notes that most corporations have multiple affiliates in offshore tax havens and hold trillions of dollars of untaxed or hardly taxed profits offshore. Figure 5.5 shows how much selected countries are losing annually to tax havens.

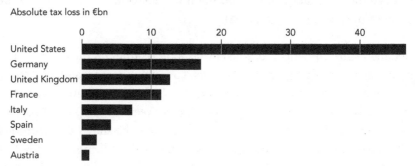

FIGURE 5.5. Countries losing more than €1 billion in tax revenue per year to tax havens.

Source: Zucman (2017). Courtesy of Gabriel Zucman.

Such evidence is leading to increasing disquiet about tax avoidance and the loss of revenue for building strong public sectors (http://www.taxjustice.net/; Murphy, 2015). An important element of fiscal governance for health is to consider the options for taxes that have the capacity to redistribute wealth. These include the following:

Global tax on capital: the French economist Piketty (2014) argues that a progressive global tax on capital, coupled with a very high level of international financial transparency, is required "to avoid an endless inegalitarian spiral and to control the worrisome dynamics of global capital concentration" (Piketty, 2014: 515). He acknowledges that this tax would require a very high level of international cooperation.

Financial transaction tax: Murphy (2015), as part of his case for the ideal taxation system, says the case for a financial transaction tax is "overwhelmingly strong" because it would enable banks to be taxed and would reduce the high volume of financial transactions, which are widely seen to destabilize the world economy.

National wealth taxes: Murphy (2015) argues for the merits of wealth taxes and suggests a sliding scale starting at 1% per annum on wealth of more than £1 million, along with measures designed to make a dramatic reduction in tax avoidance.

Inheritance and estate tax/death duties: the progressive think tank The Australia Institute has argued that an estate duty on deaseased estates is more palatable "because it is levied at a time when the one who accumulated the assets no longer needs them and the beneficiaries have not got used to owning them" (Richardson 2016: i). Within the OECD, 19 countries have such taxes and 15 do not. Most crucially, however, it is vital to have an effective taxation system that has the overall intent of being redistributive and in which opportunities for avoidance are minimal.

Minimum Wage

Setting a minimum wage can make a signifcant contribution to reducing inequities and improving health. Low income has long been associated with a range of poor health outcomes, including diabetes, obesity, and low birthweight. The World Economic Forum (Samons et al., 2015) argues that as inequality usually starts in the labor market, a broad package of coherent labor market policies, including a minimum wage, is vital to tackle inequality and helps to spread the benefits of economic growth. The American Public Health Association's (2016) policy position paper on minimum wages provides evidence of how it benefits health in multiple ways, including allowing better access to other social determinants such as housing, food, and energy. The introduction of a minimum wage in the United Kingdom has contributed to improving mental heath (Reeves et al., 2017). The International Labour Organization reports that more than 90% of their member states have one or more minimum wages set through legislation of binding collective agreements (ILO, 2018). Globally there are differences in the extent to which minimum wages are set at a livable level. Where they do provide a livable level, then they become an essential part of a healthy and equitable society.

Social Protection and Health

A major argument of neoliberal economics has been that welfare states undermine productivity efficiency and economic growth, and so governments that aim at economic prosperity should not invest in such provision. This encourages the belief that in economic terms there is a trade-off between efficiency and equality. However, recent empirical and historical research contradicts this assertion. In a summary of the evidence, Lundberg et al. (2016) note that large welfare states do not hamper economic growth. Rather, they may even increase economic wealth. They do this, as well as fostering health, well-being, and social equality. So rather than seeing social protection systems as a fiscal drain, the evidence indicates that social protection and welfare state policies should be viewed as important investments that provide the social infrastructure necessary for high employment rates. Strong systems provide cradle-to-grave protection against social and economic shocks, including support for parents, unemployment, disability, and old age. The Commission on the Social Determinants of Health (2008) noted that it would be financially feasible to provide social protection coverage for all citizens on earth if the political will were present.

There is evidence that social protection protects the health of people in vulnerable situations. For example, an analysis of longitudinal data on unemployment and health outcomes points to the differences between the institutional mechanisms in different types of capitalist states. Germany, as a coordinated market economy, contrasts with the United States as a liberal market economy. The more generous unemployment benefits in Germany mean that unemployment has less severe health impacts. The gradient is much steeper in the United States, where people with minimum levels of skills are 7 times more likely to die than the highly skilled employed, whereas the difference is only 2.7 times in Germany (McLeod et al., 2012).

Conditional cash transfer programs have been introduced in many Latin American and some African countries and have been trialed in New York. Recipients have to comply with certain educational (e.g., school attendance of children) or disease-prevention measures (e.g., vaccination) to receive the cash. Questions have been raised about the paternalism of such programs (Popay, 2008). Evidence is emerging that they can reduce poverty and can result in some limited educational and other health benefits in New York City (Riccio et al., 2016). A review of evidence suggests that they can improve maternal and infant health and encourage healthier behaviors (Lagarde et al., 2007; Ekezie et al., 2017).

Increasingly, arguments are being made in favor of a universal basic income (UBI) (see, e.g., Ermano, 2013) and the idea is attracting political attention from the right and left. This is partly as a response to the looming automation of much labor and the subsequent prospect of rising unemployment rates, and partly as a means of simplifying welfare systems. In an editorial in the *British Medical Journal*, Painter (2016) argues that a UBI would be good for health, citing some experiments that have been conducted in Canada. Others argue (Foster, 2016) that it would encourage people not to work, would cause inflation in the price of essential goods, and would entail high administrative costs. Finland is running a trial of UBI that will conclude in 2018 (Chakrabortty, 2017a). The value of a UBI has to be judged alongside the availability of other social, welfare, and health benefits and broader fiscal policies to reduce inequities.

Conclusion

Progressive and redistributive fiscal policies are foundational to governing for health. Such policies provide resources to promote health and create economic equality, which is important to health equity and to promoting solidarity and a sense of citizenship. In the absence of this fiscal underpinning, a healthy society will be much more difficult to achieve.

6

Education

ESSENTIAL INVESTMENT IN HEALTH

Education is the most powerful weapon which you can use to change the world.
—NELSON MANDELA MADISON PARK HIGH SCHOOL, *Boston, 23rd June 1990*

Introduction

Education is a vital determinant of health. If you work in the education sector, you are likely to make a greater contribution to promoting population health than many other professionals, including doctors. This is because you have the opportunity to establish the building blocks for good health by encouraging children to maximize their social, emotional, and educational skills, each of which is vital to good health. You can both prevent problems before they occur and create the conditions for good health. This potential for teachers is perhaps why Finland, the country that achieves the best educational outcomes internationally, holds teachers in such high regard and where teaching is a much desired profession to enter (Sahlberg, 2013).

This chapter demonstrates why education is so important to health and provides examples of public policies that enable education to maximize its health-promoting potential through people's life course, including early childhood development, primary, secondary, and tertiary education, and lifelong learning.

The Intrinsic Link between Education, Health, and Equity

Education has multiple benefits for health which operate for individuals (e.g., increased life expectancy) and for society (e.g., reducing crime, increasing social engagement and combating inequities). These benefits are elaborated on below.

Individual Benefits from Education

Education is a great predictor of life expectancy. For example, Lleras-Muney (2005) found that for individuals born in the United States between 1914 and 1939, an additional year of schooling reduces the probability of dying in the next 10 years by 3.6 percentage points. The OECD (Feinstein et al., 2006) cites a PhD dissertation by Spasojevic, which found that for Swedish men born between 1945 and 1955, an additional year of schooling reduces the risk of poor health by 18.5%. A study in Indonesia used the government's implementation of a primary school construction project between 1973 and 1979 to identify the causal effect of education and found that an increase in the average number of years of education in the household reduces child mortality (Breierova and Duflo, 2004). Given these figures, it is not surprising that the lower life expectancy of low- and middle-income countries is paralleled by lower educational achievement. In Finland 98% of girls complete primary school, while in Uganda and Mozambique only 54% and 46% do so, respectively. There is an increasingly robust evidence base linking early childhood experiences to later life achievements, social adjustments, mental health, physical health, and longevity of individuals (Shonkoff et al., 2009; Herzman, 2010; Currie & Rossin-Slater, 2015; National Scientific Council on the Developing Child, 2016).

Thus educational systems are vital to healthy societies and individuals. Some of the key reasons why education is good for the health and longevity of individuals are as follows:

- Education opens the door to better quality and higher paying jobs and gives cultural and social capital, which provides opportunities and the skills to be socially and economically mobile. A higher paying job mean you are more likely to be able to afford a healthy lifestyle.
- Education brings a sense of control and enables people to gain employment in areas where they have more control (which is good in itself for health).
- Education is likely to enable you to have high levels of health literacy.
- Education helps people provide more stimulating learning environments for their children.
- Education enables people to negotiate the complexity of modern society (welfare systems, dealing with financial matters, energy suppliers, etc.).

My own personal experience of the transformative effect of free public education is described in Box 6.1.

BOX 6.1

Education as a Vital Social Determinant of Health

My own story shows how education can be transformative and greatly influence the social determinants of health. My parents were relatively poor. Dad worked in various jobs in the hotel industry—as a porter, barman, and waiter. I received a good UK public-sector education, which was completely free. I gained entry to university in 1972 when tuition was free, and my local education authority provided me with a living grant on which it was possible to live frugally away from home. My mother felt I should be "out earning a living" rather than "wasting my time on studying history." If it hadn't been for the free tuition and living grant, I would not have been able to go to university. At university I learned not just about history, but also how to think critically and how to conduct myself in middle-class circles—something of which I had little experience. Thus I accumulated cultural capital, in addition to being able to gain employment that was much higher paying than would have been possible without it. School and university were completely life changing for me and have given me opportunities that have enhanced my health throughout my life.

Societal and Equity Benefits of Education

For societies, education is an investment. It produces people with multiple skills and people who are likely to be healthier as employees, parents, and active participants in society—who have the necessary skills to navigate periods of illness and to maintain their health. Education is intimately tied to a range of other social determinants, including employment, social networks, a range of literacies (including health and digital), and income and wealth. The absence of education can have a very significant impact on other determinants. Hankivsky (2008) pointed to the multiple pathways by which it affects health. She estimated that $7.7 billion would be saved if there was a 1% increase in the Canadian high school graduation rate. Her calculations combined the cost-savings for social assistance, crime, annual earning loss, annual tax revenue loss, annual revenue loss in employment insurance, employment insurance cost, and intangible costs. Such evidence lends strong support to the case that education is a vital societal investment, and a health lens suggests that it should be seen as such, rather than as a cost.

Better Education Builds Life Satisfaction, Health, and Social Engagement

The OCED (2016) notes that education contributes to stronger and better societies through the creation of wealth, through knowledge and innovation, through jobs, and through lower dependency on social welfare services. Their data show that education, cognitive skills, and social and emotional skills all play a role in increasing health outcomes and life satisfaction. OECD data indicate that over an individual's lifetime, governments receive around €100,000 more than they invest per graduate through greater tax revenues and social contributions. On average across OECD countries participating in the Gallup World Poll, 92% of tertiary-educated adults were satisfied with their life in 2015, compared to 83% of those with upper secondary or post-secondary non-tertiary education. While the building blocks of life satisfaction are complex, research shows that social and emotional skills can play a large role in determining life satisfaction, much of which stem from education in schools, as well as from family and cultural environments. These skills in turn may play a role in improving the economic and social outcomes of education: lower unemployment rates, higher earnings, better health, and greater civic and political engagement, all of which influence individual well-being (OECD, 2015).

Education's Role in Combating Rising Inequity

Most governments recognize the vital importance of education to economies, especially in post-manufacturing economies where much manual labor has been mechanized and robots are taking over more and more functions from people. More jobs require education. Rising inequity threatens social stability, and inequities may increase as those without educational qualifications will be less employable and so less able to gain the resources necessary for a healthy lifestyle. Education helps social mobility, which means that a society is more likely to be using all its assets. When education is restricted to a particular class of people, then much talent is wasted. Evidence from the United Kingdom (Figure 6.1) indicates that this is exactly what happens. Children who have low cognitive scores at 22 months of age but who grow up in families of high socioeconomic position improve their relative scores as they approach the age of 10. The relative position of children with high scores at 22 months but who grow up in families of low socioeconomic position worsens as they approach age 10. This reflects a

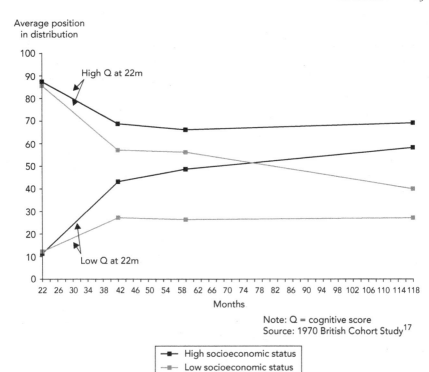

Average position
in distribution

FIGURE 6.1. Inequality in early cognitive development of children in the 1970 British Cohort Study, at age 22 months to 10 years.

Note: Q = cognitive score.

Source: Marmot, Allen, et al. (2010: 17).

range of factors, but primarily concerns resource-poor environments and the ways in which these environments make good parenting much harder, thus excluding some children from developing to their full potential.

Furthermore, research comparing the reading and vocabulary scores of Canadian and US children at age 4–5 indicates that Canadian children have outpaced US children in regard to their reading and vocabulary skills before they begin formal schooling, indicating that the comparatively poor results for US children on international education assessments are not the result of school-related factors, but rather the result of poorer social conditions during the early years (Merry, 2013).

The same is true if we compare children in low-income compared to high-income countries. Educational opportunities are near universal in most high-income countries but are lacking in many low- and middle-income countries, especially for girls. In most countries, girls are less likely to complete primary school. The example of the "low income, high health" countries (Sri Lanka, China, Kerala State in India, Cuba, and Costa Rica) demonstrates that women's education, together with comprehensive primary health care, can result in very high life expectancies without high economic development (Irwin and Scali, 2007). In low- and middle-income countries, children will be pressured to leave school and contribute to the family income instead, and girls are less likely to be kept in school (Commission on the Social Determinants of Health, 2008).

Effective early childhood education is crucial to breaking intergenerational poverty, and its crucial role is discussed in more detail in the following.

Educational Public Policies for Health

The United Nations Sustainable Development Goals (SDGs) (United Nations, 2017) set out global goals for education (Box 6.2).

Public Funding for Public Education Gives Better, More Equitable Outcomes

If the SDG education goals were achieved, the world would be much healthier. The goals stress the concept of quality, and that needs to be defined in each national context. Achieving the SDGs will require public policy that establishes and maintains strong educational sectors which provide equitable and high-quality opportunities from early childhood to tertiary education. School systems in countries pursuing neoliberal polices (particular pronounced in the United States, the United Kingdom, Canada, and Australia; see Chapters 1, 2, 3, and 5 for more details of neoliberalism) have stressed market-driven competitive school systems that test children frequently, encourage competition between schools and students, attempt to standardize teaching and learning in schools, and use public funds to subsidize private schools. For preschool, primary, secondary, and tertiary education, funding issues are vital in determining how equitable educational systems are. Containing the investment of public funds to public rather than private educational institutions is important, yet the drive in recent years has been to market-driven systems, just as we have seen in Chapter 4 in relation to the health sector. An example of the impact has been noted by Friendly (2016) in commenting on the trends toward privatization of early childhood services in Canada.

Sustainable Development Goals

Sustainable Development Goals to be achieved by 2030 mean that countries would

- Ensure that all girls and boys complete free, equitable, and quality primary and secondary education, leading to relevant and Goal-4 effective learning outcomes
- Ensure that all girls and boys have access to quality early childhood development, care, and preprimary education so that they are ready for primary education
- Ensure equal access for all women and men to affordable and quality technical, vocational, and tertiary education, including university
- Substantially increase the number of youth and adults who have relevant skills, including technical and vocational skills, for employment, decent jobs, and entrepreneurship
- Eliminate gender disparities in education and ensure equal access to all levels of education and vocational training for the vulnerable, including persons with disabilities, indigenous peoples, and children in vulnerable situations
- Ensure that all youth and a substantial proportion of adults, both men and women, achieve literacy and numeracy
- Ensure that all learners acquire the knowledge and skills needed to promote sustainable development
- Build and upgrade education facilities that are child, disability, and gender sensitive and provide safe, nonviolent, inclusive, and effective learning environments for all
- Substantially expand globally the number of higher education scholarships available to developing countries
- Substantially increase the supply of qualified teachers.

Source: http://www.un.org/sustainabledevelopment/education/ (accessed January 4, 2017).

There the absence of strong political will to provide a policy framework for early childhood education and care has left Canada without an effective system. Where public policy leads to public investment in private education, the result will, inevitably, be inequities. What is striking about the Finnish educational success story is that the country turned around its education performance by creating a system that aimed for equitable outcomes, as well as creating a knowledge-based economy through a cooperative system. A senior Finnish policymaker (Sahlberg, 2015) notes that the aim of the reforms was to build "good, publicly financed and locally governed" schools for every child. The reforms also rested on developing respectful and inspiring working conditions for principals and teachers, and giving them power to control curriculum, student assessment, school improvement, and community involvement. He commented that "cultivating trust, enhancing autonomy and tolerating diversity" were crucial to the Finnish reforms and that education is seen as a public good that makes a strong contribution to nation building. By contrast, the United States (which is in the middle of OECD rankings) has a highly competitive system, with extensive testing of students, and private schools with fees of up to $35,000 per annum (Partenan, 2011). Finland also offers all students free school meals, easy access to comprehensive health care, psychological counseling, and individualized student guidance. In addition, the country also offers generous parental leave and has very low levels of child poverty. Sahlberg notes that Finland has hardly any private schools, so all children are educated in the same system. While many would dismiss the Finnish example as having lessons only applicable to Nordic countries, it demonstrates very convincingly that an overall supportive nationwide political and economic context is vital to equitable educational outcomes. This point is further supported by the experience of Denmark, Finland, Norway, and Sweden of reporting high levels of life satisfaction regardless of educational attainment levels, and their inclusive social policies that result in lower earning advantages from higher education (OECD, 2016a).

Public funding can also be used to provide extra support for schools in areas of disadvantage—proportionate universalism. Such investments will help prevent the downward drift in school performance for children from low socioeconomic sectors that is illustrated in Figure 6.1. The countries that do well in producing high learning outcomes over time regardless of students' socioeconomic status are Finland, Canada, Japan, and Korea (OECD, 2016). A summary of the features of such systems that encourage both quality and equity are given in Box 6.3, drawn

---

BOX 6.3

Features of Education Systems That Encourage Quality and Equity

Publicly funded and provided system (versus public support for private and high percentage of students in private system)

Progressive universalism to gain equity of outcome (versus parent 'choice' of public or private school)

Local control (versus centralized)

Whole child focus (rather than solely on literacy and numeracy)

Local trust-based assessment of student progress—(versus imposed national testing and league tables)

Professionalism (versus accountability)

Collegiality (versus focus on individual teachers)

Pedagogy (versus technology)

Systems thinking (versus fragmented strategies).

Sources: Drawn from Fullan (2010); Hargreaves and Shirley (2012); Sahlberg (2015).

---

from three different reflections on educational reform. It is noteworthy that the factors in this box are also those that are compatible with good health outcomes, including public trust-based systems that give local control and holistic approaches.

Beyond funding issues, the constituents of healthy educational policy at each stage of the life course are discussed in the following.

Early Childhood Development

Emerging evidence on neuroscience is strengthening the evidence for the importance of early childhood education. Mapping of brain structures suggests that socioeconomic environments affect brain development (Brito and Noble, 2014). As with other inequities, there is a gradient of how well children flourish that largely follows the economic circumstances of families. Systematic interventions early in children's lives is vital to health equity and has been recommended in successive reviews (Commission on the Social Determinants of Health, 2008; Marmot et al., 2010; Marmot Allen et al., 2012). The reduction of poverty and health inequities will require the fostering of environments for babies and children that are stimulating, supportive, and nurturing. Such environments will benefit children regardless of geography, ethnicity, language, or societal circumstances. Evidence from the Early Childhood Knowledge network of the Commission on Social Determinants of Health indicates that what children experience during the early years sets a critical foundation for their entire life course and will influence their learning ability, school success, economic participation, social citizenry, and health (Irwin et al., 2007). Poverty expresses itself through family, neighborhood, and community life, as well as through the broader political and social structures that shape poor people's lives (Maggi et al., 2005).

Early learning has a huge impact on language and numerical ability. This impact is lifelong, affecting people's job prospects and earning potential and thus contributing to breaking down intergenerational poverty cycles. Mental stimulation in the early years is vital for children's cognitive, social, and emotional development. It enhances children's ability to benefit from formal education later on. Moore et al. (2014), on the basis of a review of evidence on child development, note that learning and development are cumulative, so that skills acquired early form the basis for later skill development. They note (2014: 19) that "skills children possess when they get to school contribute to a chain of effects that either reinforces and amplifies their initial skills and dispositions, or exacerbates initial difficulties and even produces new ones." This shows clearly how inequities start from before birth and continue through childhood, with some children accumulating disadvantage unless there is planned public intervention. Examples of such intervention are provided in the following.

Quality early childhood education is one of the best social and economic investments possible and is shown to produce a great return on investment (Kalil et al., 2012). A US presidential report calculated that for every $1 invested in early learning initiatives, $8 were returned. Numerous systematic reviews and meta-analyses have also demonstrated that high-quality early childhood education and care (ECEC) programs are especially beneficial for children from disadvantaged backgrounds (Moore et al., 2014). Friendly (2016) defines high-quality ECEC programs as having the following characteristics:

- They employ staff who are well educated for their work and have decent working conditions and wages;
- They organize children into groups of manageable size with adequate numbers of adults;

- They provide challenging, non-didactic, play-based, creative, enjoyable activities;
- They ensure consistent adult and peer groups in well-designed physical environments.

There is overwhelming evidence that the positive effects of ECEC programs occur only if they are high quality and that, indeed, poor-quality programs may have a negative effect, especially for children from low-resourced families. Thus, it is the quality of ECEC programs that is critical in determining how developmentally effective they are, not merely whether children participate in them (Shonkoff and Phillips, 2000).

Educational interventions in early childhood will be aided by policies in other sectors. Mercer et al. (2013: 110) stress that "through child and family friendly policies, governments must assist families to fulfil their obligations to their children" by making available time (e.g., adequate paid parenting leave), resources (adequate income assistance), and services (child care and education). Mechanisms to promote early learning include home visiting programs, community playgroups, and center-based programs (such as nurseries or preschools).

Education initiatives need to be part of an intersectoral approach to early childhood development.

Early Childhood Development Education—A Public
Responsibility: Inclusive, Universal, and Multisectoral

Many different policies are in place around the world, ranging from those that provide no early childhood education to the Nordic model, which provides the most comprehensive. In Sweden, for example, early learning and care programs (attended by 80%–90% of preschool-aged children), which are funded and monitored nationally and organized and delivered locally, are run by university-educated staff and are based on a gradual transition from play-based to formal learning (Mercer, 2013: 110). South Africa has recently adopted an impressive policy framework for early childhood development based on an intersectoral approach (Box 6.4).

The South Africa policy demonstrates a public policy approach in which the state is assuming responsibility for the quality of early childhood experiences and not leaving that to parents, thus making the issue one of public rather than only private concern. Such an approach is vital to ensuring that all children have an equitable chance to benefit from

---

BOX 6.4

South African National Integrated Early Childhood Development Policy (Adopted 2015)

This policy aims to result in the best possible start in life for all children and contribute to the long term prosperity of our country. In short, the policy provides:

- An overarching multi-sectoral enabling framework of early childhood development services, inclusive of national, provincial, and local spheres of government;
- A comprehensive package of early childhood development services and support, with identified essential components;
- Identifying the relevant role players, their roles and responsibilities for the provision of the various components of early childhood development services; and
- Leadership, coordination and collaboration in the delivery of early childhood development services.

The policy embeds its early learning programs within a cross-sectoral strategy. It states that all early learning programs should be designed around two objectives:

1. To promote the resourcefulness of children
2. To promote language and cognitive development.

The policy stresses the importance of early learning environments and commits to the provision of "[e]arly learning support and services from birth in the home, community and in centres." (Republic of South Africa, 2015: 55) The strategies it proposes to do this weave early learning through home visiting and health facility based programs, childminding, community early learning groups for 0–3 year olds, early learning and development programs for 3–4 year olds which encourage emotional and social development and preparation for schooling through play based learning noting that "[p]lay is the principal means by which children learn and explore the world around them, while developing cognitively, socially, emotionally, creatively and physically Republic of South Africa, 2015: 50."

(Continued)

BOX 6.4 (Continued)

The policy also stresses the importance of inclusive policies that meet the needs of all children including those with disabilities and/or living in poverty or are incarcerated with their mothers.

The policy is being implemented by National Inter-Ministerial Committee on Early Childhood Development with an inter-departmental committee to offer support. Also the South African Inter-Sectoral Forum for ECD will be formed to serve as a national platform for engagement between the Government and the non-governmental sector involved in ECD service.

Source: Republic of South Africa (2015).

education. A key challenge for public policy is to ensure that the quality of early childhood education is of the same standard in all communities (Moore et al., 2014). Unless this quality standard is achieved, then uneven quality of the education may actually increase inequities.

School Systems: Beacons of Hope or "Prison-Houses of the Mind"?

Compulsory school attendance is arguably one of the most powerful public health interventions that can be made. Yet this measure will not automatically contribute to health equity. In developed countries it has long been recognized that schools can be a central mechanism in maintaining, justifying, and reproducing structural inequalities. Unwin and Yandell (2016: 14–15) suggest that the following reflective questions be asked about schools in education debates:

> What is the purpose or function of schools? Whose interests do they serve? How are resources allocated? Is education a route to empowerment and liberation, or is it a means of control? Are schools engines of social mobility or social justice, or merely tools that reproduce the inequalities of existing social and economic structures? Are schools beacons of hope, or prison-houses of the mind? What is the relationship between the formal education that is accomplished through schooling and the learning that happens in homes, communities and workplaces?

While education reflects the culture and context in which it is developed and implemented, there is an accelerating global trend that seeks to promote education as a commodity, with measureable outcomes for all settings. For-profit companies are moving into low-income countries and offering low-fee private schools. This expansion of private education depends on the use of tests of literacy and numeracy and claims that the private sector can outperform public schools, despite the limited evidence base (Day et al., 2014) and the problem of accounting for the socioeconomic background of students whose parents can afford private education. Market-driven systems also encourage competition between students, rather than cooperation. It has long been noted that schools can serve to encourage obedience to an unfair system, rather than inspiring students to work for social change to bring about fairer and more equitable societies (Friere, 1972; Willis, 1977). Healthy societies require citizens who will campaign and argue for the common and public goods. Factors that keep children, especially girls, out of school are social, and include family illness and the need for children to be caregivers, family violence, poverty, and the expectation that children will be economically productive members of the family as soon as possible.

The provision of school is only part of the action that governments need to take. They also need to be reflective about the quality of school education. The quality of schooling is important. For instance, Sammons et al. (2013) found that an academically effective primary school can lessen the extent to which cognitive abilities during the initial years of primary school (e.g., reading, writing) predict later cognitive abilities during the latter years of primary school. Schools also need to be inclusive of students from different cultural backgrounds, with various first languages and a range of sexualities.

OECD (2016a) reports that the quality of teachers is more crucial to quality education than the size of classes. Finland's success in education is attributed to its success in improving the quality of teachers and of the standing of teachers in society.

The answers to the questions posed by Unwin and Yandell (2016) will provide a guide to the extent to which a school system is likely to contribute to health equity and the health and well-being of a population. The Healthy Schools movement appears to have embraced this concept; it envisions schools that can become health promoting not just by providing formal education (including numeracy and literacy), but also through the ways in which the school relates to its community, as well as the relationships within the school.

Schools as Healthy Settings

Schools are central to the lives of children aged 5–18 (age range depending on country) and thus can play a direct role in promoting health by becoming a healthy setting. A healthy school environment can contribute to a strong sense of self, can help resolve gender identity issues, and can promote the development of self-esteem. The development of such an environment is shown in a Canadian comprehensive school health initiative that supports improvements in students' educational outcomes while addressing school health in a planned, integrated, and holistic way through the entire organization and practice. The approach is implemented through a formal partnership between education and health ministries (see Box 6.5).

The impressive features of the Canadian program are that it is part of a national program and covers the school within its community, aims to make the organization as a whole health promoting, and pays attention to the quality of relationships within the school. A further criteria for a healthy schools approach should be that it seeks to bring about equity between schools. A possible pitfall of a settings approach is that schools in affluent areas will have the resources to mount a more effective healthy schools initiative than those in lower socioeconomic areas, where the human, social, and cultural capitals of the school and its community are likely to be lower; thus compensatory measures are required.

Tertiary Education

Postsecondary education is increasingly important, as an increasing amount of employment requires higher education qualifications. In most OECD countries, the percentage of people with post-secondary education has increased dramatically. In 2016 the OECD average showed that whereas 26.5% of 55–64-year-olds had tertiary education, this increased to 43.1% among 25–35-year-olds (OECD, 2017b). People who experience the worst health also are less likely to engage in postsecondary education. The policy challenge is to ensure equitable access to this education. One crucial issue is who pays for higher education. Countries vary considerably in what students have to pay. In Anglo-Saxon countries, higher education is increasingly subject to market forces and rising fees (see, e.g., in the United States, Sellingo, 2016). This has resulted in many students being crippled with student debts, with the consequent health effects. Other

---

BOX 6.5

Healthy Schools Initiatives: Comprehensive School Health Initiative

This initiative seeks to implement a health-promoting environment in all aspects of a school's operation. The approach has been developed in Canada through the Pan-Canadian Joint Consortium on School Health (JCSH), which is a partnership of 25 Canadian Ministries of Health and Education designed to promote a Comprehensive School Health approach to student wellness/well-being and achievement/success for all children and youth.

It is based on four pillars:

Relationships and Environments: which concerns (a) the social environment, such as the quality of relationships and emotional well-being, and (b) the physical spaces in the school, such as buildings, equipment, and outdoor areas.

Teaching and Learning: making available teaching and learning opportunities, both inside the classroom and out, that help to build knowledge and skills to improve health and well-being.

Community Partnerships: between the school and the community, including parents, other schools, community organizations, and health professionals. This pillar can also refer to partnerships within the school, such as between-class partnerships.

School Policies: This pillar refers to provincial, district, school, or classroom policies, rules, procedures, and/or codes of conduct at all levels that help to shape a caring and safe school environment and promote student health and well-being.

Source: Healthy Schools BC, http://www.healthyschoolsbc.ca/ and the Pan-Canadian Joint Consortium on School Health www.jcsh-cces.ca/.

---

countries have seen higher education as a means of investing in citizens and so have made higher education free. In some European countries, including Germany, Sweden, Finland, and Italy, university education is free. In the past it also was free in the United Kingdom and Australia; the dominance of neoliberalism on public policy in those countries has seen fees introduced, but at least along with a public loan system that only requires repayment when an individual's salary exceeds a certain amount.

Universities are a double-edged sword when it comes to health equity. On the one hand, universities have been associated with the reproduction of privilege. They have served to educate primarily middle- and upper-class people in rich countries and to introduce them to well-paying professions, including law and medicine. On the other hand, universities have contributed to social mobility when they are opened up to a broader group of people who then are able to gain the education that leads to improved employment prospects and the life skills that a university education also provides. Social mobility doesn't, however, necessarily follow in the wake of an expansion of those who are able to attend university.

Lifelong Learning

Why should society feel responsible only for the education of children, and not for the education of all adults of every age?
—Erich Fromm, 1955: 346

The health benefits of lifelong learning have been documented. For instance, one study (Hammond, 2007), based on 145 detailed biographical interviews, concluded that lifelong learning affected a number of health outcomes, detailed as well-being, protection and recovery from mental illness, and the capacity to cope with potentially stress-inducing circumstances, including the onset and progression of chronic illness and disability. These effects were mediated by relatively immediate impacts of learning on the following psychosocial qualities: self-esteem, self-efficacy, a sense of purpose and hope, competences, and social integration.

Lifelong learning beneficial to health should be about more than workforce skills; it also should include skills that encourage people to live a better life and that encourage reflection. One example is parenting education, which has been shown to lead to significant improvements in parent mental health, confidence and stress levels, parenting skills, child behavior problems, and children's emotional adjustment (Barlow et al., 2006; Piquero et al., 2008; Furlong & McGilloway, 2012). In Australia a population-wide trial of the Triple P parenting program, including media and primary health-care intervention, led to a significant reduction in the number of children with clinically elevated and borderline behavioral and emotional problems, and reduced parent depression, stress, and coercive parenting within a community facing multiple disadvantage (Sanders et al., 2008).

Learning to question the status quo will be vital in an era when a market-dominated view of the world has come to dominate so much of discourse and ways of viewing the world. Education is also a way of introducing alternative worldviews. A prime example is indigenous knowledge, which stresses a "strong sense of unity with the environment" (Durie, 2005: 303) and emphasizes a holistic ecological worldview. Such a view is a counterbalance and challenge to the dominance of the positivist scientific perspective on reality.

Paulo Friere's approach to adult education is about enabling people without power to analyze their situation in order to understand the nature of the hegemonic ideas and so be in a position to strive to transform the existing state of affairs (Mayo and Craig, 1995). Radical ideas in lifelong learning can offer ways of overcoming repressive regimes and colonial mindsets, and have been used in situations of struggle by helping people understand the reasons why they live under repression (Smith, 2000). Lifelong learning can also encourage people to lead an examined life (as recommended by Socrates) and to contemplate questions such as the following, which are considered vital to well-being: What is the meaning of life? How can I best face the inevitability of death? What does a good life consist of? An example of an educational institution offering such opportunities is the Haven Institute, British Columbia, Canada (www.haven.ca).

The policy question is how lifelong learning can be best fostered and made available to people equitably; community houses, NGOs such as the University of the Third Age, and workplace training and development are all important mechanisms by which to accomplish this.

Conclusion

Education is a vital social determinant of health. Ensuring access to high-quality and free education represents a major investment in people's health. The investment is likely to bear fruit in reduced demand for hospitals, prisons, and welfare. It will also enable people to lead more productive, satisfying, and happy lives, as education brings with it economic, cultural, and social benefits. It also enables people to have more control over their life and health.

7

Urban Planning

VITAL FOR HEALTHY CITIES AND COMMUNITIES

Healthy Urban Planning means planning for people. It promotes the idea that a city is much more than buildings, streets and open spaces but a living, breathing organism, the health of which is closely linked to that of its citizens.

—BARTON AND TSOUROU (2001: PREFACE)

Introduction

Urban planning is vital to quality of life in the twenty-first century, which is the first urban century. In 2007, for the first time, a majority of human beings lived in urban areas (Starke, 2007); in 2017 there were 4.028 billion urban residents (World Bank, 2018), and this number is expected to rise to 6.3 billion by 2050. Ensuring that these urban residents live in healthy environments will require seeing urban planning as a form of preventive medicine (Corburn, 2015). The social, physical, and environmental qualities of urban environments are a vital determinant of health. In recognition of this, the United Nations' Sustainable Development Goals (SDGs) have an overarching goal to "make cities and human settlements inclusive, safe, resilient and sustainable" (SDG 11 https://sustainabledevelopment.un.org/sdg11). The SDGs also emphasize the "capacity for participatory, integrated and sustainable human settlement planning and management in all countries." (SDG Target 11.3 https://sustainabledevelopment.un.org/sdg11). The United Nations' adoption of a "New Urban Agenda" at the Habitat III conference in Quito, Ecuador (United Nations, 2016a), has the intention of making the relevance of the SDGs to urban development explicit and is further evidence of international commitment to healthy and sustainable urban planning. The New Urban Agenda provides a 20-year road map to guide urban sustainable development globally. It stresses the importance of low carbon development, urban resilience, and the development of in-clusive public spaces.

This chapter explains why urban planning is vital to health, discusses the symbiotic relationship between urban planning and public health, examines the features of healthy and sustainable urban environments, lays out the governance requirements for healthy and sustainable urban planning, provides positive examples of healthy urban planning, and details the blocks to conducting such planning.

Why Urban Planning Is Vital to Health

There are direct and indirect pathways through which urban and transport planning and design decisions influence health, well-being, and equity, as shown in Figure 7.1. These pathways are created by policies and practices relating to transportation, open space, housing, and urban design, which in turn shape transport modes and daily living conditions, which then can increase or decrease risk conditions for health and well-being. So, for example, city planning that led to high dependency on privatized trans-portation discourages exercise and in turn contributes to populations with higher average weight and consequently greater susceptibility to a range of chronic diseases (Friel et al., 2011). Stevenson et al. (2016) mod-eled the health impact of making cities more compact and concluded that the benefit would be 420–826 disability adjusted life years (DALYs) per 100,000 population in terms of reduced diabetes, respiratory disease, and cardiovascular disease. Cities designed with sprawling anonymous suburbs encourage social isolation and loneliness and do not easily sup-port vibrant community life, which can have an adverse effect on mental health. Urbanization often disrupts traditional social, community, and family networks, leading to an increase in anomie and loneliness and con-sequent mental illness. There are also very significant health inequities within cities. For example, in many low- and middle-income countries, residents in slum areas have far worse health than those in other urban or rural areas (Friel et al., 2011), and in rich countries, urban areas are characterized by distinctive socioeconomic divides. Urban planning policy decisions are vital in determining how healthy, sustainable, and equitable cities are.

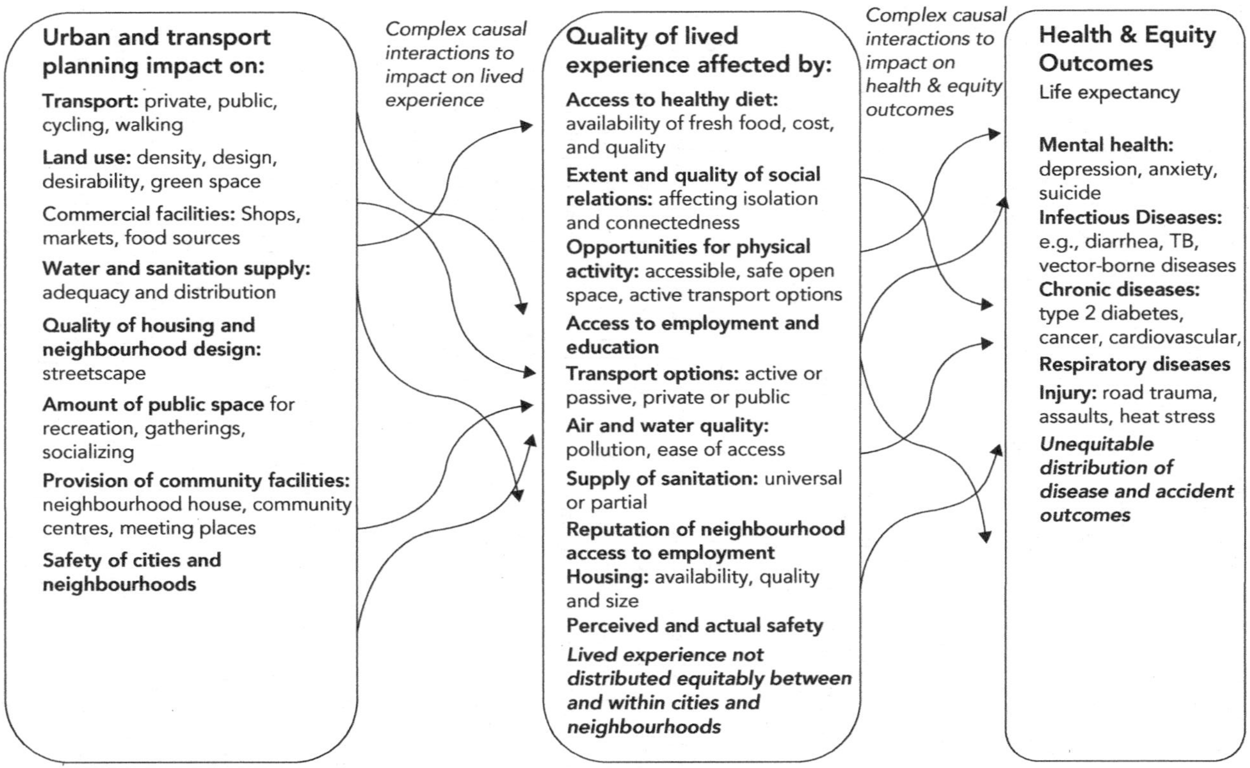

Urban and transport planning impact on:

Transport: private, public, cycling, walking

Land use: density, design, desirability, green space

Commercial facilities: Shops, markets, food sources

Water and sanitation supply: adequacy and distribution

Quality of housing and neighbourhood design: streetscape

Amount of public space for recreation, gatherings, socializing

Provision of community facilities: neighbourhood house, community centres, meeting places

Safety of cities and neighbourhoods

Complex causal interactions to impact on lived experience

Quality of lived experience affected by:

Access to healthy diet: availability of fresh food, cost, and quality

Extent and quality of social relations: affecting isolation and connectedness

Opportunities for physical activity: accessible, safe open space, active transport options

Access to employment and education

Transport options: active or passive, private or public

Air and water quality: pollution, ease of access

Supply of sanitation: universal or partial

Reputation of neighbourhood access to employment

Housing: availability, quality and size

Perceived and actual safety

Lived experience not distributed equitably between and within cities and neighbourhoods

Complex causal interactions to impact on health & equity outcomes

Health & Equity Outcomes

Life expectancy

Mental health: depression, anxiety, suicide

Infectious Diseases: e.g., diarrhea, TB, vector-borne diseases

Chronic diseases: type 2 diabetes, cancer, cardiovascular,

Respiratory diseases

Injury: road trauma, assaults, heat stress

Unequitable distribution of disease and accident outcomes

FIGURE 7.1. The impact of urban planning on health.

Source: Baum

Close Relationship between Urban Planning and Public Health

The nineteenth-century onslaught of industrialization resulted in a close relationship between urban planning and public health as it became clear that the worsening health of the newly urbanized residents in cities like Manchester, England, would only be improved by ensuring that the urban environment was supportive of health. There was particular concern about the working classes whose health suffered so greatly from the poor working and living conditions that in the north of England, in the early, chaotic days of the industrial revolution, life expectancy was as low as 28 (Lewis, 2003). Simon Szreter (1995) describes the way in which in England municipal consciousness increased through the nineteenth century, creating civil society organizations that advocated for policies to clean up cities and make them supportive of human health and well-being. Urban planning developed in response to this consciousness and from its beginnings had roots in the desire to improve health and equity (Corburn, 2009).

In high-income countries, as the death rate from infectious diseases declined and living conditions improved, the link between urban planners and public health weakened. More recently, chronic disease (including cancer, heart disease, diabetes, asthma, and depression) and risk factors for chronic disease, especially obesity, reached epidemic proportions (Rydin et al., 2012) affecting ". . . people of all ages, nationalities and classes" (Daar et al., 2007: 494). Evidence has accumulated that individual behavior change is not very effective in changing people's lifestyles (Baum and Fisher, 2014) and that the environments in which they live have powerful influence on behavior (Jackson et al., 2013). Urban planners once again increasingly appreciate that their work planning, building, and managing urban areas has a profound impact on human health (Kent and Thompson, 2014), reviving the close relationship that public health and urban planning had in the nineteenth century. Public health actors now equally recognize the need to influence land-use policy in order to achieve better population health outcomes (Corburn, 2015; Giles-Corti et al., 2016; Harris et al., 2016). The Commission on the Social Determinants of Health included a chapter on "Healthy Places—Healthy People," which recommended placing "health and health equity at the heart of urban governance and planning" (Commission on the Social Determinants of Health, 2008: 4). The WHO Healthy Cities program has played an important part in the revival of the urban planning –public health relationship, especially in

Europe, where the 66 cities involved have placed a focus on healthy urban planning, recognizing its importance to health. Globally, urban areas are stressed because of relentless population growth, economic development, and the pressing need to mitigate and prevent climate change. Urban planning has the capacity to integrate health considerations into policy and practice and encourage all sectors in cities to work together to improve health, well-being, and quality of life.

What Are the Characteristics of a Healthy Urban Environment?

There are some generic qualities of healthy and equitable urban environments that are common across time and space (see Box 7.1).

Urban planning is vital to ensuring that urban environments are planned in accordance with the qualities in Box 7.1, as planning is central to the ways in which land and buildings are used and developed in cities. Urban environments can be shaped through various planning and

---

BOX 7.1

Generic Qualities of a Healthy Urban Environment

Urban sprawl contained

High-quality infrastructures for solid and other waste disposal and access to utilities (water, power, Internet)

Urban form encourages public transportation, walking, and cycling (rather than privatized motorized options) and "tames the car"

Environmentally sustainable built environment

Mixed-used neighborhoods

People-friendly streets and convivial urban spaces that encourage social connectedness

Green spaces including urban farms, parks, community gardens

Equitable outcomes considered as part of city design

Democratic governance of the city, which limits the influence of capital on development decisions

Opportunity for democratic debate about the development of the city form.

Sources: Multiple sources, including SDGs (United Nations, 2017b), UN New Urban Agenda (United Nations, 2016a); NSW Department of Health (2009); Harvey (2012); Baum (2016).

design processes: urban planning (integrated citywide planning/spatial planning/land use management); urban design/landscape architecture (design of public spaces); civil engineering (planning and design of infrastructure, e.g., roads and sanitation); architecture (building design); transport planning and governance (Smit et al., 2011). Together, these activities will determine whether urban planning results in healthy, sustainable, and equitable outcomes.

Healthy Urban Planning

Creating healthy cities and towns is a major task for those responsible for urban and transport planning. Globally, the context for such planning varies immensely. In most low- and middle-income countries, cities are expanding, often uncontrollably, like many Indian and Chinese cities, or Bangkok, Manila, Dhaka, and Jakarta. In rich countries, experiences differ, ranging from global cities like London, New York, Vancouver, Paris, and Sydney, which are expanding and struggling to cope with the growth and skyrocketing land prices, to cities and towns that are experiencing deindustrialization with static or declining populations, like Detroit, Adelaide, and areas in the north of England. Urban living experiences range from living in high-end areas, such as the Upper East Side of New York or Notting Hill in London, to living in an informal slum settlement on the edge of a mega-city like Manila or Delhi, lacking basic water and sanitation infrastructures. While the challenges faced in establishing healthy cities with the qualities listed in Box 7.1 are different, many of the considerations are the same. Urban planning can contribute through ecosystems, and built, economic, and social environments (Figure 7.2). Each of these interact in a dynamic system to determine how healthy, equitable and ecologically sustainable urban areas are.

Four factors are crucial to realize urban planning's role in creating healthy and sustainable cities (Figure 7.2):

- Establishing models of healthy governance
- Making urban areas ecologically sustainable and adaptable to climate change
- Creating equitable cities that meet people's social needs
- Juggling the complexities of urban planning.

These issues are examined in the following.

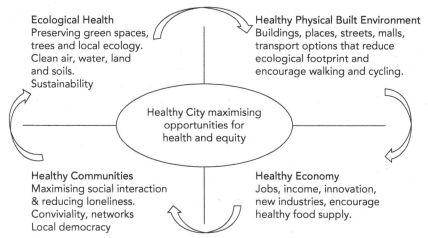

Ecological Health
Preserving green spaces,
trees and local ecology.
Clean air, water, land
and soils.
Sustainability

Healthy Physical Built Environment
Buildings, places, streets, malls,
transport options that reduce
ecological footprint and
encourage walking and cycling.

Healthy City maximising
opportunities for
health and equity

Healthy Communities
Maximising social interaction
& reducing loneliness.
Conviviality, networks
Local democracy

Healthy Economy
Jobs, income, innovation,
new industries, encourage
healthy food supply.

FIGURE 7.2. Urban planning's role in creating healthy and sustainable cities.
Source: Baum

Governance for Healthy, Equitable, and Sustainable Urban Spaces

Governance of cities is shaped by laws, institutional practices and policies, and a myriad of government, nongovernment, private-sector, and citizen actors. Urban planning is almost always devolved to regional and/or city authorities but is conducted in a context that reflects national policies and politics. How cities are governed is particularly vital to determining how equitable they are. Understanding governance in cities requires appreciation of power distribution and power relations and a knowledge of the historical, social, and economic factors that have shaped social relations in specific local, national, regional, and global settings (Barten et al., 2011). Sainsbury (2013) argues that there is an ethical mandate for urban planners and other actors to construct the urban environment in a way that promotes health and that they should be trained how to do so. The examples of good governance provided here demonstrate the ways in which governments and municipal authorities are able to intervene in the public good to create healthy urban environments. The blocks to implementing good governance are considered in the final section of the chapter.

Making Healthy Urban Planning the Law

Laws are an effective means of influencing planning in cities. Burris et al. (2010) see that they are the pathways along which broader social determinants can have an effect on the health of entire populations.

Legislation affecting cities comes from public health and urban planning. In Australia, two states—Tasmania and South Australia—have enshrined the consideration of health in planning legislation. The South Australian Integrated Planning, Development and Infrastructure Act (Government of South Australia, 2016: 29) states that "neighbourhoods and regions should be planned, designed and developed to support active and healthy lifestyles and to cater for a diverse range of cultural and social activities." While such a statement is a long way from a defined plan to achieve this goal, the vision it provides is important in guiding the work of urban planners. Gaining this kind of acceptance in legislation has not proved to be easy. In Sydney, New South Wales, a group of public health activists have worked over many years to argue the importance of making health goals a standard part of urban planning, yet despite some progress, they have not achieved this goal (Kent et al., 2017). Legislation that is more specific is also important. For instance, Boulder, Colorado, now known for being a healthy city, was the first city in the United States to enact an open space ordinance that taxed city residents so that the city government could purchase thousands of acres of land around the city that would be exempt from development (Jackson and Sinclair, 2011). This led to the development of cycling and walking trails that encourage people to be physically active.

Public health legislation can also be helpful if it has a broad mandate requiring governments to plan for healthy urban environments (Reynolds, 2011). Norway, Quebec province in Canada, and South Australia are examples of jurisdictions that have adopted progressive public health legislation updated from a focus on infectious disease to also mandate consideration of how social, urban, and natural environments can contribute to reducing noncommunicable disease, including diabetes, cardiovascular disease, and mental illness.

Participatory Planning

Participatory planning can democratise governance in all settings. The importance of participatory planning to improving living conditions in the rapidly growing cities in low- and middle-income countries has been well recognized by the United Nations. Goal 11 of the SDGs is to "[m]ake cities inclusive, safe, resilient and sustainable." (SDG 11 https:// sustainabledevelopment.un.org/sdg11). People living in slums worldwide number 828 million, and their number keeps rising. Experiments to improve slums through participatory processes are happening in many settings. Such an exercise took place in three slums in Kenya (Majale, 2008). The processes used were combined with local economic development so that community members (with special efforts to involve women and young people) were involved in upgrading the slum infrastructure in a way that created jobs for local people, and involved capacity building and income generation, and thus the initiative was empowering in several ways.

Good planning processes should be open to input from resident action groups, which are able to bring local knowledge to planning processes and offer some counterweight to the power of capital and developers. Citizens may be concerned about the impact of new developments on their existing environment (the Not in My Backyard [NIMBY] syndrome) or may wish to object to a development on ecological sustainability grounds. So, for example, in Sydney communities objected to the building of a new freeway because they believed public transportation would be better for the environment (Harris et al., 2017). The risk of token participatory processes are considered later in the chapter.

Healthy Cities and Health in All Policies

There a number of initiatives that have evolved with the intention of improving urban governance for health.

The Healthy Cities movement has been an initiative of WHO for over three decades (Tsourou, 2015; Baum, 2016) and there are thousands of cities worldwide that participate. From the outset, Healthy Cities has stressed the vital importance of linking urban planning to health goals, and many city projects emphasize this role (Barton and Tsouros, 2013). A review of the European Healthy Cities (Barton and Grant, 2013) found that the initiatives had certainly increased awareness, and in some cases, planning practice, but that the power of market forces in cities made healthy planning difficult.

A further initiative has been Health in All Policies, which was introduced by the European Union and WHO (2015b). In South Australia this initiative has been used to influence the agenda of urban planning and, for instance, encourage transport-oriented developments that take health considerations, such as healthy food choices and walkability, into account (Baum et al., 2017). In Nambia a HiAP framework is being used to bring health considerations into planning for the improvement of slums and to improve transport and road safety (Tibinyane, 2017).

Leadership

Finally, good governance can be much more effective when underpinned by strong leadership working for health, equity, and sustainability. A great example of such leadership is Bill De Blasio (2016: 1), the mayor of New York, who showed a great appreciation of equity when he said, "A person's access to a great park and, by extension, to potential health benefits, should not be determined by his or her zip code." The story of the transformation of Bogata Colombia (see later in the chapter) is also a story of inspirational leadership from two mayors, Mockus and Peñalosa. In London, Mayor Sadiq Khan used urban planning laws to ban fast food outlets within 400 meters of London schools (Crerar, 2017). Also, all new fast food outlets will have to sign up to minimum healthy food standards before getting planning permission. Khan's aim is to stem the tide of childhood obesity.

Leadership can also come from local community leaders who advocate and fight for an environmentally friendly and sustainable environment. While leadership can come from all communities, and Davis (2006) provides examples from low-income slum communities, the voice of middle-class communities is often more easily heard given their greater social and economic power.

Making Urban Areas Ecologically Sustainable and Adaptable to Climate Change

> Failing to provide the necessary infrastructure to decarbonise Australian cities today will place a social, environmental and economic burden upon future generations. . . .
>
> —Matan and Newman (2013: 1)

Cities will only be able to support human health if they use less carbon and become more environmentally sustainable. Achieving this requires changes in urban form and transport planning, which moves away from high carbon transport and toward mass transit, which encourages active transport.

City Form: Density and Sprawl

Many cities, especially in North America and Australia, were designed with sprawling suburbs, perceived in the 1950s and 1960s to be healthy as they moved people away from congested city centers to green and spacious areas (Stretton, 1972). Such low-density suburbs created social and mental health problems (described further later in the chapter) as they can isolate people, especially women. Suburban sprawl, combined with poor public transport, means that many cities suffer from heavy traffic congestion and are high consumers of carbon. Cities, which have much denser concentrations of people, use much less carbon and can create the pathways that lead to improved health (see Figure 7.1). They can also offer a high quality of life, as is shown by Singapore and Hong Kong, which are two of the densest cities in the world but are consistently rated well for livability (The Economist, 2017). Many cities are now focusing on infill developments . Such developments rely on knocking down older houses on large blocks and then replacing them with a number of smaller homes on the same block so increasing density and sustainability. A balance has to be maintained, however, in ensuring that infill development does not result in total reduction of trees and green areas.

A New Paradigm of Transport Planning

Creating sustainable urban areas with a much lower carbon footprint is vital to health and will require transformative change (United Nations, 2016a). These changes will include new styles of housing, increased green space and green commercial activity. Planning for low carbon urban transport systems will, however, be vital to sustainability. Transport planning is moving from an old paradigm that evaluated transport system performance primarily on the basis of private car travel convenience, speed, and affordability to a new paradigm that examines a broader range of impacts and options (Litman, 2013: 218). The new paradigm evaluates transport system performance on the basis of accessibility rather than mobility, and is more supportive of integrated and multimodal planning. The cycle of automotive dependency that the new paradigm seeks to break is shown in Figure 7.3, which demonstrates the ways in which planning dominated by the private car is reinforced by emphasizing provision for private cars (for example, ample parking) and reducing the attractiveness of alternatives by not providing effective public transport or more compact cities.

Sustainable and Healthy Transport Infrastructure

Transforming transportation systems will have a very beneficial impact on human and environmental health. These benefits are shown in Box 7.2.

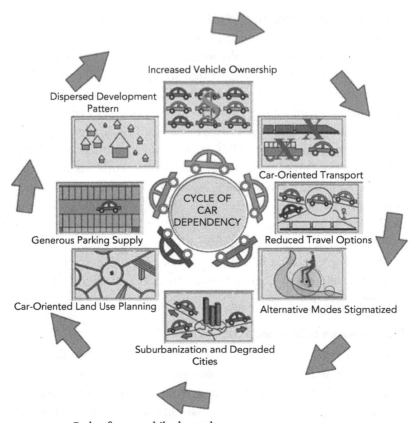

FIGURE 7.3. Cycle of automobile dependency.
Source: Used with permission of West Northamptonshire Joint Planning Unit.

Some city governments are in the lead in promoting sustainable transport. New York City has various programs to encourage environmental sustainability, attract businesses and tourists, and improve population health. It doubled its miles of bike lanes to almost 500 over three years in order to attract more cyclists and to make streets safer. On average, bike lanes reduce injury resulting from crashes for all road users by at least 40% (Sarmiento, 2013). New York has also developed pedestrian plazas to eliminate gridlock, including in Times Square, and express bus service to the outer boroughs, to reduce the number of cars. In Europe the Local Governments for Sustainability movement (see http://iclei-europe.org/home/, accessed Jan 9, 2018) is promoting multiple ways of making mobility more sustainable, including taxing private transport and promoting pedestrian and bike-friendly urban areas.

BOX 7.2

Human Health and Environmental Benefits in Cities That Plan for Fewer Cars

- Improved public transportation, available and affordable for all citizens, will be more equitable
- Less atmospheric pollution
- Contributes to low carbon futures
- Quieter cities with reduced traffic noise
- More relaxed because less congestion
- Safer cities because less motor vehicle accidents
- Encourages more active forms of transportation, like walking and cycling, which have direct mental and physical health benefits
- Improves mental health because less traffic encourages social contact, chance encounters, and people-friendly spaces, and use of public transportation encourages social contact.

Zurich, Switzerland, one of the world's richest cities, has one of the best public transportation systems (World Wildlife Fund, 2016). In 2010, Zurich's population covered some 60% of its transport needs by train, tram, trolleybus, bus, and bicycle, or on foot. An estimated 44% of Zurich residents travel to work by public transport (World Wildlife Fund, 2016). The public transportation system was planned and implemented with extensive public consultation. Zurich citizens also voted for restrictions on cars, rejecting plans to build more car parks in the city center. Over the last 20 years, the city has seen a significant reduction in greenhouse gas emissions, falling from around 6.6 tons per person in 1990 to around 5.5 tons per person in 2010.

Bursa is the fourth largest city in Turkey with a population of 2.4 million. The city has a historic center and has grown by twentyfold in the last 50 years. The urban planning challenge was to protect the historic city center and also create urban environments that would contribute to a healthier population while reducing the pressures brought by an expanding population and increasing car usage. Mayor Recep Altepe (2015: 113) noted, "When we design our cities, we need to do it in a way that makes it easier for people to be active. Sports fields, walking trails, bicycle roads, a mass transport system supporting active travel and a city that will be inviting people to go out, to walk and to be active are all in the hands of mayors." The changes in the city include a new tramway and new green spaces that would be attractive for socializing, recreation, and physical activity. One of the main streets in the historic center was closed to cars, creating a popular recreational area where people walk, shop, eat, and meet friends (Fidan and Yilmaz, 2015). The transformation of the street is shown in Figures 7.4.

Perth in Western Australia has invested $2 billion in a 280-kilometer modern electric rail system with 72 stations, a strategy designed to reduce oil dependency (Newman, 2006). Singapore, where traffic control is strict, has given rise to innovative ways of offering lower-carbon car ownership, such as car cooperatives.

It is vital for global health (because of global warming and subsequent climate change, pollution levels, and oil depletion) that the growing economies in low- and middle-income countries are given every incentive to build effective public transportation systems and to discourage private car ownership. In countries with historically low car ownership, policy direction is needed to maintain the current low dependency on private transport and encourage the provision of good public transport infrastructure. Encouragingly, China is investing in a network of high-speed trains. Bogotá, Columbia, provides an outstanding example of a low-income city that has transformed its transportation system with the aim of creating a more livable and healthy environment. Three developments underpined Bogotá's achievement:

1. *The Recreational Ciclovía* involved temporarily closing streets to motor-vehicle traffic in order to offer safe and free spaces for recreation and physical activity classes. The measures have increased the amount of physical activity in the city. The measures met with some opposition from local businesses, but the mayor argued that expanding the Ciclovía meant putting the general public's interests ahead of private interests. Since 2007 the Ciclovia has been included in the National Public Health Plan recommendations (Decree 3039) and in the 2009 Law on Obesity (1355) as a strategy to prevent non-communicable disease risk factors (Torres et al., 2013).
2. *CicloRutas* are permanent lanes dedicated to bicycle traffic that are separated from motor-vehicle roads. There are approximately 344

(a)

(b)

FIGURE 7.4 A–B. Street in Bursa, Turkey, before and after traffic calming.
Source: Used with permission of Bursa Metropolitan Municipality.

kilometers of CicloRutas, the most extensive network in Latin America.
These cycle routes are enshrined in law, but assessment indicates that
they could be more effective with some extra planning to encourage
use and increase safety, especially for women at night (deNazelle
et al., 2011).

3. *TransMilenio* is a public–private partnership bus rapid transit system (BRT) with dedicated lanes that operate in ways similar to rail with exclusive stations. In 2011 the BRT carried 463 million passengers, making it the largest rapid bus network in the world. This system developed because of cooperation between urban and transport planners, the creation of a regulatory frame for urban planning that provided new public instruments, strengthened local institutions, transport policy that privileged public transport over car infrastructure, and a political and economic context that supported a dense, transit-oriented city (Bocarejo and Tafur, 2013).

The Bogotá example illustrates the kind of changes required for a new paradigm of transport planning very well.

Walkable Cities

Cities in which walking is attractive are becoming more common. Encouraging people to walk in cities has many health benefits. Walking is beneficial for physical and mental health, it can lead to casual social encounters, and it makes city streets safer (Public Health England, 2017). Walking can be encouraged through interesting and engaging urban design. Public Health England (2017) reviewed the evidence and found that improved street connectivity, mixed land use, and compact residential design are important features of a walkable neighborhood. People are more likely to walk if they live near a river, the sea, green spaces, or interesting destinations. Most major cities in Europe provide examples of attractive areas to walk: the Thames in London, or the Seine in Paris, the Ramblas in Barcelona, Venice's narrow lanes, or Rome's boulevards with layers of history all provide examples of environments that make walking enjoyable. Contrast these examples with freeway-dominated Los Angeles or Dallas, where walking is unattractive and unsafe. In many low-income cities, walkable streets are alive with people selling food, conversing, and walking to destinations such as work and schools. Yet as car ownership in these countries increases, more cities are marginalizing pedestrians in the interests of the cars, and planning systems do not prioritize people's health and well-being. Transit-oriented developments (TODs) (Calthorpe, 1993; Francis et al., 2012) have become common in many cities. The principles of TODs include walkability, with the pedestrian as the highest priority, and a medium-density, high-quality, mixed-use development within a 10-minute walk of public transport, with reduced and managed parking inside the 10-minute walking area (Dannenberg et al., 2011).

Thus there are many ways in which cities are planning to be more ecologically sustainable and adapted to climate change. Much more action will be required in the coming decade to ensure that our cities face sustainable futures. There are also considerable barriers to implementing the positive examples given here. These are considered in the final section of the chapter, but first, the following section considers the needs people have for cities that encourage convivial social lives and activities.

Creating Livable and Equitable Cities That Meet People's Social Needs

Healthy cities need to be livable cities, which provide for people's social, cultural, and economic needs. Through the twentieth century, urban planning in rich countries came to focus on the need to be convivial and socially connected and to provide access to green environments (for example, the British Garden cities of the 1930s), as well as the traditional focus of combatting infectious diseases. By the 1950s and 1960s, especially in North America and Australia, urban planners, in an effort to create green, clean environments, developed sprawling suburbs. These suburbs were car dominated, quite soulless, impersonal, and created an epidemic of loneliness and community disconnection. In the 1950s and 1960s, women especially, many of whom spent their time childrearing without jobs outside the home, could feel marooned in suburbs that offered little social contact or few community facilities to encourage conviviality. While this situation reflected broader social factors that excluded women from the labor force and made the nuclear family the norm for childrearing, the suburban form also contributed to the adverse mental health effects of isolated suburban living. Alexander (1967: 88) said of the suburb, "The house stands alone: a collection of isolated, disconnected islands. There is no communal land and no signs of any functional connection between different houses." Feminist urban planners (Harman, 1988; Fincher, 1990) from the 1970s argued for more convivial planning, with community spaces that encouraged connection. Since then, planners have paid more attention to the social needs of neighborhoods (Frumkin, Frank, and Jackson, 2004) and people prize living in areas that offer local conviviality and opportunities for connection. This means that housing is usually most affordable away from city centers, and so cities have become segregated by socioeconomic status. Low-income people increasingly live further away from the jobs and cultural and social opportunities of city centers. Urban planners then face the challenge of creating cities that provide job opportunities, community facilities, and opportunities for meaningful social interactions that are not dictated by people's postal codes. The challenge is to make all city communities socially sustainable. that Five key measurable aspects of social life contributing to community sustainability are the following: (i) social interaction and networks, (ii) participation in community groups and networks, (iii) community stability, (iv) pride or sense of place, and (v) safety and security (Bramley et al., 2009).

In many countries, "place making" has developed as a mean of achieving these characteristics. Place making is promoted as a process through which people regain control of their streets, participate in civic life, and influence how public spaces look, function, and feel. This process is claimed to result in the creation of urban villages, or TODs (described earlier). In undertaking place making, city planners have to consciously ensure that all socioeconomic areas have access to its benefits. Areas with better off and more educated populations are better placed to lobby for and achieve great places. As a consequence, in terms of the five criteria that support community sustainability, poor areas typically do less well, especially in terms of community stability and safety. Thus urban planners need to mitigate this risk by taking extra steps to ensure that citizens in lower socioeconomic areas are given particular encouragement to participate in local planning. Most important, local government officials also need to commit extra resources to such communities in order to encourage fair urban development that reduces rather than increases the gaps between different socioeconomic areas. Designing equitable cities and towns remains a big challenge for urban planners.

Issues of equity come to the fore in terms of improving lower socioeconomic areas of cities. In the 1960s in British cities there were many slum clearance projects. Old nineteenth-century housing was demolished, and people were moved to new housing units of 20 or more floors. While the new housing was modern and offered better physical conveniences, like indoor toilets, the dislocation of generations of social networks had significant health effects (Young and Willmott, 1957). People were lonely in the new buildings and could no longer rely on their social networks. Similar dislocation is evident in contemporary low-income cities. Slums are people's homes, and they invest effort in fixing up their shelter and creating supportive social networks. Yet frequently the policy response is to turn a slum area over to developers who displace people, clear it, and then build housing to be sold for profit (Davis, 2006). While the urban area is improved, the slum dwellers are left homeless, lose their social networks and proximity to employment, and are forced to move further out of the city. A better option may be to opt for upgrading the existing slum area in a way that is people-friendly and is likely to result in health improvement. Measures that can be taken to meet social, economic, and physical safety needs include (Davis, 2006; Majale, 2008) the following:

- regularizing security of tenure;
- installing or improving basic infrastructure (e.g., water supply, sanitation; waste collection, storm drainage);
- roads and footpaths, security lighting, and electricity;
- home improvement;
- removal or mitigation of environmental hazards;
- constructing or rehabilitating community facilities such as health clinics, nurseries and schools, community centers;
- open space;
- providing incentives for community management and maintenance;
- enhancement of income-earning opportunities through training and micro-credit;
- building social capital and the institutional framework to sustain improvements; and
- relocation/compensation for those displaced by the upgrading interventions.

Juggling Complexity

So far in this chapter we have seen the extent to which the quality of people's lives reflects the physical environments in which they live. Promoting health through effective urban planning requires good governance and leadership, a commitment to making cities ecologically sustainable, and creating cities that meet people's social needs for convivial and strong communities. Experience demonstrates that juggling the different requirements for healthy cities is complex. These complexities have been recognized by Rydin et al. (2012: 2102 who note that "[u]rban planning efforts should be based on a complexity approach that recognises multi-directional causality, feedback loops, and unintended consequences." The complexities are not only about the current reality and physical forms of cities. They also reflect the history of cities; as Goodling et al. (2015: 590) note, "the particular urban form and demographic makeup of particular parts of the city are far from historical happenstance; rather, both are shaped by cycles of capital accumulation and devaluation and by the social processes (including policymaking and planning) that mediate them." Cities are the focus of economic investment. Thus many players see cities as places to make money and accumulate capital through the development of the physical form of the city, including housing and transportation infrastructure. These players include local businesses as well as TNCs. Their primary aim is to make profits, not to promote health and well-being. Urban planning is greatly influenced by the activities of developers, and the profit motive often directly threatens the quest to create healthy and sustainable cities (Harvey, 2012). Thus while it has been possible to point to some positive examples of urban planning for health, it is equally important to note that in the complexity of urban planning there are many factors that impede achieving healthy, equitable, and sustainable urban environments, and these are considered next.

What Impedes Achieving Healthy and Sustainable Urban Environments?

Cities are contested ground on which developers seek to maximize profits, often at the expense of urban residents. This is particularly the case in an era in which public–private partnerships dominate and infrastructure projects are frequently seen as profit generating, rather than public good enterprises that put people's health and well-being at the fore.

Profits or People?

Urban planners are charged with the responsibility of ensuring that decisions about urban environments are made with the public interest in mind (Barton, 2016). Yet there are many forces in city development that work against the interests of people and in favor of the interests of capital and those who seek to make a profit from urban development (Harvey, 2012). This has been very evident in cities in the Global South, such as Mumbai, where the rights of slum dwellers to remain on their land over which they only have informal title have been disregarded as the value of urban land has increased and developers have sought to make a profit out of developing the previously undesirable land. In high-income countries, there are numerous examples where the needs of developers are seen to conflict with those of local residents. Matan and Newman (2013) note the inertia stemming from current practices of the high-cost, risk-averse construction, engineering, and development sectors that inhibit the development of more sustainable urban environments. They point to the irony whereby long-term economics necessitate ecologically sustainable urban areas, while short-term economic gain and short-term political cycles impede their development. Out-of-date regulations also discourage sustainable innovations.

Harvey (2012) has written extensively about the role of capital accumulation as a driver for investment in the built environment and infrastructure. He re-examines Marxist political theory and as a result sees the city as a generator of capital accumulation. On this basis, he argues that capitalism increasingly focuses more on profit to be made from land, rent, and speculation, rather than production. Those seeking to develop housing and new neighborhoods contend that, as well as making a profit, they are providing vital services, and in their view, "any delays, requirements, restrictions, and levies are seen as unnecessary limitations imposed by an inefficient, nanny-state bureaucracy" (Sainsbury, 2013: 45). Such varying views mean that the stakes surrounding planning decisions are often very high, and when this is the case, community voices are often drowned out and consultations are token (see Box 7.3).

The Commission on Social Determinants of Health (2008: 63) called for new models of governance to plan cities that "are designed in such a way that the physical, social and natural environments prevent and ameliorate the new urban health risks, ensuring the equitable inclusion of all city dwellers in the processes by which urban policies are formed." This recommendation has rarely been implemented, and urban planning is still usually dominated by the needs of the commercial sector for profit, rather than the quest to make the city as livable as possible. Of course, sometimes the concept of livability may be adopted by a developer when it can be a marketable commodity. In low-income cities, the people living in informal settlements rarely have the chance to shape broader urban-planning agenda. Yet good planning depends on democratic decision-making whereby structures are set in place that give communities a genuine voice against the more powerful interests of developers and others. Participatory processes are hard to implement. An analysis of participatory urban governance in Mumbai indicated that the new processes had helped empower the middle- and upper-middle class to exert their claims on the city and the political space, but that the urban poor have

---

BOX 7.3

The Hitchhiker's Guide to the Galaxy: Token Consultation

Earth was to be demolished, and the Vogons insisted they had consulted with Earthlings, but the hero Arthur Dent questions the value of the participation:

"But the plans were on display. . . ."

"On display? I eventually had to go down to the cellar to find them."

"That's the display department."

"With a flashlight."

"Ah, well, the lights had probably gone."

"So had the stairs."

"But look, you found the notice, didn't you?"

"Yes," said Arthur, "yes I did. It was on display in the bottom of a locked filing cabinet stuck in a disused lavatory with a sign on the door saying 'Beware of the Leopard.'"

Source: Douglas Adams, *The Hitchhiker's Guide to the Galaxy* (1979).

---

not benefited (Zerah, 2009). An analysis of Portland, Oregon, shows that while the core of the city has been made more sustainable, this has been at the expense of the east side, where "planning and policy decisions aggregate to structure serious disparities across race and space" (Goodling et al., 2015: 521). Many African-American residents have been displaced from the city center through processes of gentrification. The authors call for the use of tools such as an equity lens to reduce the risk of uneven urban development. Equity considerations should be central to healthy urban planning, and this will mean political actors being committed to putting people's needs before those of developers seeking profits. If the political commitment is present, then urban planners will be free to plan for health.

Example of Conflicts of Interest: Maintaining Car Domination

One of the greatest challenges of planning cities lies in building cities that are not dominated by cars in an era in which urban planning has been dominated by their needs. The health impacts of car-dominated cities are many, including road trauma, air pollution, mental health impacts of stressful traffic, the dehumanizing impact of freeways on urban form, intensive carbon use, and low physical exercise. Despite such health effects, there are significant pressures on planners to continue to plan for cars. These pressures include those from the automobile industry and construction companies that benefit from large from infrastructure projects.

Public transportation is a much healthier and more inclusive option, as recognized in the SDG transport target (11.2) (United Nations, 2017b), which calls for the achievement of the following by 2030:

> access to safe, affordable, accessible and sustainable transport systems for all, improving road safety, notably by expanding public transport, with special attention to the needs of those in vulnerable situations, women, children, persons with disabilities, and older persons.

Yet, despite this goal, the UN Road Safety Collaboration (coordinated by WHO) is a global public–private partnership with intergovernmental bodies, governments, NGOs, and private-sector entities. Among the latter are a tire and steel manufacturer, the international Motorcycle Manufacturers Association, and the Fédération Internationale de L'Automobile. Thus the United Nations is working closely with the automobile industry, which might explain why the WHO agenda stresses safer roads, safe cars, and safe drivers. This is instead of arguing for better urban planning and public transportation, which could also reduce the burden of disease (including road trauma, physical activity, and air pollution), as well as reducing greenhouse gases (People's Health Movement, 2016). This example of the influence of the automobile industry illustrates the powerful international forces that shape advice relating to health and urban planning. The influence of industry is also evident in national and local government policies, often through lobbying and, in some cases, corruption through bribing local officials. Healthy and sustainable options are often not the profitable options and may threaten vested interests. Strong and participatory public governance that gives voice to and takes seriously citizens' concerns is required to overcome such influence.

Conclusion

Urban planning is vital to creating urban forms that will maximize the opportunities for people to live flourishing lives. Such lives require the protection and support of physical health, the ability to move around the city in a way that supports sustainability, and urban spaces that maximize social contact and interaction. All these considerations need to be applied equitable so that everyone is given the chance to flourish. Good urban and equity is not possible without good urban planning.

8

Creating an Ecologically Sustainable World to Support Environmental and Human Health

Here is your country. Cherish these natural wonders, cherish the natural resources, cherish the history and romance as a sacred heritage, for your children and your children's children. Do not let selfish men or greedy interests skin your country of its beauty, its riches or its romance.

—THEODORE ROOSEVELT

Introduction

Our planet's ecosystem is greatly threatened by human activity. Industrialization has ravaged the natural environment to the point that soon it may no longer support human life. The impact of human activity is now so great that Steffen et al. (2011) label the current era "the Anthropocene" because human activity is influencing earth systems in potentially irreversible ways, and this activity will leave its mark for millennia. Earth scientists have dubbed the period from the 1950s until the present the "Great Acceleration" because of the increasing space and impact of human activity on the planet (Steffen et al., 2015). The threat comes from population growth with high-carbon consumerist lifestyles in rich countries (Crocker, 2017), the overuse of nonrenewable resources, increasing air and water pollution, and the loss of biodiversity. While the details of the changes and the precise nature of the strain on the planet are disputed, there is increasing consensus that business as usual will result in ecological disaster. This chapter explains the impact of environmental threats on human health, considers the urgency for action in a context of disputed politics, argues the need for an ecosystems perspective, and assesses policy action in the areas of global warming (climate change), renewable energy, sustainable food and water, and the need for humans to reconnect to nature and land.

Why Urgent Action Is Needed: Environmental Impacts on Human Health

> Climate change is the defining health issue of the 21st Century. . . .
> A ruined planet cannot sustain human lives in good health.
> —Dr. Margaret Chan (2016a: n.p), director general of WHO

Industrialization has contributed to increasing life expectancies, population growth, and more comfortable material lives for many. Yet alongside this, economic and health inequities between people and nations have grown, and industrialization has greatly disrupted many of the earth's natural systems, including rivers, oceans, and forests. Every corner of the planet is affected by chemical and other forms of pollution that degrade the soils, air, groundwater, and animals, including people. The health threats created by the disruptions to our natural environment are summarized in Table 8.1. Underpinning each of these is a capitalist system that encourages consumerism and endless growth, despite the planet's natural limits to growth. Many countries, especially those that are rich, have developed a throwaway society that is fueled by an aggressive advertising industry (Crocker, 2017). The ecological footprint of countries like the United States, Canada, and Australia is much higher than those of low- and middle-income countries, and the footprint of the richest in these societies is higher still (Global Foot Print Network, 2018). Yet it is low-income countries and poorer people that are most affected by the environmental disasters. They are more likely to live in threatened areas and have fewer resources with which to respond to threats. Environmental impacts in the future will obviously affect younger generations more, raising important policy questions of intergenerational equity. Thus major inequities have been created and are playing out through the various threats detailed in Table 8.1.

Point of No Return?

> The future holds only two possibilities. First ecological destruction; the second, radical, systemic, transformative, epochal change.
> —Weston (2014: 197)

Table 8.1 Major Environmental Threats Faced by Planet Earth
and Health Consequences

Environment Threat	Health Impacts
Carbon pollution, leading to warming of the planet. Modest global warming has occurred since the 1970s and has led to increased severity of weather disasters	*Direct* Direct injury risks and follow-on outbreaks of infectious diseases resulting from extreme weather events Mass displacement and disruption of livelihoods in low-lying coastal areas and small island states due to storm surges and sea level rise Lack of nutrition and mental stress resulting from extreme weather events Excessive heat exposures resulting in heat stroke, which may lead to deaths Heat exhaustion that reduces work productivity and interferes with daily household activities *Indirect* Malnutrition and undernutrition due to failing agriculture, loss of employment, income Spread of vector-borne diseases and other infectious diseases, mental health and other problems caused by forced migration from affected homes and workplaces Changes in access to clean drinking water (particularly in conditions of crowding and poverty) that can cause diarrheal diseases and other water-related diseases, including cholera Mental illness and conflict-prone tensions caused by forced migration from affected homes and workplaces Potentially increased risk of violent conflict associated with resource scarcity and population movements by forced migration from affected homes and workplaces
Human population growth	Competition for resources leading to increased conflicts, food shortages, infections, decline in biodiversity
Air and water pollution	Increase in respiratory, infectious, and diarrheal diseases WHO (2018c) estimated that around 3 million premature deaths were attributable to ambient (outdoor) air pollution in 2012, with about 88% of these occurring in middle- and low-income countries. Further, they say that 92% of the world's population live in places exceeding WHO air quality guidelines.

(*continued*)

Table 8.1   Continued

Environment Threat	Health Impacts
Loss of link to nature and of biodiversity	Mental illness, loss of traditional cultural practices tied to land
	Species extinction affects health directly and indirectly, including through loss of seed diversity and threats to entire ecosystems

Some scientists argue that the point of no return has been reached in terms of environmental damage, especially concerning global warming, or climate change. Most others argue that significant and drastic action is required to protect and restore the environment to a state where it can continue to support human life. Martin Rees (former president of the United Kingdom's Royal Society) sees the problem as so dire that the odds "are no better than fifty-fifty that our present civilisation on Earth will survive to the end of the present century" (Rees, 2003) and Australian writer Clive Hamilton (2010) pessimistically entitles his book on climate change *Requiem for a Species*. Tim Flannery (2005: 209) concludes, "If humans pursue a business-as-usual course for the first half of this century, I believe that collapse of civilisation due to climate change becomes inevitable." *The Lancet* is so concerned about the threat that climate change poses to global health that it has established a website—www.lancetcountdown.org—which is dedicated to tracking progress on climate change. Its 2017 report (Watts et al., 2017) notes that the human impacts of climate change are unequivocal and potentially irreversible, and the delayed response to climate change over the past 25 years has jeopardized human life and livelihoods.

Given these assessments, the main game for policy actors is to ensure that the environmental issues do not lead to the predicted collapse and that issues of equity are considered in policy responses. This is a very tall order—daunting, overwhelming, and requiring urgent action that challenges much of the status quo that has been taken for granted over the last two centuries. The enormity and pressing nature of the problems we face mean that there is no shortage of guidance concerning what needs to be done in technical terms. But disputed politics and the power of those who wish to hang on to the status quo impede the needed action.

Disputed Politics Makes Policy Action Difficult

Major political powers globally do not accept the need for urgent action on many environmental issues. This includes the most pressing—global warming, or climate change—for which the science is disputed by some policy actors. Most significantly, in 2016 the Trump administration in the United States was elected on a climate change denialist platform. The absence of response to what nearly all scientists who have studied the issue see as a crisis is likely because the problem is "invisible, long-term and unfamiliar" (McMichael, 2017: 255). The other dilemma is that action to respond to the many environmental issues faced will require significant changes to the dominant status quo mode of neoliberal economic thinking (see Chapter 5). Making these changes means challenging powerful ideologies, and financial and political interests. This means it is unsurprising that action on most environmental issues, including climate change, faces powerful opposition and concerted action against it. Despite such formidable opposition, there are examples of positive action and promising environmental policies and actions, and it is to those that the rest of the chapter is devoted.

New Perspective Needed: Ecosystems for Health

The concept of Planetary Boundaries has been introduced by Rockstrom et al. (2009), who concluded that three of nine critical boundaries has been already crossed (loss of biodiversity, disruption of the global nitrogen cycle, and global climate change). They concluded that radical change is needed to maintain a safe operating space for humanity, and that this must be done in such a way that low-income countries could achieve material and social development. Given that each of the human-induced changes to the earth systems are not happening in isolation, but affect and are affected by other changes, only a systems view of the problem will enable effective policy responses. The existence of the UN's Sustainable Development Goals (SDGs) demonstrates an approach to policy, which takes a society-wide systems approach, and considers the interaction between different policy areas. These goals are far from perfect and have been criticized for accommodating the dominant neoliberal economic model too much (see summary of critiques in Kenner, 2015). This model encourages capital to exploit natural resources, including fossil fuels, by advocating small government and reducing the state's regulatory capacity for environmental management. The SDGs see poverty as the problem, rather than the growing accumulation of wealth by the top richest 1% who benefit from the free-market neoliberal regime. The SDGs also do not challenge the consumerism that drives market accumulation and contributes to environmental degradation. Despite these critiques, the SDGs *do* provide an overarching global structure for action that can be adapted to low-, middle-, or high-income countries and do view environmental problems within a broader systems approach.

Just as in the other areas of governing for health that we have reviewed, keeping the planet fit for human health will require policy decisions that put environmental considerations above those of economic growth and short-term profit. Such policies appear likely to require a new zeitgeist that privileges nature, environmental protection, biodiversity, and human health (Weston, 2014; McMichael, 2017). Systems thinking, which considers the whole ecosystem, will be vital to bring this about. A transformative change in thinking will be required, as incrementalism appears insufficient to maintain the planet as supportive of human life. Systems thinking will need to be informed by new ways of measuring human progress that value natural capital and offset the environmental "externalities" caused through profit-seeking activities like extractive industries and large-scale agriculture. Various methods have been tried to value ecological and environment services, including Payment for Environmental services (PES), and while they work in some circumstances, their application needs to be done with care (Muradian et al., 2013) so that the trap of the "neoliberalization of nature" (McAfee and Shapiro, 2010) is avoided. A systems view also allows calculation of the co-benefits that stem from environmental action. Thus a study in the United Kingdom to assess the co-benefits from action to meet the legally binding UK carbon budgets assessed them as providing a net present value of more than £85 billion from 2008 to 2030 (Smith et al., 2015). The benefits arose from reduced congestion, pollution, noise, and road accidents as a result of avoided journeys, and health benefits from increased exercise from walking and cycling instead of driving. Co-benefits have also been identified in terms of reduced air pollution by introducing energy efficiency into the cement industry in China (Yang et al., 2013). It is vital to our survival on this planet that a generation of environmental policymakers emerge who do take a systems view and see their task as environmental stewards and guardians of the environment, rather than seeing nature as something to exploit for profit. Their job will be to monitor the changes and convey these to the citizens they serve in such a way as to encourage existing environmental activism and mobilize additional support for the policies needed to avert environmental disaster. The policies required will protect the environment from human activity and ensure that we "transform our environmentally damaging way of living to accord with the limits of the Earth's biocapacity. This will require a transition that is "global, deliberate and rapid" (McMichael, 2017: 270).

A movement toward an ecosystems view of health has started (Hancock, 1993; Dakubo, 2010). Parkes (2010: 2) notes that there has been a shift from seeing "the environment as a 'natural resource' (to be exploited, or as a possible source of 'hazards') to a view of the ecosystem as life source, and a non-negotiable foundation for all life." She notes that this view is entirely compatible with Indigenous knowledges concerning the importance of connection with nature and land. The Great Acceleration in human economic activity, which for the most part is continuing (Steffen et al., 2015), is essentially a capitalist, neoliberal acceleration that privileges profit-making above other factors in the ecosystem and in human health. Changing this will require a significantly different worldview. Such a new worldview is seen in the Latin American movement Buen Vivir, which calls for a new paradigm of relationship with the environment. Buen Vivir stresses the importance of community rather than individuals and aims for ecological balance and cultural sensitivity (Gudynas, 2011; Balch, 2013). Its philosophy is enshrined in the new constitutions adopted by Ecuador and Bolivia.

This sea change to an ecosystem approach to policy is vital to effective governing for health. This change is unlikely to occur without significant pressure from civil society environmental groups. Examples of such advocacy and activism are provided in Chapter 10.

Policy Action on Specific Environmental Issues

Crucial international, national, and city actions on global warming, advances in renewable energy, sustainable food and water, and efforts to maintain and restore connections with nature and land are occurring and are described in the following. These will all be vital to restoring a healthy and sustainable ecosystem.

Global Warming

The UN 2015 Paris Climate Change Conference (COP21) agreed to the goal of limiting warming to 2°C above preindustrial levels and to try to keep them below 1.5°C, thus strongly encouraging low-carbon economies. This requires governments around the world to reduce reliance on fossil fuels; nearly all signed the agreement, and 147 have formally ratified it. A major exception is the United States, which announced in 2017 that it would withdraw from the agreement. McGlade and Ekins (2015) calculate that if an average temperature rise above 2°C is to be avoided, then one-third of oil, half the gas, and 80% of coal reserves need to remain unused. This challenges the economic growth to which most governments aspire and a powerful fossil fuel industry that makes its profit from extraction of those fuels. Renner and Prugh (2014: 36) note that "leaving the bulk of the world's fossil fuel deposits untouched will require quasi-revolutionary change," including regulation, litigation, shareholder activism, dogged divestment, and civil disobedience campaigns. However, some major institutions *are* beginning to divest from fossil fuels. For example, the development of a new coal mine in Queensland, Australia, by the Indian company Adani has met with significant opposition, including a campaign to persuade banks not to invest in the mine. Some governments are increasingly intervening to encourage low-carbon use through taxes, regulation, the introduction of carbon markets, and energy-efficiency standards for industrial equipment, buildings, motor vehicles, and consumer goods. Many cities around the world are committing to reducing carbon emissions and even are aiming to become zero-carbon (see further discussion in Chapter 9). Binding emissions limits are another option, such as the carbon pollution standards for US power plants proposed by President Barack Obama that would have effectively ruled out conventional coal units. In 2015 decarbonization was at the highest level since 2000 at 2.8%. However, to reach the 2°C level, a rate of 6.5% per annum is required (PricewaterhouseCoopers, 2016). Thus, despite some progress, not enough has happened yet to meet the COP21 targets. More efforts to increase the use of renewal non-carbon energy are required, and promising developments are described in the following.

Renewable Energy

To avoid climate disaster, the world needs to rapidly shift from high consumption of fossil fuels to renewable non-carbon energy. If the world does not decarbonize, then a huge social, environmental, and economic burden will be placed on future generations. Massive national, international, and intergenerational inequities of the kind not seen before will create major social tensions. Renewables are now a mainstream solution that makes economic sense and which more governments are promoting through low-carbon policies. China is leading the world in the uptake of most renewables, and the United States is not far behind, although it is likely to fall further behind given the Trump administration's avowed intention to promote coal and reduce investment in renewables.

Overall, renewable energy use has nearly doubled during 2006–2015 (Figure 8.1). Hydro power is the predominant source, followed by wind power.

The Climate Council of Australia (2017) has reviewed the global uptake of solar photovoltaic (PV) power and concluded that it is surging and has continually falling costs. Key facts they noted are as follows:

- A projected 70 GW (gigawatts) of new solar power capacity was added globally in 2016, breaking the 2015 record of 50 GW new capacity. China (34.2 GW), the United States (13 GW), and Japan (10.5 GW) led 2016 growth in new solar PV capacity.

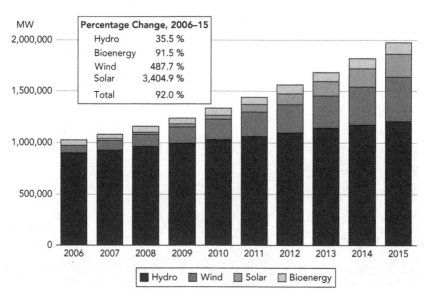

FIGURE 8.1. Global renewable energy: installed capacity by technology (in megawatts, 2006–2015).

Source: Bartlett (2016).

- The solar sector employed 2.8 million people globally in 2016, outnumbering coal jobs. In the United States, solar provided twice as many jobs as coal.
- Solar costs have dropped 58% in five years and are projected to fall by a further 40%–70% by 2040 and large, industrial-scale solar plants provide cheaper power than new fossil and nuclear power.
- Solar will become even more viable with the development of energy-storage technologies such as the Tesla lithium ion batteries (the largest in the world in 2018) being deployed in South Australia (Parkinson, 2017) (see Figure 8.2).

Like solar power, wind power is expanding rapidly, with China as the world's largest generator of wind power (Figure 8.3). The Global Wind Energy Council (2017) estimated that in 2015, wind power avoided over 702 million tons of CO_2 emissions globally.

Geothermal energy is also a policy option where conditions permit. Roughly half the world's installed geothermal-generating capacity is in the United States and the Philippines, and there is great potential for further expansion (Ampri, 2012). South Korea and New Zealand have invested in tidal power, and Scotland has invested in wave power. Wave power could

FIGURE 8.2. South Australian Tesla lithium ion battery (the largest in the world in 2018).
Source: Used with permission of Telsa Australia.

FIGURE 8.3. Windfarm, South Australia.
Source: Courtesy of Lloyd Thornton.

generate 10,000 GW of electricity (double the current world electricity capacity from all sources).

Distributed renewable energy (DRE) systems are also increasing steadily, especially in China, India, and parts of Africa, where they already provide energy to millions of people. DRE systems are power, cooking, heating, and cooling systems that generate and distribute services independently of centralized systems (REN21, 2017). An example is a stand-alone pollution-free solar cooking system.

Policymakers need to ensure that they are aware of the potential of renewable energy and the many benefits it brings in terms of contributing to a low-carbon economy and protecting population health. Using renewables is difficult in a situation where there is no policy consensus. For example, South Australia has one of the highest rates of renewables in the world and aims to increase this. Yet in 2017 its aim was not supported by the Australian federal government, and when a fierce storm brought down power lines in early 2017 the prime minister blamed the resulting power cuts on the high level of renewable energy in South Australia. Subsequent investigation confirmed the innocence of the renewables. Policy actors need to do whatever they can to encourage, cajole, and support investment in and use of renewable energy, even in the face of opposition from those invested in a high-carbon economy. There is some hope for optimism. The global accounting firm RSM (2016: n.p) noted in a review of renewable energy, "Recent changes in the commercial and technological landscape signal a transformative moment for renewable energy, which now presents a credible challenge to fossil fuels in the competition for global investment."

Additionally, globally there are numerous groups supporting and advocating the move to renewable energy. These groups are sometimes able to force the hand of government and business.

Ensuring Food for All in a Way That Protects the Environment

Access to good-quality, nutritious food is vital to good health. Yet supplying the world's population with such food is increasingly diffi-cult in the face of climate change, increasing population, and growing demand for animal protein and biofuels. Climate change, loss of bio-diversity, desertification, deforestation, waterlogging, and salinization of land are all threatening food supply. McMichael (2017) predicts that food shortages are likely this century unless there are radical changes in food systems toward greater sustainability. Research on the effects of climate change on agricultural areas suggests they will be uneven: some areas may become drier, while others will get more rain. The 2014 IPPC report noted that 75% of the available studies predict yield declines of up to 50% by the 2030s, with impacts on major crops including wheat, maize, and rice. Oxfam (2014) quotes the Intergovernmental Panel on Climate Change (IPCC) as concluding that it is "very likely" that climate impacts will result in estimated food price increases between 3% and 84% by 2050. The fifth of the world's population that suffers from malnutrition will become more vulnerable. The world also faces an epidemic of obesity, which is largely caused by a growing supply of high-fat and high-sugar food (Freudenberg, 2014). This will make the intersection of environmental, agricultural, and health policy vital for the twenty-first century. The key questions faced by policy makers are as follows:

- Will food production primarily encourage the provision of local food and ecological sustainability? Or will it aim to satisfy an increasingly commodified global food market?
- How can sustainable agricultural practices be encouraged?
- How can food systems be altered to reverse the current epidemic of obesity?

- How can genetic diversity be maintained in seed supplies when trans-national corporations are creating less diversity and a narrow range of selectively bred staple plants?
- How can small farmers be supported to use locally suited methods of food production for local consumption?
- What balance needs to be struck between the need for land for food production and that for environmental use?

Posing and encouraging debate and discussion on these questions will be vital to ensure that our societal systems adapt to put sustainable food supply above a single-minded pursuit of profits made through food supply.

Water: Vital to Humans and the Environment

Clean drinking water is a central public health issue for humans, and ensuring adequate water to protect ecosystems and biodiversity is vital for the environment. The United Nations reports (2017a) that 1.8 billion people globally use a source of drinking water that is fecally contaminated, which is estimated to cause more than 500,000 diarrheal deaths each year. The United Nations (2014) also estimated that around 700 million people in 43 countries suffered from water scarcity in 2014. Fresh water is becoming a scare resource for two key reasons: population growth is leading to more water-intensive agriculture and industry; and climate change is reducing rainfall in some existing dry regions. Schlosser et al. (2014) predict that 5 billion of the world's 9.7 billion people (52%) will live in water-stressed areas by 2050. Brown (2013) has argued that unsustainable extraction from major aquifers and rivers has led to a "peak water" scenario and that fresh water reserves are diminishing at an unparalleled rate. Large-scale corporate agricultural production consumes 70% of the world's fresh water. As a result, intra-national water conflict and conflicts between local communities and global corporations are likely (Balch, 2014). Examples are Coca-Cola's excessive extraction of groundwater at its Mehdiganj bottling plant in India, which triggered vigorous and persistent protests, resulting in its closure (Hansia, 2014), and with other water-hungry industries such as pulp mills and agribusiness projects such as large palm oil plantations. The conflict between Australian states over management of and illegal theft of water from the threatened Murray River is another example, with any effective action to stop unsustainable over-extraction for irrigation stymied by intransigent state governments for many years, despite a national agreement (Thompson, 2017).

Community groups facing water shortages argue that access to clean water is a human right and that water should be regarded as a resource held in common. These rights are threatened by the increased privatization and corporate control of water resources. This conflict between interests is at the heart of contemporary policy debates about water. A human rights and public health view both argue for the control of water to be in public hands (see discussion in Chapter 5 about the myth of privatization). Thus policymakers should resist the pressures to privatize water supplies and ensure sound public management of the resources.

Providing clean water to the world's population is as much a political as technical issue. It does not require any technological breakthroughs. Yet it would yield massive health gains in low- and middle-income countries. Similarly, reducing the amount of water that goes to irrigation and industry and increasing the amount devoted to the environment also should be an overarching policy aim. Political commitment will be vital to ensuring that water remains or is restored as a public good, rather than a source of private profit.

Restoring Nature and Biodiversity to Human Lives and the Environment

All those concerned with the health of people must then ask, will our species be able to engineer itself a secure place in the fraying tapestry of life?

—Bernstein (2014: 162)

Importance of Links to Nature

Policymakers are waking up to the importance of restoring and, in some cases, re-establishing the link between humans and the natural environments they live in—and depend on—for a sustainable future. Hartig et al. (2014) outline the importance of nature to air quality, physical activity, social cohesion, and stress reduction. They make the point that while effect sizes are likely to be small, a small beneficial effect on a large number of people is a significant contribution to population health. Moughtin et al. (2009: 7) note that "since humanity evolved in close association with nature, indeed as part of it, people therefore have an affinity for, and are comforted by nature." They go on to note that industrialization had the impact of putting people out of this crucial contact with nature to the detriment of their health. The importance of contact with nature has never been lost to Aboriginal people, who see contact with their land as central and vital to their well-being and culture.

> It is through the song cycles that we acknowledge our allegiance to the land, to our laws, to our life, to our ancestors and to each other. . . . It is a form of torture for a Yolngu person to see the loss of our life: every word, every note, every slip in the song is pain; every patch of land taken. Galarrwuy Yunupingu (2016: n.p)

Around the world, Indigenous peoples speak of the importance of connection with land and nature as vital to well-being and health. Parkes (2010) reviewed evidence on eco-health and concluded that restoring links with land and country is vital to restoring health for Indigenous peoples. In Australia a study found that those involved in caring for the land had better health, judged by a variety of measures including blood pressure, diabetes, cholesterol level, and cardiovascular risk (Burgess et al., 2009).

The importance of contact with nature is also being increasingly realized by mainstream agencies in industrialized countries. A healthy public policy originating from the environment sector is the Healthy Parks, Healthy People initiative, which has been launched in many places around the world, including Australia, Europe, the United States, Canada, and South Africa. Parks Victoria (2017) has produced an engaging video that explains why this program is important to both health promotion in individuals and to protecting the environment through bringing people and nature closer together. A review of the evidence concluded that "access to safe, high quality green space benefits individuals across every stage of the lifespan, enhancing their physical, mental, social and spiritual health and wellbeing" (Townsend et al., 2015: 4).

Biodiversity

Healthy ecosystems rely on biodiversity and its maintenance.

> Biological diversity—or biodiversity—is the term given to the variety of life on Earth and the natural patterns it forms. The biodiversity we see today is the fruit of billions of years of evolution, shaped by natural processes and, increasingly, by the influence of humans. It forms the web of life of which we are an integral part and upon which we so fully depend. (Convention on Biological Diversity, 2018: n.p)

In all natural environments—including wetlands, salt marshes, mangroves, bushland, and inland creeks—the destruction of habitat is causing a dramatic loss of biodiversity. Despite a UN-sponsored global convention and a 2010 strategic plan for protecting and enhancing biodiversity, the 2014 Global Biodiversity Outlook 4 (Convention on Biological Diversity, 2014: 10) report found that little progress had been made toward the 2020 targets, and indeed that, in key areas, biodiversity continued to decline. The report noted the vital role that achieving key biodiversity targets would make to meeting sustainable development goals, including reducing hunger and poverty, improving human health, and ensuring a sustainable supply of food and clean water. Of 55 target elements, only five are on track for 2020. For example, global rates of deforestation have slowed, but are still at unsustainable levels.

Species extinction is continuing at an unprecedented rate, and understanding is increasing of how the loss of biodiversity affects human health (Chivian and Bernstein, 2008). Cebellos et al. (2017) have examined patterns of species loss and population loss within species, calling it a "biological annihilation" that is likely to result in the sixth great extinction on earth and to threaten human life. They blame this on human overpopulation and excessive consumption, especially by the rich. The ways in which the loss of biodiversity affects systems is demonstrated by Bernstein (2014), who examines its role in new medicines, biomedical research, the provision of food, and the distribution and spread of infections. He notes that once biodiversity is lost, it is lost forever and he recommends that far more attention be paid to understanding the web of life and its vital importance to human health. While the link between biodiversity loss and human health is hard to prove empirically, who doesn't cringe inside when another species is reported as being on the endangered list—usually because of human activity? Whether it is whales, tigers, a rare bird, or polar bears, something important is lost with each species the earth loses. Vandana Shiva has written for many years about the impact of the loss of seed diversity on indigenous communities and has argued that the loss is not only practical, in terms of food supply, but also spiritual, as something sacred is lost when communities lose control of resources vital to their traditional ways of life and sustenance.

The task for policy actors seems massive in the face of the biodiversity loss that has already happened and that which is threatened. The Convention on Biodiversity establishes three main goals:

- conservation of biological diversity,
- sustainable use of its components, and
- fair and equitable sharing of the benefits from the use of genetic resources.

Asking how business-as-usual responds to these three goals is vital. When current practice fails to do so, establishing effective new policies and practices is essential. In doing this, it is crucial to remember that species being lost have few advocates and compete with the power and resources of TNCs and governments that seek to maintain the status quo. Traditional communities who want to protect their rights to seeds used for generations require legal protection against trade agreements that give patent control to TNCs. Public policy that ensures legal recognition of the rights of traditional owners of knowledge can be part of that protection.

Conclusion

The drafting and implementation of environmental policies highlights the conflicts between economic development and ecosystem and the need for human health protection. Despite the importance of a diverse and vital biosphere in ensuring access to the requirements for good health, including clean water, nutritious food, clean air, and a viable climate, the drive for profits is still undermining polices that would secure such a biosphere. The state of the environment also raises many issues of intergenerational, national, and international equity, which grow in importance as signs of deterioration grow, along with awareness that the coming generations will have to deal with the accumulated environmental impact of two centuries of industrialization. Current policy actions are inadequate to deal with environment threats, despite some promising developments. Imagination, deep understanding of the threats to ecosystems, courage, and radically new ideas will be required to produce the policies needed to ensure a future for sustainable healthy human life on planet earth. Policymakers who are committed to building such a future will need to move their governments away from alliances driven by economic growth and private profits and find their popular support from those community civil society groups who share their concerns.

9

Local Government and Health Governance

Local government is the leading local democratic institution and as such is responsible for shaping the way that citizens are involved in their own wellbeing, can improve wellbeing in their communities, and hold local health and wellbeing services to account.

—SOUTH, Hunter, and Gamsu (2014: summary)

Introduction

The purpose of local government is to build sustainable human development (Hancock, 2017). It is vitally important to the quality of life in cities and communities. It is the level of government that is closest to people and, at its best, can govern to encourage health, equity, and sustainable environments (Collins and Hayes, 2010), and it is well placed to encourage citizen involvement. Local government includes mega-cities of over 10 million as well as small rural towns with only a few thousand people. Local governments vary considerably in terms of the functions devolved and jurisdictional powers. Some city governments (for example, New York City, London) are more powerful than many countries. In other settings (e.g., rural Australia and the United States), local governments have relatively few powers. Local governments provide social, cultural, natural, built, and economic services and facilities, and through these can contribute to health and well-being. In nineteenth-century industrializing cities in Europe, city governments were vital to the sanitary revolution that led to improved living environments and human health. Local governments usually are responsible for urban planning and designing healthy cities. In regional and rural areas, they can mobilize their residents, protect their communities from external threats, and plan proactively. More recently, local government has been the focus of a number of movements that have seen the huge potential for it to be a powerful force in improving health and equity.

These include the UN New Urban Agenda and the WHO Healthy Cities movement. This chapter examines how local governance can be most effective in promoting health, and then reviews developments in first urban and then rural and regional governance in terms of contributions to health equity, well-being, and sustainability.

Ensuring Local Governance for the Public Good

This chapter focuses on the ways in which local government can be a positive part of the governance for health and presents examples where this is a reality. It is important to recognize, however, that local government is not always benign. It can be captured by vested interests whose aim is to profit from development in a city, rather than acting in the interests of the public good. Some of the ways in which this may happen were shown in Chapter 7 on urban planning, where we saw that unsustainable development can dominate over ecologically and socially sound planning. Harvey (2012) observes that capital domination of decision-making in city governments can mean that cities are very often undemocratic. This situation means that local government requires safeguards to ensure that those who have only a profit motive in mind are not able to capture local authorities or exercise undue influence over them. These safeguards are best provided by sound governance processes, the characteristics of which are set out in Box 9.1. The Global Network of Cities and Local and Regional Government (UGLC) note that

> [g]overnance is most effective when these processes are participatory, accountable, transparent, efficient, inclusive, and respect the rule of law. Good governance is particularly important at local level, where governments interact with citizens and communities on a daily basis. (UGLC, 2017: n.d)

The United Nations Development Programme (UNDP) (2014) has noted that effective local governance for sustainability should include diverse local stakeholders and thus ensure broad-based accountability and ownership of initiatives. Local government is well-placed to develop meaningful resident participation, and UNDP (2014) stresses that the SDGs will depend on a bottom-up approach that leads to local ownership of the development goals. To realize such an approach, governance needs to be

BOX 9.1

Main Characteristics of Good Local Governance

ACCOUNTABILITY

Accountability is a fundamental requirement of good governance. Local government has an obligation to report, explain, and be answerable for the consequences of decisions it has made on behalf of the community it represents.

TRANSPARENT

People should be able to follow and understand the decision-making process. This means that they will be able to clearly see how and why a decision was made—what information, advice, and consultation council considered, and which legislative requirements (when relevant) council followed.

FOLLOWS THE RULE OF LAW

This means that decisions are consistent with relevant legislation or common law and are within the powers of council.

RESPONSIVE

Local government should always try to serve the needs of the entire community while balancing competing interests in a timely, appropriate, and responsive manner.

EQUITABLE AND INCLUSIVE

A community's well-being results from all of its members feeling that their interests have been considered by the council in the decision-making process. This means that all groups, particularly the most vulnerable, should have opportunities to participate in the process.

EFFECTIVE AND EFFICIENT

Local government should implement decisions and follow processes that make the best use of the available people, resources, and time to ensure the best possible results for the community.

PARTICIPATORY

Anyone affected by or interested in a decision should have the opportunity to participate in the process for making that decision. This can happen in several ways—community members may be provided with information, asked for their opinion, given the opportunity to make recommendations, or, in some cases, be part of the actual decision-making process.

Source: Governance Institute of Australia (2017).

inclusive of groups who are often marginalized in local government, including women, young people, indigenous peoples, migrants, and those with disabilities (Reddy, 2016). The importance of participatory governance was stressed by the Commission on the Social Determinants of Health (CSDH, 2008: 63), which recommended that "[l]ocal government and civil society, backed by national government, establish local participatory governance mechanisms that enable communities and local government to partner in building healthier and safer cities."

Another form of participatory governance that is spreading around the world after its first experiment in Porto Alegre, Brazil, is participatory budgeting; 1,500 cities in Latin America, North America, Asia, Africa, and Europe have used the process. Participatory budgeting, in which people decide together how a portion of a government's (or organization's) budget is spent, appears to be an effective way to give decision-making power to the people. It enables citizens to play an active role in shaping their community and creates more transparent governance. The Shareable website (Johnson, 2014) includes recent examples. New York City has steadily expanded its participatory budgeting since its first experiment in 2011. Council members choose to join Participatory Budgeting New York City (PBNYC), giving at least $1 million from their budget for the entire community to participate in decision-making. The process, which includes public meetings, take a year to ensure that people have the time and resources to make informed decisions. Community members discuss local needs and develop proposals to meet these needs. Through a public vote, residents then decide which proposals to fund. Melbourne City Council (2017) used a citizen jury process to shape their 10-year budget-setting process. The People's Panel of 43 randomly selected Melburnians made recommendations to the Council on its spending and revenue strategy for the next decade. In Porto Alegre, Brazil, participatory budgeting was designed to be pro-poor, to increase equity, and to result in redistribution. This social justice focus has not always been evident in subsequent applications. In the United States the exercise is often concerned with funding of particular projects, rather than setting the budget of the entire local government. Pape and Lerner (2016) examined its implementation in the United States and noted that while equity was generally an implicit or explicit assumption, in practice this focus was not always maintained.

Local models of governance differ between forms of local government. In some cities, mayors are directly elected, while in others they are appointed from among the councilors. Elected mayors are likely to have more power. In the United Kingdom, elected mayors (except in London) are a new phenomenon, and the question of whose interests they are likely to serve is debated. Some see the move as likely to be democratic and to lead to increased civic accountability. Others (Hambleton and Sweeting, 2014) claim it leads to an executive leadership style and greater concentration of power in the office of the mayor, and thus is likely to serve the needs of global capital as mayors may be more likely to make developer-friendly deals behind closed doors.

The global network United Cities and Local Governments (UCLG)—formed to represent and defend the interests of local governments globally (https://www.uclg.org/en/organisation/about, accessed June 19, 2017)—recognizes that the ability of city and local governments to contribute to health and well-being depends on national enabling environments with adequate legal frameworks and resources. They also argue for decentralization in regions that have not already achieved it. Most important, they argue that national governments should involve city and regional governments in responses to the SDGs and ensure that models of decentralization enable local government, with sufficient resources to enable action. Another global network of local governments—ICLEI, or Local Governments for Sustainability—is dedicated to sustainability and includes health and well-being in its core agenda (http://www.iclei.org/agendas.html, accessed March 2, 2018). Reddy (2016) notes that local government associations are critical as they provide a platform for local and intergovernmental relations, as well as enabling capacity-building in critical areas, including participatory transparent governance and budgetary management. The UGLC also argues for greater involvement of local government in global issues and stresses the value of city-to-city cooperation, learning, and knowledge sharing. The WHO Healthy Cities initiative does this well and examples are provided in the following.

The ability of local government to govern for health and well-being is constrained by its relationship with higher levels of government. If a higher level of government sees a minimalist role for the state, then local governments will have little room to move. The style of local government may also vary over time in response to the external environment. Thus in the 1970s in the United States, there was considerable interest in a more radical progressive local government that promoted community power (Young, 1975). In the United Kingdom, local government fortunes have been tied to the changing views of the state from the central government; these changes provide a good example of central and local government relations. Under the Thatcher Conservative government, local government suffered cutbacks and was the battleground for the very unpopular and regressive poll tax. In the United Kingdom in the 1980s, the Greater London Council under "Red Ken"—Ken Livingston, the elected mayor—was the site of very progressive and pro-equity policies. The Blair Labour government also saw a more progressive role for local government to support place-based initiatives designed to promote health and equity in areas of disadvantage. This period saw local government enmeshed in policy networks and leading progressive policy development. The Conservative (Cameron and May) governments have imposed severe austerity on local government and have placed education and social services under considerable strain. Local government was forced to resort to outsourcing services as a means to cut costs, but with reduced service quality and accountability. This has meant that functions that were once core to local government were outsourced, usually to major corporations. Problems with privatization were outlined in Chapter 5. The 2017 Grenfell Tower fire disaster, in which the apartment building burned rapidly, highlighted some of these problems. The fire has been attributed to the lack of fire safety measures such as sprinkler systems and the failure of local and central government politicians and officials to listen to tenants' concerns about the danger of fire. The management of social housing was outsourced to a management organization, which was unaccountable to tenants and gave a contract to a builder who covered the building in banned unsafe cladding, resulting in the loss of 71 lives (Chakrabortty, 2017b).

The progressive weakening of UK local government by ongoing cycles of budgetary cuts and retrenchment of staff has reduced its powers to pursue oppositional politics (Ward et al., 2015) and has been a key part of the winding back of the welfare state, as many of the functions that citizens took for granted as core to local government have been eroded. The UK example demonstrates how local government is beholden to the central and state or regional governments for resources and power, and how its ability to govern in the interests of health reflects wider institutional constraints on its actions.

Central and regional governments can provide administrative and legal frameworks to encourage local governments to take action to promote health and sustainability. In the Australian states of South Australia, Western Australia, and Victoria (Victorian State Government, 2017) and the Canadian province of Quebec (Quebec, 2017), local governments are mandated by law to prepare healthy community plans. These plans encourage them to focus on issues of health, sustainability, and equity.

The issues that urban and rural local governments face are different. Globally, many urban areas are growing, and the governance challenges concern managing this growth. By contrast, many rural areas are facing loss of population and often of services and facilities. Given these differences, we will first look at urban local government and then rural.

Urban Local Government

Many urban local governments are planning for growth and are seeking to create ecologically sustainable and livable cities. The importance of cities to sustainability, health, and well-being has been recognized internationally by initiatives such as the UN New Urban Agenda and the WHO Healthy Cities movement. Both are discussed in the following.

Rapid Urbanization

City governments are becoming powerful in the wake of rapid urbanization. In 1800, only 3% of the world's population lived in urban areas. At the beginning of the twentieth century almost 14% did so, although only 12 cities had 1 million or more inhabitants. By 2008 half of the world's population lived in urban areas, and there were more than 400 cities with a population of over 1 million, and 19 cities had over 10 million inhabitants (Population Reference Bureau, 2017). In 2016 there were 31 mega-cities with a population of more than 10 million (United Nations, 2016b). Projections suggest that by 2030 60% of people globally will live in cities with at least half a million inhabitants (United Nations, 2016b). City governments have been primarily responsible for handling the growth within the world's burgeoning cities. This has required planning for growth, providing sufficient housing and infrastructure, encouraging economic development, and, at the same time, maintaining sustainable ecosystems and livability. In low- and middle-income countries, the magnitude of the growth and lack of resources have led to the development of huge informal settlements in which people live without adequate water supply or sanitation and in shanty housing.

Inequities and the New Urban Agenda

Inequities are massive in most cities, as shown by the following contrasts: favelas and rich areas of cities in Brazil; informal settlements like Khayelitsha and wealthy areas of Cape Town like coastal Clifton; harborside Sydney and its sprawling working-class western suburbs; the middle-class areas of Mumbai and its many slum settlements. Such inequities are mirrored in urban areas across the globe. The extent of these has been recognized by the United Nations through Habitat III, a United Nations Conference. Habitat III adopted a New Urban Agenda (see Box 9.2), which responds to these inequities and also demonstrates the magnitude of the very many challenges faced in urban areas, including instituting effective urban planning, halting climate change, and responding humanely to refugees.

This New Urban Agenda recognizes the importance of local government to achieving equity, sustainability, and health. It reflects a long process, from the Rio Declaration on sustainable development, after which a localized movement developed—Local Agenda 21—which focused on the ways in which local action could be effective. Despite this, local government was not involved in the negotiation of the Millennium Development Goals (MDGs), even though many of the areas covered by the goals are local government responsibilities. The lack of local ownership of the goals, as well as insufficient resources at local level to implement them, were identified as major weaknesses of the MDGs. In the lead-up to the SDGs, a thorough consultation was held, which has meant that city and local governments have been more central to the development of the goals and actions for local governance, and the global network, United Cities and Local Governments (UCLG), has become a powerful advocate. Thus, the importance of cities to achieving healthy people and environments is increasingly recognized. The importance and ability of cities to take independent action was shown in 2017 when the President Donald Trump withdrew the United States from the Paris Climate Agreement. A grouping of mega-cities (C40 Cities, http://www.c40.org/cities) has committed to implementing the Paris Agreement and cooperate to encourage and share their progress. This network includes US cities that have vowed to continue to implement the agreement. The mayor of Pittsburgh tweeted, following President's Trump's announcement, saying, "As the Mayor of Pittsburgh, I can assure you that we will follow the guidelines of the Paris Agreement for

BOX 9.2

United Nations New Urban Agenda

PROVIDE BASIC SERVICES FOR ALL CITIZENS

These services include access to housing, safe drinking water and sanitation, nutritious food, health care and family planning, education, culture, and access to communication technologies.

ENSURE THAT ALL CITIZENS HAVE ACCESS TO EQUAL OPPORTUNITIES AND FACE NO DISCRIMINATION

Everyone has the right to benefit from what their cities offer. The New Urban Agenda calls on city authorities to take into account the needs of women, youth, and children, people with disabilities, marginalized groups, older persons, and indigenous people, among other groups.

PROMOTE MEASURES THAT SUPPORT CLEANER CITIES

Tackling air pollution in cities is good both for people's health and for the planet. In the Agenda, leaders have committed to increase their use of renewable energy, provide better and greener public transport, and sustainably manage their natural resources.

STRENGTHEN RESILIENCE IN CITIES TO REDUCE THE RISK AND THE IMPACT OF DISASTERS

Many cities have felt the impact of natural disasters, and leaders have now committed to implement mitigation and adaptation measures to minimize these impacts. Some of these measures include better urban planning, quality infrastructure, and improving local responses.

TAKE ACTION TO ADDRESS CLIMATE CHANGE BY REDUCING THEIR GREENHOUSE GAS EMISSIONS

Leaders have committed to involve not just the local government but all actors of society to take climate action, taking into account the Paris Agreement on climate change, which seeks to limit the increase in global temperature to well below 2°C. Sustainable cities that reduce emissions from energy and build resilience can play a lead role.

(Continued)

BOX 3.1 *(Continued)*

FULLY RESPECT THE RIGHTS OF REFUGEES, MIGRANTS,

AND INTERNALLY DISPLACED PERSONS (IDPS) REGARDLESS

OF THEIR MIGRATION STATUS

Leaders have recognized that migration poses challenges, but it also brings significant contributions to urban life. Because of this, they have committed to establish measures that help migrants, refugees, and IDPs make positive contributions to societies.

IMPROVE CONNECTIVITY AND SUPPORT INNOVATIVE AND

GREEN INITIATIVES

This includes establishing partnerships with businesses and civil society to find sustainable solutions to urban challenges.

PROMOTE SAFE, ACCESSIBLE, AND GREEN PUBLIC SPACES

Human interaction should be facilitated by urban planning, which is why the Agenda calls for an increase in public spaces such as sidewalks, cycling lanes, gardens, squares, and parks. Sustainable urban design plays a key role in ensuring the livability and prosperity of a city.

Source: http://www.un.org/sustainabledevelopment/blog/2016/10/newurbanagenda/ (accessed June 19, 2017).

our people, our economy & future." In addition, the US Conference of Mayors announced that it strongly opposes Trump's withdrawal from the climate accord and vowed to continue plans to reduce greenhouse gas emissions to reduce the effects of global warming (Thomsen, 2017). In July 2017 the first "global covenant of mayors" was held to devise standard measures of emission reduction and to share ideas for carbon-free transportation and housing (Boffey, 2017). UN special envoy Michael Bloomberg told this meeting that the United States is already halfway to their goal of a 26% reduction in emissions by 2025, and that cities had been central to this.

Cities also have been at the forefront of adopting tobacco-free policies before other levels of government, with bigger cities adopting policies first and then small cities following suit (Shipan and Volden, 2006). Thus, local government can be in the vanguard of policy innovation.

The WHO Healthy Cities Movement

The WHO Healthy Cities movement has reinforced the importance of local jurisdictions in public health, noting their potential to improve health, reduce health inequities, build community capacity, and take intersectoral action to promote health. The Ottawa Charter for Health Promotion provided the range of strategies for the Healthy Cities movement, and its founders saw it as one of the ways in which the Charter could be implemented (Hancock and Duhl 1986; Ashton, 1988). The first healthy cities were in Europe and Canada, but the movement soon spread to become global. The WHO European Healthy Cities Network comprises nearly 100 cities and towns from 30 countries that are committed to health and sustainable development. They are also linked through national, regional, metropolitan, and thematic Healthy Cities networks. A city joins the WHO European Healthy Cities Network based on criteria that are renewed every five years. Phase VI (2014–2018) has been focused on reducing health inequities and improving leadership and participatory governance. WHO-Euro (2017) defines healthy cities as a process, not an outcome:

- A healthy city is not one that has achieved a particular health status.
- It is conscious of health and striving to improve it. Thus, any city can be a healthy city, regardless of its current health status.
- The requirements are a commitment to health and a process and structure to achieve it.
- A healthy city is one that continually creates and improves its physical and social environments and expands the community resources that enable people to mutually support each other in performing all the functions of life and developing to their maximum potential.
- Successful implementation of this approach requires innovative action addressing all aspects of health and living conditions, and extensive networking between cities across Europe and beyond. This entails explicit political commitment, leadership, institutional change, and intersectoral partnerships.
- The Healthy Cities approach recognizes the determinants of health and the need to work in collaboration across public, private, voluntary, and community-sector organizations. This way of working and thinking includes involving local people in decision-making, requires political commitment and organizational and community development, and recognizes the process to be as important as the outcomes.

One of core themes in the previous phase was "Healthy Urban Environment and Design" (HUED). Grant (2015) conducted an assessment of self-reported case studies from this theme and found considerable activity in the cities. His study found a range of citywide activities, including:

- citizen participation in a new waste disposal system;
- the application of the WHO Health and Economic Assessment Tool (HEAT) to assess the benefits of more cycling provision;
- place-based activity, which included health urban design and planning;
- healthy transport (e.g., ecological Sundays in Modena in which areas of the city were car-free for a day);
- housing regeneration and projects that increased livability and safety (e.g., disability access to beaches).

Another evaluation of Healthy Cities Phase V in Europe found that the cities involved were adopting comprehensive multisectoral approaches to local health policy development.

The Alliance for Healthy Cities (2018: n.p) formed in Asia includes around 200 cities and organises biannual conferences. Typical projects of cities include (Alliance for Healthy Cities, 2018) the following:

- the healthy villages initiative from Healthy Cities Kuching, which involves 90 villages and the Kuching healthy longboat project, which has led to improved "physical surroundings, the organisation and administration of the longhouse, the gotong royong (team) spirit, health and safety consciousness, and the most notable of all—their success in kicking their smoking habit."
- workplace breastfeeding (Jeju City, Republic of Korea);
- promotion of the safety of agricultural products (Wujian City, China);
- planning for emergency preparedness and response (Marikina City, Philippines);
- tackling gender-based violence (Kunshan, Jiangsu, China);
- equity enhancement in access to health-care services (Seoul, Republic of Korea).

In the Americas, Canada is at the forefront of the Healthy Cities movement. Cities there have been involved in healthy cities since the 1980s and have developed a depth of experience about the ways in which healthy cities work. British Colombia provides a good example (see Box 9.3).

BOX 9.3

British Colombia: Healthy Communities

The PlanH was developed in British Columbia as a response to an extensive consultation held by the BC Healthy Communities Society, which found that local government wanted more support and opportunities to learn, share resources, and partner with other sectors and community leaders to promote health. The program supports local government engagement and partnerships across sectors to create healthier communities. Recognizing that community policy, plans, and decisions affect health and well-being, PlanH provides learning opportunities, resources, and leading-edge practices for collaborative local action. Their website contains lots of information about making healthy communities, including an excellent introductory video about the role of local government in health promotion (http://planh.ca/resources/videos/local-governments-healthy-communities, accessed July 5, 2017).

As part of PlanH, the City of Vancouver has developed the Healthy City Strategy and Action Plan. This is a long-term plan for healthier people, healthier places, and a healthier planet. It addresses health in the broadest sense by integrating elements that influence well-being and involving diverse sectors in a shared vision of a healthy city for all residents. A key feature of the Vancouver initiative is their 30-member leadership team, composed of a diverse group of leaders from the public, private, and voluntary sectors. The council staff and council members give strong support to achieving the plan. The plan has 13 goals supported by indicators to show if they have been achieved by 2025:

A good start	Active living and getting outside
A home for everyone	Lifelong learning
Feeding ourselves well	Expressing ourselves
Healthy human services	Environment to thrive in
Making ends meet and working well	Getting around
Being and feeling safe and included	Collaborative leadership
Cultivating connections	

(Source: City of Vancouver, 2017).
A video describing the initiative is available (Plan H, 2017).

The healthy cities movement has been successful in engaging local governments in population health planning and action on a range of social determinants, especially those concerning the design of local neighborhoods. While applying indicators of outcomes to healthy cities projects has long been recognized as challenging, local governments generally use more sophisticated measures of progress than the GDP used at the national level (see critique of this in Chapter 5). Hancock (2017: 96) notes that "I do not know any city that measures its progress solely in economic terms. Instead, they tend to use a suite of 'quality of life' indicators that cover a variety of domains, including many aspects of human development as well as the quality of their built and natural environments and social and economic conditions." That this is the case underlines that local government is very well placed to promote health and sustainability.

Rural and Regional Local Government

While urban areas have been magnets for people, rural and regional areas around the world are most typically experiencing depopulation and the aging of their populations. Rural populations also usually experience worse health status than their urban counterparts and have less comprehensive service provision than in urban areas. Agriculture is also less of a contributor to GDP than in the past, increasing the need for rural areas to diversify their economies. The CSDH (2008) report noted that strengthening rural areas and making them more attractive places to live could help deal with the crisis of rapid urbanization. Local government has a central role to play in this strengthening.

The OCED (2014) has reviewed the experience of many countries in encouraging rural development and has used these experiences to produce "A New Rural Development Paradigm for the 21st Century." This report notes that rural populations do not necessarily have lower incomes. Some OECD countries with the highest average GDP per capita (including Finland, Sweden, and Ireland) are also those with the highest percentage of rural populations, thus contravening "the idea that 'rural' is synonymous with backwardness" (OECD, 2014: 83). The report recommends that the new paradigm for rural development should be based on eight components:

Governance: To ensure capacity and integrity at all levels.
Multiple sector: That moves beyond a sole focus on agriculture and that includes in particular the renewable energy and tourism sectors.

Infrastructure: Including connectivity across rural areas and between urban and rural areas, and improved access to education and health.

Urban-rural linkages: Recognizing that successful rural development strategies do not treat rural areas as isolated entities, but as part of a system in which rural livelihoods depend on urban center for their access to goods, services, new technologies, and exposure to new ideas.

Inclusiveness: Poverty and its social determinants (including health and nutrition, education, infrastructure) need to be targeted, and the exclusion of certain groups eliminated.

Gender: Inclusion and empowerment of women are vital, and their property rights need to be respected and access to resources ensured.

Demography: Differs from context to context; generally rural populations are aging, but low- and middle-income countries have high fertility rates, so the service mix needs to be tailored to local requirements.

Sustainability: Rural areas are vulnerable to climate change and energy, food, and water scarcity.

Rural local governments often lack the capacity and resources to deal with this complex set of issues. From the 1990s onward, there has been increased recognition of the need for effective local government, and national governments have recognized the need for a micro-regional, bottom-up approach, in which national government provides support for local strategies. The OECD (2016b: 89) comments, "it is clear that the idea of a bottom-up approach is not something that comes easily to national governments. Most national governments continue to play the dominant role in rural development. Local governments may be allowed to choose among a set of policy options, but their decision-making power is limited to these alternatives." Very often, rural local governments have not had the opportunity of training and capacity development. Some examples of success in doing this do exist. Box 9.4 highlights two examples from Korea and the United States, which highlight the need for local ownership of issues and resources.

Effective rural local government depends on national policies that support rural communities so that they are more attractive to live in and the push to move to cities is reduced. These policies need to encourage investment in infrastructure, including energy, health, education, stable employment, and land ownership and tenure reform. These needs were summarized in recommendations from the Federation of Canadian Municipalities (2017: 1) to the federal government process for the newly allocated infrastructure funding. The report noted:

BOX 9.4

Rural Local Governance for Well-Being: Examples from Korea and the United States

KOREA

The OECD identified Korea's Saemaul Undong as a successful example of combining bottom-up and top-down approaches to building government and institutional capacity. They were designed to mobilize people and resources to achieve Korean President Park's vision for rural development through poverty reduction, rural modernization, community-building, and self-reliance. Saemaul village leaders (who were ideally equally male and female) were trained to manage and coordinate development activities and so built local capacity to design and implement projects and help drive local participation in and commitment to development. In addition, the creation of local offices to monitor progress and of a coordinating body comprising various ministry heads ensured coherence across government levels, led to better integration of projects across sectors, and facilitated monitoring and evaluation.

Source: OECD, (2016b: 199)

MISSISSIPPI (UNITED STATES)

In the United States, environmental justice is an important issue for rural local government. In the state of Mississippi, rural communities facing common issues (including high rates of poverty, low median incomes, and aging, inadequate water infrastructure) regularly meet with federal agencies. The Mississippi Conference of Black Mayors recognizes that their communities have poor access to health care, water infrastructure, and other resources. Their communities' struggles are compounded by the cleanup efforts from the damage caused by Hurricane Katrina and extreme weather events related to climate change, such as flooding. Local government leaders are dealing with these issues by forming coalitions among small towns to encourage innovative partnerships aimed at overcoming these challenges and building sustainable solutions. Despite these local efforts, these rural communities still suffer from structural disadvantages that would require addressing by national leadership through redistributive fiscal and other policies.

Source: EPA Local Government Advisory Committee (2015).

From coast to coast, rural communities are central to Canada's economic, social and environmental well-being. But with limited fiscal capacity, rural governments face formidable challenges providing the infrastructure that's needed to sustain local economies and ways of life.

The report notes that municipalities in Canada have responsibility for 60% of the nation's infrastructure but have access to only around 8%–10% of each tax dollar. Yet they are delivering many public services and playing a growing role in public safety and climate change adaptation. The report recommended more support for the capital priorities of rural local government (roads, bridges, water treatment, septic system upgrades), predictable funding allocation models, streamlined administration, reliable broadband, new housing investment, and adaptation to local contexts. These requirements would echo those of rural local government globally.

Conclusion

Local government is a vital part of the infrastructure for health in rural and urban areas for countries at all levels of development. It can have a large impact on how equitably resources are distributed, how sustainable the local living environment is, and the extent to which citizens can participate in decisions that affect their lives. Mega-cities in particularly are increasingly important players in responses to climate changes, and they challenge nation-states in terms of their influence. Achieving sound local governance is vital for health and requires high levels of accountability, transparency, and participation. Creative and innovative thinking from a diverse range of participants will also be vital in the future as a means of increasing the contribution of local government to equity, sustainability, and human health.

10

Civil Society

HEALTHY GOVERNANCE FROM BELOW

If we can be positive in a crazy world,
And respond with heart, maybe
We can make a small difference
That ripples. . . .

—JOCK MCKEEN AND BEN WONG (2012: 401)

Introduction

Civil society has been vital to many measures that have improved governance for health. Advocates outside government have inspired many policy and law changes that have resulted in improved health and well-being. Examples include the abolition of slavery, women's voting rights, and marriage equality. Civil society is also vital to maintaining good governance through mechanisms including representative boards of management, watchdog functions, and formal processes of participation. This chapter reviews each of these to demonstrate that civil society is vital to good governance for health. The chapter also takes the position that governance for health is much stronger and more likely to come about when there is top-down action from government, combined with bottom-up pressure for change that can force the hand of governments to act in favor of health, equity, and sustainability. I have previously called this the "nutcracker effect," as illustrated in Figure 10.1.

FIGURE 10.1. The health equity nutcracker.
Source: Conceived by Fran Baum and drawn by Simon Kneebone, reproduced in Baum (2007, 2016).

Health Reforms Thanks to Civil Society Bottom-Up Pressure

The history of the last two hundred years is replete with examples of how civil society has helped bring about progressive reform through bottom-up pressure to force change through a "nutcracker" action. The nineteenth-century anti-slavery movement was vital in the decision to legislate against slavery in the United Kingdom and United States. The early twentieth-century suffragette movement was instrumental in winning the support for women's right to vote. The anti-apartheid movement in South Africa campaigned for decades before it finally triumphed in 1994.

Rapidly industrializing nineteenth-century England provides an example of the nutcracker effect in action. Szreter and Woolcock (2004) observe that it was pressure from a range of civil society groups, including trade unions and civic associations, that forced the hand of government to clean up cities and provide clean water and sanitation. The government established a Health in Towns Commission, which revealed the appalling unsanitary conditions in fast-growing cities like Liverpool, York, and Nottingham (Ashton and Ubido, 1991). A Health of Towns Association then advocated strongly for major changes. As a consequence of their and other civil society advocacy, living conditions improved through the nineteenth century, and in their wake, so did health. For example, life expectancy in Manchester went from 27 years in 1841 to near 50 by the end of the century (Szreter, 1995).

Another example of this nutcracker effect is the struggle for affordable drugs in South Africa in the face of a tsunami of HIV/AIDs in the 1990s. Sanders (2009) describes how in 1997 Nelson Mandela's government passed a law that aimed to lower drug prices through "parallel importing"—that is, importing drugs from countries where they are sold at lower prices—and "compulsory licensing," which would allow local companies to manufacture certain patented drugs in exchange for royalties. A number of pressures (e.g., threats of trade sanctions and legal action) were brought to bear on the South African government by the US government and pharmaceutical companies to repeal the legislation. These threats were met by effective campaigns by local and international AIDS activists and progressive health NGOs (particularly the South African Treatment Action Campaign) and an uncompromising South African government. Thus the nutcracker effect forced a backdown by both the US government and the multinational pharmaceutical companies (Bond, 1999). The result of the campaign was that the new anti-retroviral drugs have been brought within the reach of all people living with HIV/AIDS and so extended millions of lives, especially in Africa.

Current Civil Society Campaigns

Current campaigns that are arguing for improved governance for health include the following.

Anti-privatization Movement

Many civil society groups are arguing against privatization, including the People's Health Movement (PHM) and Public Service International (PSI), both of which have had very active campaigns against the privatization of health services. PHM-UK is fighting to save the National Health Service (Figure 10.2). PSI is running a campaign #PublicHealth4All (http://www. world-psi.org/en/right-health-campaign-better-future-publichealth4all, accessed December 28, 2017). One of the priorities of the PHM is organizing protests against the privatization and commercialization of health care. In 2018 they organised a People's Health Day on April 7 (WHO's World Health Day) to protest privatization with the slogan "Our health is not for sale."

FIGURE 10.2. PHM-Europe anti-privatization campaign.

Source: European Network against Health Commercialization. "Our Health is Not for Sale"- campaign at World Social Forum 2015, Tunis.

Opposition to Neoliberal Economic Models

Many groups fall under this rubric. The Occupy movement, which started in the wake of the global financial crisis, has argued against the concentration of wealth in the hands of the 1%. Oxfam (2017) has been an active campaigner against the rapidly growing inequities. Corporate Accountability International (https://www.stopcorporateabuse.org/, accessed June 8, 2017) runs a campaign against corporate abuse. A protest against the consumerism inherent in capitalism is run by Adbusters, which holds an annual Buy Nothing Day and a Buy Nothing Xmas. (http://buynothingxmas.org/, accessed June 8, 2017).

Equity and a Fair Society

There are a number of groups that campaign for a fairer and more just society, and in doing so, run multiple campaigns using many different strategies. The Australian GetUp movement (GetUp, 2018: n.p) has one million members from all walks of life and come together around a "shared belief in fairness, compassion and courage". Their website says "It is GetUp members who set our movement's agenda on issues they care about, in the fields of Environmental Justice, Human Rights, Economic Fairness and Democratic Integrity. Our work is driven by values, not party politics".

Avaaz has been established as an international membership movement that "empowers millions of people from all walks of life to take action on pressing global, regional and national issues, from corruption and poverty to conflict and climate change." (Avaaz, 2017: n.p). In April 2018 they had just under 47 million members in 195 countries. Their actions (https://secure.avaaz.org/page/en/highlights/) have influenced climate debates, challenged the media monopolies, won battles over the use of glyphosate in agriculture, and stopped the expansion of Monsanto into Argentina (Figure 10.3). Avaaz and GetUp's agendas are driven by consultation with their supporters about what their key priorities are for each year. The effectiveness of such mass democratic organizations is made possible through rapid communication enabled by the Internet.

FIGURE 10.3. Avaaz-sponsored demonstration about the health dangers of chemical agriculture.

Source: Avaaz.org, Argentina.

Environmental Movements

There are numerous environmental movements around the globe that campaign to protect nature, protect wild animals from extinction, and protect the planet from global warming and subsequent climate change. Their work is important to health because of the increasing evidence that contact with nature and spending time in natural places is good for mental and physical health. Also, as we saw in Chapter 8, the threat of global warming and subsequent climate change and the many impacts of the Anthropocene age on the environment is creating more threats to health. Groups that campaign globally include Greenpeace, Friends of the Earth, and Sea Shepherd. International groups also get involved in local campaigns; Figure 10.4 shows a Greenpeace protest about the Fukushima nuclear plant disaster of 2011, urging the company that owns the plant to take responsibility. There are also nationally and locally based campaigns. Local campaigns often focus on one issue, for example the Australian anti-fracking of coal seam gas group Lock the Gate which encouraged landowners and farmers to lock their gates against coal seam gas speculators (http://www.lockthegate.org.au/), or the US protests against the XL Pipeline. Other groups take a broader approach,

FIGURE 10.4. Greenpeace protest about the cleanup following the Fukushima Daiichi nuclear power plant accident.
Source: Bernd Arnold/Greenpeace. European Hitachi headquarters in Duisburg, 2016.

such as the Australian Conservation Council or the National Trust in the United Kingdom. Some environmental groups take an explicit focus on the human health impacts of environmental change. One example is the Australian Climate and Health Alliance (http://www.caha.org.au/), which is a network of health-care organizations whose commitment "is based on the understanding that further global warming poses grave risks to human health and biodiversity and if left unchecked, threatens the future of human civilisation" (CAHA, 2017: n.p).

Strategies Used in Civil Society Campaigns

Civil society is able to effect change when political systems are open to influence from policy entrepreneurs who can be ready to exploit windows of opportunity (Kingdon, 2011). Such policy entrepreneurs from civil society can exert bottom-up pressure that, when combined with support from government, results in change (Figure 10.1).

Civil society activists and organizations use a range of strategies, detailed in the following.

Lobbying Politicians

Writing letters, emailing, and meeting with politicians and cabinet ministers are all activities vital to advocacy campaigns. Experienced campaigners note that stories are vital to this advocacy (Ganz, 2009). The Australian Asbestos Network (2017) website contains stories of victims that bring to life the devastating effects on people's lives and have been effective in bringing about bans on the use of asbestos.

Civil society competes with powerful commercial vested interest when it lobbies governments. The power of this commercial lobbying has been acknowledged by Dr. Margaret Chan (2015b: n.p), former director general of the World Health Organization:

> When crafting preventive strategies, government officials must recognize that the widespread occurrence of obesity and diabetes throughout a population is not a failure of individual willpower to resist fats and sweets or exercise more. It is a failure of political will to take on powerful economic operators, like the food and soda industries.

A US group, OpenSecrets.org (Center for Responsive Politics, 2017), estimates that in 2016 the agribusiness industry (including food and beverage) spent US$32 million, the pharmaceutical industry US$246 million, and the oil and gas industry US$119 million on lobbying, with total spending on lobbyists estimated at US$31.1 billion. Corporations hire public relations firms to set up phony grassroots advocacy groups. Examples include (Monbiot, 2016) the Competitive Enterprise Institute, which argues against the reality of climate change and is funded by the Koch Brothers and large corporations. A Coalition for Safe Affordable food (2018) (funded by food corporations) used deceptive tactics to undermine campaigns for the labeling of genetically modified foods (Rosebro, 2015).

Boycotts

Boycotts involve not using, buying, or dealing with a person, organization, or country. A successful boycott against Nestle's marketing of infant formula was the first successful international boycott of a TNC. This boycott resulted in the first United Nations Code of Marketing, setting standards for the entire industry. Many other examples of successful boycotts are given at http://www.ethicalconsumer.org/boycotts/successfulboycotts.

FIGURE 10.5. US boycott of Safeways in the 1940s.
Source: Used with permission of Crisis Publishing. District of Columbia, USA, 1941.

aspx (accessed June 8, 2017). In the 1940s the food chain Safeways was boycotted because they refused to employ African Americans (Figure 10.5).

Disinvestments

Disinvestments were a vital part of the anti-apartheid struggle in the 1980s, where banking sanctions made doing business in South Africa very difficult and made a significant contribution to bringing down the regime (Farrell, 2014). More recently, disinvestment campaigns have become increasingly popular as a means of combating potentially environmentally damaging developments. In the United States and Canada, an Indigenous Alliance has launched a disinvestment campaign against the expansion of tar sands mining. The campaign is urging banks to stop funding the pipelines and to "develop ethically sound banking policies" and is asking bank customers to withdraw from banks that don't disinvest (Kestlet-D'Amours, 2017).

Public Protests

Protests take many forms, including street marches of thousands of people, street theater, or other staged events. On January 21, 2017, a Women's March took place globally as a protest against the inauguration of Donald Trump as US president and the comments he had made that

FIGURE 10.6. Washington, DC, Women's March, protesting after the inauguration of President Donald Trump, January 21, 2017.
Source: Flickr/Mobilus in Mobili.

were adverse to the rights of women, migrants, the natural environment, gay and lesbian people, and of citizens' rights to health care. It was largest single-day protest in US history. Estimates indicate that over 500,000 marched in Washington, DC (see Figure 10.6), and an estimated 5 million protested globally (Hartocollis and Alcindor, 2017).

Mass protests marked the period before the COP21 Paris meeting with large rallies around the world, including 300,000 in the People's Climate March in New York (September 2014). A creative range of street protests have been used, including street theater, "die-ins," and guerrilla theater. Die-ins have grown in popularity and involve volunteers pretending to die, to convey the idea that something or someone—the target of the action—is literally killing people (Figure 10.7). Those pretending to have died remain play-dead for a few minutes, or longer. The issues are explained by signs and speeches (Freudenheim, 2017).

Public Art

Art is also used as a form of protest, including graffiti, Internet games, and formal artworks at exhibitions with a political message. The BUGA Up (Billboards Utilising Graffitists Against Unhealthy Promotions) campaign

FIGURE 10.7. "Die-in" protest against immigration policy, Strasbourg, France, April 2015.

Photo: Adrian Hancu. Courtesy of iStockphoto.

FIGURE 10.8. Protest art about economic inequities from the 1980s by Michael Callaghan.

Estate of Michael Callaghan, silkscreen print 1979—redbackgraphix.com.au

organized its members to change the messages of advertising billboards in a humorous way. For example, "Welcome to Marlboro Country" was changed to "Welcome to Cancer Country." Art has been used to challenge popular misconceptions. In Australia, "dole bludger" is a term of abuse for people living on unemployment assistance (known as the "dole"), and an artist used a confronting image to highlight the inequities of a system where some rich people are able to not work at all (Figure 10.8).

Petitions

Petitions are widely used, and the Internet makes them much easier to organize than in the past. Change.org hosts many petitions on topics related to health and well-being. The site provides examples of cases where online activism has resulted in change.

Watching

Reporting on and analyzing the actions of institutions is also an effective means of civil society action to hold organizations accountable. The People's Health Movement (2017) mounts an annual watch on the World Health Organization's Executive Board and World Health Assembly. The WHO Watch website contains detailed analyses of policies and position papers. Civil society organizations may also comment on key government actions such as annual budgets. For example, the Canadian Centre for Policy Alternatives produces an annual alternative federal budget that places emphasis on equity (Canadian Centre for Policy Alternatives, 2017). A study (Robinson, 2006) of the impact of civil society advocacy on budgets in six countries (Brazil, Croatia, India, Mexico, South Africa, and Uganda) found that the processes were effective, including by improving the transparency of budgetary decisions and the budget process and increasing the likelihood that there is a social justice focus in budgets. Consumer product organizations also perform a type of watching by monitoring the activities of private firms and the products they produce.

The watching function of civil society has also been seen as part of a new form of democracy—monitory democracy. This has been described as a complex web of monitoring bodies that monitor the activities of governments and the private sector and "[b]y putting politicians, parties and elected governments permanently on their toes, they complicate their lives, question their authority and force them to change their agendas" (Keane, 2009a). In reviewing the success of the Treatment Action Campaign in South Africa, Klugman (2016: 37) notes, "at the heart of monitory democracy is the capturing of the evidence of the extent to which government is delivering on its constitutional mandate." This implies that civil society has an increasingly important role in maintaining democratic government.

Media, Including Social Media

Media are a vital means of social movements drawing attention to their cause. Keane (2009b: n.p) notes that "groups using mobile phones, bulletin boards, news groups, wikkies and blogs sometimes manage, against considerable odds, to publicly embarrass politicians, parties and parliaments, or even whole governments." The 2018 the Stoneman Douglas Shootings led to an organized social-media-driven campaign by students from the school, arguing for greater gun control and using very sophisticated social media savvy. A National school walkout was organized (see Figure 10.9). The students used the hashtagh #neveragain and around 850,000 marched in Washington, DC, and many thousand more at other locations in the United States and internationally. *The New York Times* (Yee and Blinder, 2018) reported that this student movement had unsettled a gun debate dominated by the powerful National Rifle Association that had previously been impervious to gun control lobbies.

Freedom of the press is vital to civil society using media, and this freedom is not guaranteed in many countries. There are also increasing concerns about the domination of the press in some countries by a handful of media owners who, as a result of this concentration, gain considerable power and influence. In Australia, for instance, all major capital city newspapers are owned by two companies—Newscorp and Fairfax. Public interest journalism, free from commercial interest (Simons, 2017), is vital to civil society being able to contribute to public debate about crucial health issues. Yet as the means of communication multiply, the mainstream media outlets are devoting less resources to investigative journalism. This gives less scope for advocacy groups to receive coverage for their issues in the mainstream media. Box 10.1 describes South African and Australian social journalism experiments that provide new outlets for advocacy on crucial public health issues.

FIGURE 10.9. Students leading rallies advocating gun control.
Source: Rob Crandall/Shutterstock.com. Washington, DC, USA, 24th March 2018.

Civil Disobedience and Nonviolent Direct Action

Civil disobedience draws on the philosophy of Mahatma Ghandi and has been an important part of many successful civil society campaigns, including that in India for self-rule. Martin Luther King, Jr., (1963: n.p) said, "one has a moral responsibility to disobey unjust laws." The Lock the Gate campaign in Australia is using peaceful blockades to protest the development of gas and coal mining. Members lock themselves to obstruct mining equipment and have met with some success (http://www.lockthegate.org.au/, accessed June 8, 2017). The campaign is reflective of the importance of nonviolent direct action (see http://csgfreenorthernrivers.org/nonviolent-direct-action/, accessed July 12, 2017) and has developed a code of conduct and training to support the code's implementation. In the United States, 350.org is leading nationwide protests against the building of the Keystone XL pipeline, which will stretch from Nebraska to Texas to take oil from the tar sands in Alberta to the Gulf of Mexico (Figure 10.10). These have included protest camps by Native Americans where up to 10,000 people have joined the camps to protest the pipeline (Sylvester, 2017). The Standing Rock Sioux tribe maintain that the pipeline is a threat to their drinking water and traverses sacred burial grounds. Authorities have used water cannons to deter the protesters.

Picketing

Picketing originated as an action by trade unions against employers to persuade workers from entering a worksite where there was a strike, but it has been used to draw attention to other causes as well. In the Philippines, tobacco trade fairs have been picketed as a protest against the continued marketing of their products (Teves, 2012). In Kerela State in India, the Coca-Cola factory has been picketed through round-the-clock vigils outside

FIGURE 10.10. Tar Sands protests.
Source: 350.org

BOX 10.1

Media for Health

In South Africa, Health-e has been developed to encourage investigative journalists; the initiative combines deep technical knowledge and expertise and a strong commitment to justice and equality. The journalists investigate stories in places and about people who seldom gain coverage, and then these stories can get picked up by mainstream media. They also train citizen journalists who produce their own stories and use social media (website, Facebook, and Twitter). In the 10 years preceding 2014, Health-e wrote 1,860 stories, 6,650 of which were written by citizen journalists. The South African Broadcasting Corporation used 664 of these stories. An evaluation of Health-e concluded that it catalyzes action by producing "a health-related news cloud which draws the public, advocacy groups' and decisions makers' attention to otherwise barley covered issues." (Klugman, 2015: iii). It does this through a dynamic processes in which Health-e's investigations spur advocacy groups and the government into action, and then this action leads to further stories.

The Australian social journalism venture Croakey was the brainchild of journalist Melissa Sweet (@croakeyblog). Croakey is described on its website "as an ever-evolving journalism project that aims to provide a public service for those who care about the community's health and well-being." It goes on to say that it aims to "hold power to account." Its platform provides a venue for progressive views on health-care sector issues and the social determinants of health. Examples of recent story headlines from Croakey include the following:

"Medical students taking action on Australia's humanitarian crisis"
"New report: a damning indictment of health system's failure to care for women"
"Pathways to justice pass through health: six ways the health sector can help reduce the harms of over-incarceration"
"The situation is catastrophic: Time to prioritise the planet's health?"
"Cycling and walking are short-changed when it comes to transport funding in Australia."

Croakey is funded by a range of organizations, including the Public Health Association of Australia and individual donations. It offers a the factory gates, protesting the impact the factory had on taking ground water. Coca-Cola and its subsidiaries were accused of creating severe water shortages for the community by extracting large quantities of water for their factories, affecting both the quantity and quality of water and thus threatening local livelihoods. Global activists picketed the company's annual general meeting on April 19, 2006, in Wilmington, Delaware, United States. The protesters stood outside the meeting, waving banners with messages such as "Coca-Cola: Stop De-Hydrating the World" and "Coca-Cola: Destroying Lives, Livelihoods and Communities" (The Right to Water and Sanitation, 2017).

Revolutions

Revolutions happen when enough citizens strongly believe that their government is damaging health and well-being. The two most famous in history are the French and the American revolutions. The French Revolution resulted in the out-of-touch monarchy being replaced by a republic advancing the cause of equality, fraternity, and liberty. The American Revolution resulted in the overthrow of British rule and the establishment of the Declaration of Independence, which asserted the unalienable right to "Life, Liberty and the pursuit of Happiness." This document also noted the mandate for the revolution: "whenever any Form of Government becomes destructive of these ends, it is the Right of the People to alter or to abolish it, and to institute new Government, laying its foundation on such principles and organizing its powers in such form, as to them shall seem most likely to effect their Safety and Happiness" (US history. org, 2017: n.p.). Revolutions in Latin America have also led to repressive regimes being replaced by more democratic ones that have provided much improved health, education, and welfare services. Most famously, the Castro Revolution in Cuba resulted in the provision of universal health care, a strong primary health-care network (Hamblin, 2016), and free education. As a result, life expectancies are as high as in the United States and literacy rates are higher, at 99.8% (UNICEF, 2017).

All of the strategies listed in the preceding are used by civil society to bring about healthy, sustainable, and equitable change. Of course the influence of civil society is much greater if governments are prepared to enter into partnerships and be receptive and open to civil society. Conversely, governments that resist and isolate civil society groups may build social dissent and popular pressure. A healthy society will be characterized by participatory systems and productive partnerships. These are discussed in the following section.

Governance to Support Civil Society Actions and Campaigns

Good governance requires establishing political and legislative regimes in which the activities of civil society in favor of health and well-being are protected and encouraged. International law protects the rights of civil society (see Box 10.2).

To be effective, civil society requires the rights outlined in Box 10.2. Yet these principles apparently are being violated in many places around the world. Defending Civil Society (International Center for Not-for-Profit

---

BOX 10.2

International Principles Protecting Civil Society

1. The right of CSOs to entry (that is, the right of individuals to form and join CSOs);
2. The right to operate to fulfill their legal purposes without state interference;
3. The right to free expression;
4. The right to communication with domestic and international partners;
5. The right to freedom of peaceful assembly;
6. The right to seek and secure resources.

Source: International Center for Not-for-Profit Law (2012).

Law, 2012) notes the serious threats civil society is facing. These include traditional forms of repression, such as imprisonment, harassment, disappearances, and execution. In addition, they note that many governments have become subtler in their measures to restrict the space in which civil society, especially democracy and human rights groups, operate. These measures include "legal or quasi-legal obstacles, such as barriers to the formation of organizations, barriers to operational activities, barriers to advocacy and public policy engagement, barriers to communication and cooperation with others, barriers to assembly, and barriers to resources" (International Center for Not-for-Profit Law, 2012: 5). Overall, they conclude that there is a "worrying trend of increasingly restrictive environments for civil society around the world." (Ibid: 6). Civil society action may meet with "reprisals, including violence from state actors against those who challenge the status quo" (Gaventa, 2011: 425). There are numerous examples of the ways in which restrictive environments are reinforced by laws and their application, including the following:

- In **Singapore**, any gathering of five or more people for non-social purposes is considered an illegal assembly.
- The **Russian** Law on Extremist Activity (2003) prohibits advocacy of extreme political positions and relies on a vague definition of "extremist activity," inviting the government to label civil society organizations (CSOs) that advocate positions counter to the state as extremist.
- In **Malaysia**, the Anti-Sedition Act prohibits public discussion of certain issues altogether, and provides that the dissemination of false information can lead to imprisonment.
- In the **United Arab Emirates**, the Federal Law on Civil Associations and Foundations of Public Benefit (Federal Law 2 of 2008) restricts NGO members from participating in events outside the country without prior authorization from the Ministry of Social Affairs (Articles 16, 17).
- **Tanzania**'s NGO Act (2002) contains penal provisions for even minor breaches of the Act. More disturbingly, the Act places the burden of proof in a criminal trial against office bearers of an NGO on the accused, not the prosecution.

- **Australian** governments have also restricted the advocacy activities of community and nongovernment groups by building into government funding contracts clauses that prohibit advocacy.
- **Turkey's** draconian crackdown on civil society by the Erdoğan government has been extreme and has included the arrest and imprisonment of many civil society actors and academics seen to be critical of the regime (Mahfuz, 2017).

These restrictions on the voice of civil society constitute unhealthy governance because they encourage repression and restriction on democratic processes. At the extreme, of course, is state-delivered or endorsed action using detention or violent armed force, which may be used strategically to create fear and discourage dissent.

Governments that prioritize their survival and that of a democratic state need to protect the rights outlined in Box 10.1. Key measures by which citizen action can be protected and democratic participation by civil society can be encouraged are laws or constitutional guarantees of the right to join associations and engage in peaceful protest, and laws permitting freedom of information to government documents. Democratic action also needs to be supported by restricting the power of lobbyists paid by industry (see earlier discussion) and keeping publicly available registers of their lobbying activities and of donations to political parties. Such actions will protect and expand the space for citizen actions in support of health, sustainability, and equity.

Funding for civil society to conduct its advocacy work is important. This raises dilemmas; if the funding is from the government, the government will often be in the position of feeding the mouth that bites them. A trend is evident in terms of funding where funders provide money for specific projects but not for ongoing institutional sustainability. Yet ongoing support is vital if groups are going to be able to "take on and make progress in challenging and addressing intractable issues of inequity and discrimination" (Klugman, 2016: v). Civil society funding also needs to be driven by trust, rather than suspicion. Flexibility is required to ensure that groups can operate in highly complex and rapidly changing environments. For governments, civil society can play a helpful role as critical friends once trust has been established.

Civil Society's Role in Improving Governance for Health

Involving citizens in governance processes is recognized as important in ensuring responsive public services and in providing a check on the power of institutions. Most democratic governments and international organizations, including the World Bank and WHO, note the importance of citizen participation and consultation to good governance. In practice, however, the quality varies from effective participation with real power to token consultation processes. Research conducted in the 1990s (and which holds true today) noted that effective consultation by government relies greatly on the characteristics of the bureaucracy. The features that were identified as providing conditions conducive to effective consultation were as follows (Putland et al., 1997):

- Official endorsement of consultation at senior levels of the department;
- Staff with expertise, experience, and skills in consultative practices;
- Decentralized and devolved decision-making;
- Simple and clear structures and procedures;
- Stable functions and continuity of staff;
- Focus on social justice as much as economic efficiency;
- Constructive and ongoing relationships with communities;
- Representative mechanisms for diverse communities.

Many features of the neoliberal state, however, work to undermine these features. Miller (2014) notes that neoliberalism stresses individualism in government, rather than solidarity and meaningful citizen consultation. Also the disruptions to public services mean that features such as continuity of staff and ongoing relationships are not features of modern government.

Meaningful citizen participation can occur through management and advisory boards, and it is common to have citizen representation on governance boards. Examples include the boards of hospitals, health-care planning authorities, medical and other health professional regulation, and regional environmental authorities. These forms of civil society involvement can shape services so that they better reflect community needs. They may also reinforce existing inequities when the boards' memberships reflect elite and dominant groups and are not representative of, for example, women or people from minority groups, including those with disabilities, or those from different racial groups or linguistic backgrounds. Power relations for civil society are usually complicated by the exertion of invisible power, domination through hegemonic thought, and sometimes actions that may reinforce existing power relations in a society or community. Despite these complications, Gaventa (2011) concluded that civil society has an empowering influence in most studies reviewed.

Key advantages of civil society involvement in governance processes are that citizens and civil society can:

- play a watchdog function on public services and guard against corruption and maladministration;
- provide the perspective of citizens and users of services, which assists the development of more appropriate service and policy development;
- bring the voices of those on the margins of society to the table, including low-income people, indigenous people, women, and people with disabilities and a range of sexualities;
- introduce new ideas that will challenge group think within the public sector.

Deliberative Democracy

Some jurisdictions are experimenting with innovative ways of engaging citizens and civil society through deliberative democracy strategies. Thailand has developed a National Health Assembly (Rasanathan et al., 2012), which engages a range of sectors, including civil society, in a deliberative democracy process concerning key health policy issues. These include both health sector debates (for example, strategies to achieve universal access to medicines) and social determinant issues (for example, establishing a process for people's participation in free trade negotiations). The citizen jury is a widely used deliberative democracy method. A group of randomly selected citizens are invited to consider a matter of policy. Citizen juries have been used in the United Kingdom for many years to explore issues such as health-care rationing, education policy, and TV content. While some issues of concern have been raised (for example, their expense, the need for them to be supported by broader engagement and scrutiny, and the way topics are chosen), they are seen to offer citizen input to policy (Delap, 2001). In South Australia, a citizen jury process has been used to deliberate on the value of South Australia developing a nuclear waste dump and resulted in the government changing its policy position to adopt that of the jury (see Box 10.3).

BOX 10.3

Citizen Jury Response to Royal Commission

In South Australia, citizen juries were used to deliberate on whether or not the state should develop a nuclear waste dump. A report from a Royal Commission had recommended that such a dump be supported and that it would have many benefits for the state (http://nuclearrc.sa.gov.au/). The first jury, consisting of 50 randomly selected citizens, met over two weekends in July 2016, and the second, of 500 jurors, deliberated over three weekends. Seventy-five percent of these jurors voted against the dump, expressing the view that there were too many risks for the state in proceeding with the idea. In June 2017 the state's premier announced that as a result of the consultation, his party was dropping the idea of the nuclear dump.

Source: https://nuclear.yoursay.sa.gov.au/know-nuclear/engagement-process (accessed June 14, 2017).

Conclusion

A vibrant and active civil society and citizen involvement are vital aspects of good governance for health. This is not an optional extra, but central to the heart of a participatory democratic healthy system of government. The very processes of civil society are good for collective health because they provide people with empowerment and a sense of control. The functions performed by civil society as watchdogs and in monitoring the activities of government are vital to ensure that the power of market and profit-driven entities is curtailed in order that the health of people and environments assume primacy. A government that values, and acts on ensuring, the health, welfare, and human development of its population achieves that through working in concert with and listening carefully to the voice of civil society.

11

Conclusion

SIX KEY MESSAGES FOR GOVERNING FOR HEALTH

Was the earth made to preserve a few covetous, proud men to live at ease, and for them to bag and barn up the treasures of the Earth from others, that these may beg or starve in a fruitful land; or was it made to preserve all her children?

—GERRARD WINSTANLEY, *The New Law of Righteousness, 1649*

THE WELL-BEING MANIFESTO for the twenty-first century described in Chapter 3 presented my vision for the suite of policies forming a backbone for health and well-being. Governing for health should aim to enact these polices. Each chapter in this book has explained how this manifesto might be achieved. Six central points distill the essential messages:

1. Reducing inequities is the central, vital mechanism for building population health.
2. Human health is intimately connected to planetary health and needs to be viewed as part of the broader ecosystem.
3. How we govern is vitally important to how healthy, sustainable, and equitable we are: co-ordinated and joined-up government is vital.
4. Regulation is a powerful and essential tool of governing for health.
5. New ways of measuring progress are important.
6. Ubiquitous leadership is required for health, equity, and well-being.

I elaborate on each of these in the following and then end with a consideration of maintaining hope and acting with courage.

Reducing Inequities Is the Central, Vital Mechanism for Building Population Health

. . . the present levels of economic inequality are intrinsically inconsistent with the conception of a good society.

—ATKINSON (2015: 301)

Inequities are not an inevitability. People will never all be the same (that is, equal), but equity is a possible goal because it concerns addressing situations that are "avoidable, unfair and unjust" (Whitehead, 1991). The evidence presented in this book points to the conclusion that when health is shared more equally in a population, then the overall health of that population is better. This is likely part of the explanation for countries that punch above their weight when their life expectancy is compared with their per capita GDP. Thus while in 2015 Costa Rica has a GDP of $10,200 and the United States $55,000, Costa Ricans citizens live half a year longer on average than US citizens (World Bank, 2016). The healthiest country in the world—Japan—is also one with a relatively equal distribution of wealth. It is hard to pin down exactly why an equal distribution of economic resources is good for health. In part, it is that better equity means that solidarity between citizens is easier. People are less fearful of crime driven by envy and so have fewer security measures in place, which means they are more open to community interactions. By contrast, in societies with high economic inequity, security cameras and guards, increased policing, high walls, and fear of people who live in poverty create unhealthy social divisions. It also seems that countries that do distribute their economic resources more equally are also more likely to invest in health-promoting public goods, including education, public housing, and social security.

Finally, as Michael Marmot (2004) has pointed out, humans are driven by status considerations and make comparisons with their neighbors and others. More equity is likely to mean that the quest to outdo one's neighbour is reduced, thereby creating less stress and tension in people's lives. Thus another pathway to ill health is blocked by increased equity. Governing for health therefore requires governing for equity and exerting a redistributive spirit in all government decision-making.

Human Health Is Intimately Connected to Planetary Health and Needs to Be Viewed as Part of the Broader Ecosystem

Our species has become a geological force in its own right, and the Faustian bargain appears to be turning sour as overheated conditions loom menacingly. It is time we took up the option of renegotiating the deal—this time on terms acceptable to Nature.

—MCMICHAEL (2017: 21)

We have seen that human health is dependent on the health of the planet and that the planetary system is under immense threat. The pressure on natural ecosystems since the advent of the industrial revolution have continued to accelerate and currently have reached an alarming rate (Steffen et al., 2015). The earth's climate is warming, extinctions and depletions of species are hastening, air and water pollution directly threaten human health, and population growth is adding to the stresses on our ecosystem. Governing for health has to be centrally concerned with ensuring that the planet remains fit for human habitation.

One future scenario is that this ceases to be the case and the overload on our planetary systems results in irretrievable breakdown of the systems with disastrous consequences for humans. This bleak scenario should be at the forefront of the minds of all who govern. Scientific consensus is that we have but a few years in which to turn our ecological situation around. There are hopeful signs. Investment in renewable energy means that it is now a serious challenger to fossil fuels. Some nations (including the most populous, China and India) are at the forefront of such investment. There is a loud civil society voice in favor of the environment, but fossil fuel industry advocates can easily drown out this voice. Around the world, there are battles between those seeking to develop fossil fuel resources— whether coal, shale oil and gas, or offshore oil—and local communities and environmentalists who oppose these developments on the grounds of immediate impacts on local environments and communities and the longer-term impact of burning more fossil fuels on our planet.

Given these serious issues, environmental policy is more than ever central to improving population health, and the aim of policy must be to not exceed the ecological ceiling described in the doughnut model of economics presented in Chapter 2. Public health must embrace an ecological perspective as fundamental to its mission to promote human health.

Co-ordinated Government Is Vital

It is now widely recognized that diverse social and environmental determinants that lie outside of the direct control of a single ministry or government department shape population health. A new approach to integrated governance for health is therefore critical for addressing today's complex health challenges.

—Zsuzsanna Jakab, WHO regional director for Europe (2013: vi)

Population health and well-being are not possible without good governance in all sectors of government. In this book we have considered the importance of action in fiscal departments, education, urban planning, local government, the health-care sector, the environment, and the role of politicians and civil society actors. Good governance for health relies on action within all sectors and, while led by governments, also requires pressure from civil society to force the hand of government to make healthy changes and to regulate the private sector so its profit-seeking activities do not threaten health (see next section for elaboration on this point).

The main aim of good governance is to achieve policy coherence so that each sector is working in the same direction to create and maintain health in the population. This is illustrated by the policies needed to maintain a healthy food supply:

Fiscal

The taxation system should be used to encourage the production and consumption of healthy, fresh, locally produced foods and to discourage the production and consumption of ultra-processed high-fat and high-sugar foods and drinks. Advertising of such products would be restricted, especially advertising aimed at children.

Education

Educational institutions provide healthy food to students at low or no cost, students are provided with information on healthy diets, and educational institutions encourage healthy food production through school gardens.

Urban Planning

Urban gardens and farms are encouraged. Prime agricultural land is protected from development to maintain local food supply to urban areas.

Environment

Small farmers are supported, rather than providing tax and other subsidies to large agribusinesses. Meat and dairy production is reduced. Policy is used to reduce the food miles incurred in the food chain wherever possible.

Local Government

Community gardens and street fruit tree plantings are encouraged. Cities use local laws and mandates to discourage fast foods and to encourage fresh food markets with local produce.

Health-Care Sector

The food provided in hospitals is healthy, and primary health-care services encourage local food knowledge, production, and consumption. Tap water is promoted for drinking. Advocacy for healthy food supply to other sectors is led from the health sector.

If such coherence could be achieved, then it would make a significant contribution to reducing the burden of diet-related chronic disease, including cardiovascular disease and diabetes. Achieving such policy coherence will require government coordinating mechanisms to create cooperation across sectors. It will also require political leadership and fortitude in the face of pressure from industry. In the case of a healthy food supply, there is strong advocacy and lobbying against regulation by the food and beverage industry and transnational agricultural companies. Civil society has an important role to play in arguing for healthy food supplies and counteracting negative forces.

Perhaps the most fundamental change needed for co-ordinated government to promote health is for coherence between governments' fiscal agenda and the requirement for health. Currently, many fiscal policy actors argue that trickle-down economics means the only fiscal task is to produce a strong economy, and that will be good for all the population. But as we have seen, this belief is not supported by evidence. Neoliberal economics has exacerbated inequities and has led to the relentless growth and influence of TNCs. Unfettered market capitalism is good for short-term profits but has not resulted in the trickle-down of wealth that its supporters predicted. Chang (2014) notes that the aphorism "a rising tide lifts all boats" has proven not to be true under Thatcher and Reagan in the 1980s, yet the myth still holds sway among many. The evidence suggests that there has rather been a tsunami of wealth toward the top and stagnant wages at the bottom (Quiggan, 2010; Raworth, 2017; Chancel, 2018). A health and well-being agenda requires governments to abandon their love affair with neoliberalism and adopt measures that see planetary and human health accorded more importance than maximizing profits. Requiring this change addresses one of the most vital meta-narratives of the past two hundred years concerning the benefits of capitalism or socialism (and variations thereof) as ways of organizing society. At the end of the Cold War and following the fall of the Berlin Wall, Fukuyama (1989) declared the end of history—and that capitalism and the free market had won the battle. Yet as the reach of neoliberalism affects so many national and international institutions while at the same time its shortcomings become evident, a healthy future will require a rethink of this philosophy. Just one example that has been evident throughout this book is that of privatization. Many of the claims for its benefits did not have an evidence base, and when privatization measures were enacted, they have proved not to live up to their promises.

Of course, the big question is what economic arrangement will best enable governing for health? So extreme has been the domination of neoliberalism on fiscal imaginations that alternative economic arrangements are rarely seriously debated. Citizen debates that open the question of socialism versus capitalism and other economic alternatives and that consider which model will best serve the needs of the ecosystem and human health are vital. So readers, please take up this challenge. Discuss the alternatives; let your imagination run wild. How can we organize ourselves differently? How can we create a society in which governing for health can really happen? What form of economic regime will best support ecological and human health and well-being and equity?

I believe that achieving my manifesto for well-being is possible—but not unless we move away from the current neoliberal model that privileges the free market above other considerations. The neoliberal model believes that leaving things to an unfettered free market will be best for health and well-being. The following section questions this and promotes the power and value of regulation.

Regulation: The Invisible Hand of Good Governance

When healthy regulation has been in place for a while, the likelihood is that people take it for granted. Thus, when getting in a car, it is second nature to put a seat belt on. In many countries we take for granted that restaurants adopt hygienic food-safety practices and only notice when there is a breach of the regulations. Gun control is accepted in many countries without question. Compulsory school attendance is welcomed and accepted by a vast majority of most populations. In countries where there is generous welfare provision, people expect to be looked after in times of crisis, sickness, and old age. In each case, this is the invisible hand of regulation at work in defense of our health and well-being. While regulation can be cast as restricting the freedom of individuals (for example, the right to own a gun or not to send your children to school), from a public health perspective it is normally liberating for individuals. It means that they have the chance to give in a gun-safe environment, receive education, eat safe food, and be safer on the road. This public health perspective adopts a collectivist position and considers health and well-being above the absolute right of the individual to exert freedom.

Regulations can both promote health (through education and good urban planning, for example) and protect health. Some regulation is concerned with curbing the adverse aspects of business activity. Examples are through legislation to protect the environment, regulation to minimize conflicts of interest (not allowing industry representatives on public health committees), zoning to restrict industrial development to nonresidential areas and to place restrictions on the advertising and sale of unhealthy products. Governing for health requires regulation in the name of health and well-being.

New Ways of Measuring Progress Are Important

Measure what you treasure.

Good governance for health is much more likely to happen if the measures of progress valued by a society or community reflect well-being. There is increasing criticism of the GDP as a sole measure of progress. Alternatives have been proposed, including the Happy Planet Index and the Genuine Progress Indicator (GPI). These indices are designed to measure the downside of economic activity as well as its benefits, and to accord importance to protection of the environment and the promotion of human well-being. They also include measures of inequity and see greater equity as a positive.

I look forward to the day when news bulletins include such measures and value them as much as economic growth measures are currently valued.

Ubiquitous Leadership Is Required for Health, Equity, and Well-Being

It always seems impossible until it is done.

—ATTRIBUTED TO NELSON MANDELA

The vision of governance for health will evolve in response to leadership from civil society, local, regional, and national governments, and international agencies, especially the United Nations.

The Preamble of the founding Charter of the United Nations (1945: n.p) stated as one of its purposes "to promote social progress and better standards of life in larger freedom." This purpose concerns health, equity, and well-being. The Millennium Development Goals saw only a disappointing level of progress and left gaping inequities. The SDGs for 2030 made the important connection between human development and ecological sustainability and thus hold more promise. They also reflect a truly intersectoral perspective on well-being. Criticisms of the SDGs argue that they do not set out to tackle the underlying factors driving growing inequities in wealth and leave untouched the current global economic system that has allowed the inequity gap to widen in the past 30 years (McCloskey, 2016). Realizing the SDGs will require strong leadership to change the current focus on neoliberalism and tame the power of TNCs to shape our world solely for profit rather than health.

All governments need to ensure that they govern for health in the ways that each chapter of this book has laid out. Most fundamentally, national governments also need to ensure that they establish systems to ensure that taxes cannot be avoided or evaded by very wealthy individuals and TNCs. These taxes are vital to provide funding for the public sector, which will enable services and resources, which in turn will lead to improved health and well-being. As a global community, we have more than enough resources to meet every global citizen's needs for the basics for a healthy and purposeful life. Our problem is that those resources are so poorly and unequally distributed. Good governance for health would oversee a fairer distribution.

Civil society has a vital leadership role in arguing for the public good and ensuring that the United Nations and all its agencies and governments work to promote that good. The nutcracker effect described in Chapter 10 (Figure 10.1) results from concerted bottom-up pressure for change, combined with top-down policy action. A watchdog function is required to ensure that those interests seeking private profits are not able to gain sway over public policy. Conflicts of interest must be avoided, noted, and legislated against.

Hope and Courage

Hope is being able to see that there is light despite all of the darkness.
—DESMOND TUTU (2010 QUOTED IN SOLOMON, *2010: n.p)*

Governing for health will require a mix of hope and courage in the future. Inspirational stories of how hope triumphed in darkness can inspire the present. Mandela's long walk to freedom signified his immense courage at a time when hoping for a free South Africa seemed an impossible dream. Brave suffragettes who sacrificed their lives in the name of women's equality always saw the inevitability of their cause. Anti-slavery campaigners rejected those who claimed their campaign would result in economic disaster and clung to the moral rightness of their cause. Climate change scientists and environmental activists continue to point to the body of evidence in the face of irrational denialism. People of different sexualities lived with the hope that their identities would be recognized and accepted. Each campaign was laced through with hope and courageous actions. Each campaign seemed impossible at some point, only to be won through courage, and then the new norm became quickly accepted. Such will be the revolution of governing for health. One day people will look back—aghast—at how economic considerations came to dominate our public policy and how commercial interests were able to promote their quest for profit as if it were a public good. On that day we will collectively celebrate the way our society has organized itself for sustainability, health, well-being, and equity, and we will recognize the true value of governance for the public good.

References

Adams, D. (1979) *Hitchhiker's Guide to the Galaxy*. London: Pan Books.

Alexander, C. (1967) "The city as a mechanism for sustaining human contact." In W. R. Ewald (ed.), *Environment for Man*. Bloomington: Indiana University Press, pp. 60–102.

Alliance for Healthy Cities. (2018) "Putting healthy settings theory into practice: Seeing is believing." http://www.alliance-healthycities.com/htmls/innovation/index_innovation.html (accessed May 2, 2018).

Altepe, R. (2015) "Country profiles: Urban health indicators in Turkey." In L. J. Lafond (ed.), *National Healthy Cities Networks in the WHO European Region*. Copenhagen: World Health Organization, p. 113.

American Public Health Association. (2016) "Improving health by increasing the minimum wage," Policy Number: 20167, November 1, 2016. https://www.apha.org/policies-and-advocacy/public-health-policy-statements/policy-database/2017/01/18/improving-health-by-increasing-minimum-wage (accessed January 6, 2018).

Ampri, I. (2012) "Fiscal support for the efficient and sustainable management of natural resources in Indonesia: Renewable energy and forestry resources." Ministry of Finance, Jakarta Republic of Indonesia.

Anaf, J., Baum, F., Fisher, M., et al. (2017) "Assessing the health impact of transnational corporations: A case study on McDonald's Australia." *Globalization and Health* 13(7): 1–16.

Anand, S., and Segal, P. (2015) "The global distribution of income." In A. Atkinson, F. Bourguignon (eds.), *Handbook of Income Distribution*. Volume 2A Chapter 11, pp. 937–979.

Anderson, I., Robson, B., Connolly, M., et al. (2016) "Indigenous and tribal peoples' health (The Lancet–Lowitja Institute Global Collaboration): A population study." *The Lancet* 388(10040): 131–157.

Ashton, J. (1988) "Esmedune 2000: Vision or dream: A healthy Liverpool." Liverpool: Department of Community Health, University of Liverpool.

Ashton, J., and Ubido, J. (1991) "The healthy city and the ecological idea." *Social History of Medicine* 4(1): 173–180.

Atkinson, A. B. (2015) *Inequality: What Can Be Done.* Cambridge, MA: Harvard University Press.

Australian Broadcasting Corporation (ABC). (2017) "CDC ban: Alarm over reports health agency forbidden from using words like 'fetus,' 'transgender' and 'diversity,'" December 18, 2017. http://www.abc.net.au/news/2017-12-17/fetus-transgender-forbidden-words-for-us-health-officials-report/9266560 (accessed May 2, 2018).

Avaaz. (2017) "About us." https://secure.avaaz.org/page/en/about/ (accessed July 19, 2017).

Bacchi, C. (2009) *Analysing Policy: What's the Problem Represented to Be?* Frenchs Forest, NSW: Pearson Education.

Balabanova, D., McKee, M., and Mills, A. (eds.). (2011) *Good Health at Low Cost: 25 Years on: What Makes a Successful Health System?* London: London School of Hygiene & Tropical Medicine.

Balch, O. (2013) "Buen vivir: The social philosophy inspiring movements in South America," February 4, 2013, *The Guardian.* https://www.theguardian.com/sustainable-business/blog/buen-vivir-philosophy-south-america-eduardo-gudynas (accessed April 13, 2018).

Balch, O. (2014) "Water wars: A new reality for business and government," October 7, 2014, *The Guardian.* http://www.theguardian.com/sustainable-business/2014/oct/06/water-wars-business-governments-scarcity-pollution-access, (accessed November 10, 2017).

Bambra, C. (2009) "Welfare state regimes and the political economy of health." *Humanity and Society* 33: 99–117.

Bambra, C. (2012). "Reducing health inequalities: new data suggest that the English strategy was partially successful." *Journal Epidemiol Community Health* 66: 662.

Bambra, C., Garthwaite, K., and Hunter, D. (2014) "The impact of financing health care on equity. All things being equal: Does it matter for equity how you organize and pay for health care? A review of the international evidence." *International Journal of Health Services* 44(3): 457–477.

Barlow, J., Johnston, I., Kendrick, D., et al. (2006) "Individual and group based parenting programmes for the treatment of physical child abuse and neglect." *Cochrane Database of Systematic Reviews* (3): CD005463. doi:10.1002/14651858. CD005463.pub2.

Barten, F., Akerman, M., Becker, D., et al. (2011) "Rights, knowledge, and governance for improved health equity in urban settings." *Journal of Urban Health* 88(5): 896–905.

Bartlett, D. (2016) "Global trends in renewable energy," May 11, 2016, *RSM.* https://www.rsm.global/insights/economic-insights/global-trends-renewable-energy.

Barton, H. (2016) *City of Well-being: A Radical Guide to Planning*. London: Taylor & Francis.

Barton, H., and Tsourou, C. (2001) *Healthy Urban Planning: A WHO Guide to Planning for People*. London: Taylor & Francis Ltd.

Barton, H., and Grant, M. (2013) "Urban planning for healthy cities: A review of the progress of the European healthy cities programme." *Journal of Urban Health* 90(Supp 1): 129–141.

Baum, F. (2007) "Cracking the nut of health equity: Top down and bottom up pressure for action on the social determinants of health." *Promotion & Education* 14(2): 90–95.

Baum, F. (2009) "More than the tip of the iceberg: Health policies and research that go below the surface." *Journal of Epidemiology and Community Health* 63(12): 957–957.

Baum, F. (2016) *The New Public Health* (4th ed.). Melbourne: Oxford University Press.

Baum, F. (2017) "Beyond the social determinants: A manifesto for wellbeing." In A. Coopes (ed.), December 6, 2017, *Croakey*. https://croakey.org/beyond-the-social-determinants-a-manifesto-for-wellbeing/.

Baum, F., Bégin, M., Houweling, T. A., and Taylor, S. (2009) "Changes not for the faint-hearted: Reorienting health care systems towards health equity through action on the social determinants of health." *American Journal of Public Health* 99(11): 1967–1974.

Baum, F. E., Laris, P., Fisher, M., et al. (2013) "'Never mind the logic, give me the numbers': Former Australian health ministers' perspectives on the social determinants of health." *Social Science and Medicine* 87: 138–146.

Baum, F., and Fisher, M. (2014) "Why behavioural health promotion endures despite its failure to reduce health inequities." *Sociology of Health and Illness* 36(2): 213–225.

Baum, F., Laris, P., Fisher, M., et al. (2014) "Dear health minister: Tend the garden but make sure you fence the crocodiles." *Journal of Epidemiology and Community Health* 68(4): 295–296.

Baum, F., Delany, T., Macdougall, C., et al. (2017) "Ideas, actors and institutions: Lessons from South Australian health in all policies on what encourages other sectors' involvement." *BMC Public Health* 17(811): 1–16.

Beckfield, J., and Krieger, N. (2009) "Epi + demos + cracy: Linking political systems and priorities to the magnitude of health inequities—evidence, gaps, and a research agenda." *Epidemiology Review* 31: 152–177.

Bernstein, A. S. (2014) "Biological diversity and public health." *Annual Review of Public Health* 35: 153–167.

Bocarejo, J. P., and Tafur, L. E. (2013) "Urban land use transformation driven by an innovative transportation project, Bogotá, Colombia. Case study prepared for Global Report on Human Settlements 2013." Nairobi: United Nations.

Boffey, D. (2017) "US cities commit to bypassing Trump," July 7, 2017, *The Guardian Weekly*, 197(5): p. 10. https://www.pressreader.com/uk/the-guardian-weekly/20170707/textview.

Bond, P. (1999) "Globalization, pharmaceutical pricing, and South African health policy: Managing confrontation with U.S. firms and politicians." *International Journal of Health Services* 29(4): 765–792.

Bowen, A., and Casadevall, A. (2015) "Increasing disparities between resource inputs and outcomes, as measured by certain health deliverables, in biomedical research." *Proceedings of the National Academy of Sciences of the United States of America* 112(36): 11335–11340.

Braithwaite, J., and Drahos, P. (2000) *Global Business Regulation*. Cambridge, UK: Cambridge University Press.

Branas, C. C., Kastanaki, A. E., Michalodimitrakis, M., et al. (2015) "The impact of economic austerity and prosperity events on suicide in Greece: A 30-year interrupted time-series analysis." *Health Policy Research* 5: e005619.

Bramley, G., Dempsey, N., Power, S., et al. (2009) "Social sustainability and urban form: Evidence from five British cities." *Environment and Planning* 41(9): 2125–2142.

Breierova, L., and Duflo, E. (2004) "The impact of education on fertility and child mortality: Do fathers really matter less than mothers?" *NBER Working Paper Series*. Cambridge, MA: National Bureau of Economic Research.

Brito, N. H., and Noble, K. G. (2014) "Socioeconomic status and structural brain development." *Frontiers in Neuroscience* 8(276). Published online 2014 Sep 4. doi:10.3389/fnins.2014.00276

Brown, L. R. (2011). *World on the edge: How to prevent environmental and economic collapse*. London, UK, Earthscan.

Brown, L. (2013) "The real threat to our future is peak water," July 6, 2013, *The Guardian*. http://www.theguardian.com/global-development/2013/jul/06/water-supplies-shrinking-threat-to-food (accessed October 6, 2014).

Bunker, J. P., Frazier, H. S., and Mosteller, S. (1994) "Improving health: Measuring effects of medical care." *Milbank Quarterly* 72(2): 225–258.

Burgess, C. P., Johnston, F. H., Berry, H. L., et al. (2009) "Healthy country, healthy people: The relationship between Indigenous health status and 'caring for country.'" *Medical Journal of Australia* 190(10): 567–572.

Burris, S., Wagenaar, A. C., Swanson, J., et al. (2010) "Making the case for laws that improve health: A framework for public health law research." *The Millbank Quarterly* 88(2): 169–210.

Butchart, A., and Mikton, C. (2014) *World Report on Violence and Health*. Geneva: World Health Organization.

Calthorpe, P. (1993) *The Next American Metropolis: Ecology, Community, and the American Dream*. New York: Princeton Architectural Press.

Canadian Association of Community Health Centre. (2018) "About Community Health Centre." https://www.cachc.ca/about-chcs/ (accessed May 9, 2018).

Canadian Centre for Policy Alternatives. (2017) "Alternative Federal Budget 2017," https://www.policyalternatives.ca/projects/alternative-federal-budget (accessed September 7, 2017).

Canadian Index of Wellbeing. (2016) *How Are Canadians Really Doing? The 2016 CIW National Report.* Waterloo, ON: Canadian Index of Wellbeing and University of Waterloo.

Carpenter, M. (2000) "Health for some: Global health and social development since Alma Ata." *Community Development Journal* 35(4): 336–351.

Centre for Responsive Politics. (2017) "Open Sectrets.org. Agribusinesses." https://www.opensecrets.org/industries/indus.php?Ind=A (accessed September 7, 2017).

CentreForum Commission. (2014) *The Pursuit Of Happiness: A New Ambition for Our Mental Health*, July 2014, CentreForum Mental Health Commission.

Chakrabortty, A. (2017a) "A basic income for everyone? Yes, Finland shows it really can work," November 1, 2017, *The Guardian.* https://www.theguardian.com/commentisfree/2017/oct/31/finland-universal-basic-income (accessed January 6, 2018).

Chakrabortty, A. (2017b) "Over 170 years after Engels, Britain still murders its poor," June 21, 2017, *The Guardian*, p. 25.

Chan, M. (2016a) "WHO director-general addresses Human Rights Council on climate change." Human Rights Council on Climate Change. Geneva: Switzerland.

Chan, M. (2016b) "Obesity and diabetes: The slow-motion disaster." Keynote address at the 47th meeting of the National Academy of Medicine. Washington, DC: World Health Organization.

Chan, M. (2016c) "The relevance and importance of promoting health in national SDG responses, Keynote address at the 9th Global conference on health promotion." http://www.who.int/dg/speeches/2016/shanghai-health-promotion/en/

Chan, M. (2017) "Address to the Seventieth World Health Assembly." Seventieth World Health Assembly. Geneva: World Health Organization.

Chancel, L. (2018) "40 years of data suggests 3 myths about globalization." *Harvard Business Review*, March 2, 2018. https://hbr.org/2018/03/40-years-of-data-suggests-3-myths-about-globalization (accessed July 16, 2018).

Chandler, M. J., and Lalonde, C. (2008) "Cultural continuity as a moderator of suicide risk among Canada's first nations." In L. Kirmayer and G. Valaskakis (eds.), *The Mental Health of Canadian Aboriginal Peoples: Transformations, Identity, and Community.* Vancouver: University of British Columbia Press.

Chang, H. (2010) *23 Things They Don't Tell You about Capitalism.* New York: Bloomsbury Press.

Chang, H. (2014) *Economics: The User's Guide.* London: Bloomsbury Press.

Chapman, S. (2008) *Public Health Advocacy and Tobacco Control: Making Smoking History*. Oxford: Blackwell.

Chivian, E., and Bernstein, A. (eds.). (2008) *Sustaining Life: How Human Health Depends on Biodiversity*. Oxford: Oxford University Press.

City of Vancouver. (2017) "Healthy City Strategy: Our goals." http://vancouver.ca/people-programs/healthy-city-strategy.aspx (accessed July 5, 2017).

Climate Council of Australia. (2017) "State of solar 2016: Globally and in Australia." Potts Point, NSW: Climate Council of Australia.

Climate and Health Alliance. (2017) "About." http://www.caha.org.au/ (accessed July 19, 2017).

Coalition for Safe Affordable Food. (2018) "About." http://coalitionforsafeaffordablefood.org/ (accessed May 2, 2018).

Cobellos, G., Ehrlich, P. R., and Dirzo, R. (2017) "Biological annihilation via the ongoing sixth mass extinction signalled by vertebrate population losses and declines." *Proceedings of the National Academy of Sciences* 114(30): E6089–E6096. doi:10.1073/pnas.1704949114. Epub 2017 Jul 10.

Collins, P., and Hayes, M. (2010) "The role of urban municipal governments in reducing health inequities: A meta-narrative mapping analysis." *International Journal of Equity Health* 9(1): 13. doi.org/10.1186/1475-9276-9-13.

Commission on Social Determinants of Health (CSDH). (2008) *Closing the Gap in a Generation: Health Equity through Action on the Social Determinants of Health. Final Report of the Commission on Social Determinants of Health*. Geneva: World Health Organization.

Commonwealth of Australia, Department of the Prime Minister and Cabinet. (2018) *Closing the Gap:Prime Ministers Report 2017*. https://closingthegap.pmc.gov.au/sites/default/files/ctg-report-2018.pdf.

Considine, M., O'Sullivan, S., and Nguyen, P. (2014) "Mission drift? The third sector and the pressure to be businesslike: Evidence from Job Services Australia." *Third Sector Review* 20(1): 87–107.

Convention on Biological Diversity. (2018) "International Day for Biological Diversity." www.un.org/en/events/biodiversityday/background.shtml (accessed May 2, 2018).

Co-operative Group Limited. (2017a) "Membership dashboard." www.coop.co.uk/membership/membership-dashboard (accessed April 20, 2017).

Co-operative Group Limited. (2017b) "Co-op values: Principles more valuable than profits." www.co-operative.coop/about-us/values (accessed April 20, 2017).

Corburn, J. (2009) *Toward the Healthy City: People, Places, and the Politics of Urban Planning*. Cambridge, MA: MIT Press.

Corburn, J. (2015) "City planning as preventive medicine." *Preventative Medicine* 77: 48–51.

Corcoran, P., Griffin, E., Arensman, E., et al. (2015) "Impact of the economic recession and subsequent austerity on suicide and self-harm in Ireland: An interrupted time series analysis." *International Journal of Epidemiology* 44(3): 969–977.

Credit Suisse. (2017). "Global Wealth Databook 2017." https://www.credit-suisse. com/corporate/en/research/research-institute/publications.html (accessed November 2017.)

Crerar, P. (2017) "Total ban on fast-food outlets within 400m of London schools, Mayor Sadiq Khan to announce," November 27, 2017, *EveningStandard*. https:// www.standard.co.uk/news/london/total-ban-on-fastfood-outlets-within-400m-of-london-schools-a3702376.html (accessed May 2, 2018)

Crocker, R. (2017) *Somebody Else's Problem: Consumerism, Sustainability and Design*. New York: Routledge.

Currie, J., and Rossin-Slater, M. (2015) "Early-life origins of lifecycle well-being: Research and policy implications." *Journal of Policy Analysis and Management* 34(1): 208–242.

Daar, A. S., Singer, P. A., Persad, L., et al. (2007) "Grand challenges in chronic non-communicable diseases." *Nature* 450(7169): 494–496.

Dakubo, C. Y. (2010) *Ecosystems and Human Health: A Critical Approach to Ecohealth Research and Practice*. New York: Springer.

Daly, H. E., and Cobb, J. B. (1990) *For the Common Good*. London: Green Print.

Dannenberg, A. L., Frumkin, H. and Jackson, R. J. (eds.). (2011) *Making Healthy Places: Designing and Building for Health, Well-being, and Sustainability*. Washington, DC: Island Press/Center for Resource Economics.

Davis, M. (2006) *Planet of Slums*. London: Verso.

Davis, M. (2014) "Neoliberalism, the culture wars and public policy." In C. Miller and L. Orchard (eds.), *Australian Public Policy: Progressive Ideas in the Neo-Liberal Ascendency*. Bristol, UK: Policy Press, pp. 27–42.

Day Ashley. L., Mcloughlin, C., Aslam, M., et al. (2014) "The role and impact of private schools in developing countries: A rigorous review of the evidence. Final report. Education Rigorous Literature Review." London: Department for International Development.

de Blasio, B. (2016). "Healthier neighbourhoods through healthier parks." *The Lancet* 388(10062): 2850–2851. Published Online September 23, 2016. http:// dx.doi.org/10.1016/ S0140-6736(16)31579-3

de Leeuw, E., Clavier, C., and Breton, E. (2014) "Health policy—why research it and how: Health political science." *Health Research Policy and Systems* 12(55): 1–10.

de Nazelle, A., Nieuwenhuijsen, M. J., Antó, J. M., et al. (2011) "Improving health through policies that promote active travel: A review of evidence to support integrated health impact assessment." *Environment International* 37(4): 766–777.

Delany, T., Lawless, A., Baum, F., et al. (2015) "Health in All Policies in South Australia: What has supported early implementation?" *Health Promotion International* 31(4): 888–898.

Delap, C. (2001) "Citizens' juries: Reflections on the UK experience." *PLA Notes* 40: 39–42.

Doyal, L. (1979) *The Political Economy of Health*. London: Pluto Press.

Durie, M. (2005) "Indigenous knowledge within a global knowledge system." *Higher Education Policy* 18(3): 301–312.

Dwyer, J., O'Donnell, K., Lavoie, J., et al. (2009) "The overburden report: Contracting for indigenous health services." Darwin: Cooperative Research Centre for Aboriginal Health.

Ecological Footprint. (2012) "Earth overshoot day." http://www.footprintnetwork. org/en/index.php/GFN/blog/today_is_earth_overshoot_day1   (accessed September 27, 2017).

Ekezie, C. C., Lamont, K., and Bhattacharya, S. (2017) "Are cash transfer programs effective in improving maternal and child health in Sub-Saharan Africa? A systematic review of randomized controlled trials." *Journal of Global Health* (April   1).   http://www.ghjournal.org/are-cash-transfer-programs-effective-in-improving-maternal-and-child-health-in-sub-saharan-africa-a-systematic-review-of-randomized-controlled-trials/#

Elder, J. P., Schmid, T. I., Dower, P., et al. (1993) "Community heart health programs: Components, rationale and strategies for effective interventions." *Journal of Public Health Policy* 14(4): 463–479.

EPA Local Government Advisory Committee. (2015) "EJ best practices for local government."   https://www.epa.gov/sites/production/files/2015-10/documents/2015_best_practices_for_local_government.pdf (accessed May 2, 2018).

Ermano, P. (2013) "Equity, efficiency and progressive taxation." In J. Leaman and A. Waris (eds.), *Tax Justice and the Political Economy of Global Capitalism, 1945 to the Present*. New York: Berghahn Books, pp. 227–238.

Farrell, B. (2014) "Divestment helped to end apartheid in South Africa: Can it work for fossil fuels?" November 4, 2014, *Yes! Magazine*. www.yesmagazine. org/planet/divestment-helped-to-end-apartheid-in-south-africa-can-it-work-for-fossil-fuels (accessed May 2, 2018).

Farrow, K., Hurley, S., and Sturrock, R. (2015) *Grand Alibis: How declining public sector capability affects services for the disadvantaged*. Melbourne: Centre for Policy Development, December 2015.

Federation of Canadian Municipalities. (2017) "Seizing the moment for rural Canada: Municipal recommendations for Federal Budget 2017." Ottawa: Federation of Canadian Municipalities.

Feinstein, L., Sabates, R., Anderson, T. M., et al. (2006) "What are the effects of education on health?" *Measuring the Effects of Education on Health and Civic Engagement: Proceedings of the Copenhagen Symposium*, OECD, pp. 171–354.

Ferreira, F. H. G. (1997) *Economic Transition and the Distribution of Income and Wealth*. Washington, DC: Office of the Chief Economist for East Asia and Pacific.

Fidan, N., and Yilmaz, E. (2015) "The integration of health planning in Turkish Cities." In H. Barton et al. (eds.), *The Routledge Handbook of Planning for Health and Well-being*. London and New York: Routledge, pp. 497–510.

Fincher, R. (1990) "Women in the city." *Australian Geographical Studies* 28: 29–37.

Fioramonti, L. (2017) *Wellbeing Economy: Success in a World Without Growth.* Johannesburg: Pan MacMillan.

Flannery, T. (2005). *The Weather Makers: The History and Future Impact of Climate Change.* Melbourne: Text.

Foster, G. (2016) "Universal basic income: The dangerous idea of 2016." https://theconversation.com/universal-basic-income-the-dangerous-idea-of-2016-70395 (accessed May 25, 2017).

Francis, J., Giles-Corti, B., Wood, L., et al. (2012) "Creating sense of community: The role of public space." *Journal of Environmental Psychology* 32(4): 401–09.

Freeman, T., Baum, F., Lawless, A., et al. (2017a) "Case study of an Aboriginal community-controlled health service in Australia: Universal, rights-based, publicly funded comprehensive primary health care in action." *Health and Human Rights* 18(2): 93–108.

Freeman, T., Baum, F., Labonte, R., et al. (2017b) "Primary health care reform, dilemmatic space, and risk of burnout among health workers." *Health* 22(3): 1–21.

Freire, P. (1972) *Pedagogy of the Oppressed.* Harmondsworth: Penguin.

Freudenberg, N. (2014) *Lethal but Legal: Corporations, Consumption, and Protecting Public Health.* New York: Oxford University Press.

Freudenberg, N. (2015) "The 100 largest governments and corporations by revenue." http://www.corporationsandhealth.org/2015/08/27/the-100-largest-governments-and-corporations-by-revenue (accessed November 1, 2017).

Freudenheim, E. (2017) "Political street theater: How to organize a die-in to protest attacks on Medicaid, Affordable Care Act and other safety net programs." www.huffingtonpost.com/entry/political-street-theater-how-to-organize-a-die-in_us_58c1a678e4b0a797c1d39a3d (accessed May 2, 2018).

Friel, S., Gleeson, D., Thow, A. M., et al. (2013) "A new generation of trade policy: potential risks to diet-related health from the trans pacific partnership agreement." *Globalization and Health* 9(46): 1–7.

Friel, S., Akerman, M., Hancock, T., et al. (2011) "Addressing the social and environmental determinants of urban health equity: Evidence for action and a research agenda." *Journal of Urban Health* 88(5): 860–874.

Friendly, M. (2016) "Early childhood education and care as a social determinant of health." In D. Raphael (ed.), *Social Determinants of Health: Canadian Perspectives* (3rd ed.). Toronto: Canadian Scholars' Press, Chapter 9.

Fromm, E. (1955). *The Sane Society.* New York, Rinehart.

Frumkin, H., Frank, L., and Jackson, R. J. (2004) *Urban Sprawl and Public Health: Designing, Planning, and Building for Healthy Communities.* New York: Island Press.

Fukuyama, F. (1989) "The end of history." *The National Interest* 16(Summer 1989): 3–18.

Fullan, M. (2010) *All Systems Go: The Change Imperative for Whole System Reform.* Thousand Oaks, CA: Corwin.

Furlong, M., and McGilloway, S. (2012) "The incredible years parenting program in Ireland: A qualitative analysis of the experience of disadvantaged parents." *Clinical Child Psychology and Psychiatry* 17(4): 616–630.

Ganz, M. (2009) "Why stories matter," March 2009, *Sojourners Magazine*. www.sojo.net/magazine/2009/03/why-stories-matter (accessed July 30, 2014).

Gaventa, J. (2011) "Civil society and power." In M. Edwards (ed.), *The Oxford Handbook of Civil Society*. New York: Oxford University Press.

Ghebreyesus, T. A. (2018) "Health World Day," Director-General of the World Health Organization, Colombo, Sri Lanka, April 7, 2018. http://www.who.int/dg/speeches/2018/world-health-day/en/ (accessed April 27, 2018).

Ghebreyesus, T. A. (2017) "WHO Director-General Dr. Tedros." Remarks at the Sixty-ninth session of the WHO Regional Committee for Americas. Washington, DC: World Health Organization.

Giles-Corti, B., Vernez-Moudon, A., Reis, R., et al. (2016) "City planning and population health: A global challenge." *The Lancet* 388: 2912–2924.

Givel, M. S. (2015) "Gross National Happiness in Bhutan: Political institutions and implementation." *Asian Affairs* 46(1): 102–117.

Global Alliance for the Rights of Nature. (2015) "Universal Declaration of Rights of Mother Earth." http://therightsofnature.org/universal-declaration/ (accessed March 3, 2018).

Global Footprint Network. (2018) "Ecological wealth of nations." http://www.footprintnetwork.org/content/documents/ecological_footprint_nations/ecological_per_capita.html (accessed January 11, 2018).

Global Health Watch 4. (2014) *An Alternative World Health Report*. London: Zed Books.

Global Health Watch 5. (2017) *D1 Money Talks at the World Health Organization*. London: Zed Books.

Global Wind Energy Council. (2017) "Global statistics." http://gwec.net/global-figures/graphs/ (accessed April 19, 2017).

Godar, S., Paetz, C., and Truger, A. (2014) "Progressive tax reform in OECD countries: Perspectives and obstacles." Global Labour University working paper no. 27. Geneva: International Labour Office.

Governance Institute of Australia. (2017) "Good governance guide: 'What is good governance?'" www.goodgovernance.org.au/ (accessed July 24, 2017).

Government of South Australia (2016) *The South Australian Integrated Planning, Development and Infrastructure Act*. Adelaide: SA Government.

Goodling, E., Green, J., and McClintock, N. (2015) "Uneven development of the sustainable city: Shifting capital in Portland, Oregon." *Urban Geography* 36(4): 504–527.

Grant, M. (2015) "European Healthy City Network Phase V: Patterns emerging for healthy urban planning." *Health Promotion International* 30(1): i54–i70.

Gudynas, E. (2011) "Buen Vivir: Today's tomorrow." *Development* 54(4): 441–447.

Gulland, A. (2016) "Pension funds: Tobacco investment up in smoke." *BMJ* 352: i1491.

Haigh, F., Baum, F., Dannenberg, A. L., et al. (2013) "The effectiveness of health impact assessment in influencing decision-making in Australia and New Zealand 2005–2009." *BMC Public Health* 13(1): 1188.

Halstead, S. B., Walsh, J., and Warren, K. S. (eds.). (1985) *Good Health at Low Cost.* Proceedings of a Conference held at the Bellagio Conference Centre. Bellagio, Italy: The Rockefeller Foundation.

Hambleton, R., and Sweeting, D. (2014) "Innovation in urban political leadership: Reflections on the introduction of a directly-elected mayor in Bristol, UK." *Public Policy and Management* 34: 315–22.

Hamblin, J. (2016) "How Cubans live as long as Americans at a tenth of the cost: Lessons of physical prosperity in a despotic regime," November 29, 2016, *The Atlantic.* https://www.theatlantic.com/health/archive/2016/11/cuba-health/508859/ (accessed May 2, 2018).

Hamilton, C. (2010) *Requiem for a Species: Why We Resist the Truth about Climate Change.* London and New York: Earthscan.

Hamilton, C., and Denniss, R. (2005) *Affluenza.* Sydney: Allen & Unwin.

Hammond, C. (2007) "Impacts of lifelong learning upon emotional resilience, psychological and mental health: Fieldwork evidence." *Oxford Review of Education* 30(4): 551–568.

Hancock, T. (1993) "Health, human development and the community ecosystem: Three ecological models." *Health Promotion International* 8(1): 41–47.

Hancock, T. (2017) "Equity, sustainability and governance: Key challenges facing 21st century cities (Part 1)." *Cities & Health* 1(1): 95–99.

Hancock, T., and Duhl, L. (1986) *Healthy Cities: Promoting Health in the Urban Context.* WHO Healthy Cities Paper No. 1. Copenhagen: FADL.

Hankivsky, O. (2008) "Cost estimates of dropping out of high school in Canada." Ottawa: Canadian Council on Learning, Simon Fraser University.

Hansia, F. (2014) "Coca-Cola forced to shut bottling plant in India because of its 'unsustainable water extraction practices,'" July 15, 2014, *Global Research.* http://www.globalresearch.ca/coca-cola-forced-to-shut-bottling-plant-in-india-because-of-its-unsustainable-water-extraction-practices/5391271 (accessed November 17, 2017).

Hardoon, D. (2017) "Oxfam briefing paper: An economy for the 99%. It's time to build a human economy that benefits everyone, not just the privileged few," January 16, 2017. Oxford, Oxfam International.

Hargreaves, A., and Shirley, D. (2012) *The global fourth way: The quest for educational excellence.* Thousand Oaks, CA: Sage.

Harman, E. (1988) "Capitalism, patriarchy and the city." In C. Baldock and B. Cass (eds.), *Women, Social Welfare and the State in Australia.* Sydney: Allen & Unwin.

Harris, P., Kent, J., Sainsbury, P., and Thow, A. M. (2016) "Framing health for land-use planning legislation: A qualitative descriptive content analysis." *Social Science & Medicine* 148: 42–51.

Harris, P., Kent, J., Sainsbury, P., et al. (2017) "Creating 'healthy built environment' legislation in Australia: A policy analysis." *Health Promotion International*, dax055, 1–11. doi:10.1093/heapro/dax055

Harris-Roxas, B., and Harris, E. (2011) "Differing forms, differing purposes: A typology of health impact assessment." *Environmental Impact Assessment Review* 31(4): 396–403.

Hartig, T., Mitchell, R., de Vries, S. and Frumkin, H. (2014) "Nature and health." *Annual Review of Public Health* 35: 207–228.

Hartocollis, A., and Alcindor, Y. (2017) "Women's March highlights as huge crowds protest Trump: 'We're not going away.'" https://www.nytimes.com/2017/01/21/us/womens-march.html?_r=0 (accessed May 2, 2018).

Harvey, D. (2007) *A Brief History of Neoliberalism*. New York: Oxford University Press.

Harvey, D. (2012) *Rebel Cities: From the Right to the City to the Urban Revolution* (1st ed.). London: Verso.

Hertzman, C. (2010) "Framework for the Social Determinants of Early Child Development." In R. E. Tremblay, M. Boivin, and RDeV Peters (eds.), *Encyclopedia on Early Childhood Development*. [online]. http://www.child-encyclopedia.com/importance-early-childhood-development/according-experts/framework-social-determinants-early-child. Published November 2010. Accessed March 14, 2018.

Hetherington, D. (2016) "Per Capita Tax Survey 2016: Public attitudes towards taxation and public expenditure." Melbourne, Australia: Per Capita.

Hetherington, D. (2017) "From public good to profit margin: How privatisation is failing our communities." March 6, 2017, *The Guardian*.

Heywood, M., and Altman, D. G. (2000) "Confronting AIDS: Human rights, law, and social transformation." *Health and Human Rights* 5: 149–179.

Hickel, J. (2016) "Global inequality may be much worse than we think," April 8, 2016, *The Guardian*. https://www.theguardian.com/global-development-professionals-network/2016/apr/08/global-inequality-may-be-much-worse-than-we-think (accessed May 2, 2018).

Hill, M., and Verone, F. (2017) *The Public Policy Process* (7th ed.). Oxon and New York: Routledge.

history.org. US Declaration of Independence. http://www.ushistory.org/declaration/document/ (accessed June 14, 2017).

Howlett, M., Ramesh, M., and Perl, A. (2009) *Studying Public Policy: Policy Cycles and Policy Subsystems* (3rd ed.). Oxford: Oxford University Press.

Hutton, W. (1995) *The State We're In*. London: Jonathan Cape.

International Labour Organization. (2018) "1.2. How many countries have a minimum wage?" http://www.ilo.org/global/topics/wages/minimum-wages/definition/WCMS_439073/lang--en/index.htm (accessed May 2, 2018).

International Center for Not-for-Profit Law and World Movement for Democracy. (2012) "Defending civil society." *The International Journal of Not-for-Profit Law* 14(3): 1–92.

Irwin, L. G., Siddiqi, A., and Hertzman, C. (2007) "Early child development: A powerful equalizer." Vancouver: HELP, University of British Columbia.

Irwin, A., and Scali, E. (2007) "Action on the social determinants of health: A historical perspective." *Global Public Health* 2(3): 235–256.

Jackson, R. J., and Sinclar, S. (2011) *Designing Healthy Communities*. San Francisco: John Wiley & Sons.

Jackson, R. J., Dannenberg, A. L., and Frumpkin, H. (2013) "Health and the built environment: 10 years after." *American Journal of Public Health* 103(9): 1542–1544.

Jackson, H., and Shiell, A. (2017) *Preventive Health: How Much Does Australia Spend and Is It Enough?* Canberra: Foundation for Alcohol Research and Education.

Jacobs, M. (1991). *The Green Economy*. London: Pluto Press.

Jakab, Z. (2013) "Foreword." In I. Kickbusch (ed.), *Implementing a Health 2020 Vision: Governance for Health in the 21st Century*. Copenhagen: WHO Regional Office for Europe, p. vi.

Jeffrey, K. (2016) "This is the most efficient economy in the world." July 19, 2016, *New Economics Foundation*. http://neweconomics.org/2016/07/this-is-the-most-efficient-economy-in-the-world/?_sf_s=Happy+PLanet+Index&_sft_latest=articles (accessed January 2, 2018).

Jenkins-Smith, H. C., Nohrstedt, D., Weible, C. M., et al. (2014) "Advocacy coalition framework: Foundations, evolution, and ongoing research." In P. A. Sabatier and C. M. Weible (eds.), *Theories of the Policy Process* (3rd ed.). Boulder, CO: Westview Press.

Jericho, G. (2018) "What happened this week is not a shock, it is capitalism as intended." April 21, 2018, *The Guardian*. https://www.theguardian.com/business/grogonomics/2018/apr/20/what-happened-this-week-is-not-a-shock-it-is-capitalism-as-intended (accessed April 29, 2018).

Johnson, C. (2014) "15 participatory budgeting projects that give power to the people." Oct. 8, 2014, *Shareable*. https://www.shareable.net/blog/15-participatory-budgeting-projects-that-give-power-to-the-people (accessed May 2, 2018).

Kalil, A., Haskins, R., and Chesters, J. (2012) "Introduction." In A. Kalil., R. Haskins, and J. Chesters (eds.), *Investing in Children: Work, Education and Social Policy in Two Rich Countries*. Washington, DC: Brookings Institution Press, pp. 1–23.

Keane, J. (2009a) *The Life and Death of Democracy*. New York: W. W. Norton.

Keane, J. (2009b) "Monitory democracy and media-saturated societies." *Griffith Review* Edition 24, Griffith University. https://griffithreview.com/articles/monitory-democracy-and-media-saturated-societies/ (accessed May 2, 2018).

Kelaher, M. A., Ferdinand, A. S., and Paradies, Y. (2014a) "Experiencing racism in health care: The mental health impacts for Victorian Aboriginal communities." *Medical Journal of Australia* 201(1): 44–47.

Kelaher, M. A., Sabanovic, H., La Brooy, C., et al. (2014b) "Does more equitable governance lead to more equitable health care? A case study based on the implementation of health reform in Aboriginal health Australia." *Social Science and Medicine* 123: 278–286.

Kenner, D. (2015) "The politics of the Sustainable Development Goals (SDGs)." http://whygreeneconomy.org/the-politics-of-the-sustainable-development-goals-sdgs/ (accessed May 2, 2018).

Kent, J. L., and Thompson, S. (2014) "Three domains of urban policy." *Journal of Planning Literature* 29(3): 239–256.

Kent, J. L., Harris, P., Sainsbury, P., et al. (2017) "Influencing urban planning policy: An exploration from the perspective of public health." *Urban Policy and Research*: 36(1): 20–34, doi: 10.1080/08111146.2017.1299704

Kestlet-D'Amours, J. (2017) "Indigenous alliance launches divestment campaign against US and Canadian pipelines," May 25, 2017, *Truthout*. http://www.truthout.org/news/item/40707-indigenous-alliance-launches-divestment-campaign-against-us-and-canadian-pipelines (accessed June 8, 2017).

Kickbusch, I. (2015) "The political determinants of health: 10 years on (Editorials)." *BMJ* 350(h81): 1–2.

Kickbush, I., Allen, L., and Franz, C. (2016) "The commercial determinants of health." *The Lancet* 4(12): e895–e96.

Kickbusch, I., and Gleicher, D. (2012) *Governance for Health in the 21st Century.* Copenhagen: WHO Regional Office for Europe.

King, M. L. (1963) Letter from a Birmingham Jail, http://www.africa.upenn.edu/Articles_Gen/Letter_Birmingham.html (accessed July 16, 2018).

Kingdon, J. W. (2011) *Agendas, Alternatives, and Public Policies* (2nd ed.). Longman Classics in Political Science. Boston: Longman.

Kleinert, S., and Horton, R. (2017) "From universal health coverage to right care for health." *The Lancet* 390(10090): 101–102.

Klugman, B. (2015) "Media for health: Speaking truth to power." *The Atlantic Philanthropies.*

Klugman, B. (2016) "Membership-based organizations in constitutional democracies: Lessons from the treatment action campaign." *The Atlantic Philanthropies.*

Korten, D. (1995) *When Corporations Rule the World.* London: Earthscan.

Korten, D. (2015) *Change the Story, Change the Future: A Living Economy for a Living Earth.* Oakland, CA: Berrett-Koehler.

Korten, D. (2016) "How Trump's extremism may help us expose one of history's greatest political deceptions," December 26, 2016, *Yes! Magazine.* http://www.yesmagazine.org/new-economy/trumps-con-artist-economics-20161228 (accessed May 2, 2018).

Kubiszewski, I., Costanza, R., Franco, C., et al. (2013) "Beyond GDP: Measuring and achieving global genuine progress." *Ecological Economics* 93: 57–68.

Lagarde, M., Haines, H., and Palmer, N. (2007) "Conditional cash transfers for improving uptake of health interventions in low- and middle-income countries: A systematic review." *JAMA* 298(16): 1900–1910.

Lagarde, C. (2013) "A new global economy for a new generation," January 23, 2013. International Monetary Fund, Davos, Switzerland. http://www.imf.org/en/News/Articles/2015/09/28/04/53/sp012313

Lakoff, G. (2014) *The All New Don't Think of an Elephant*. White River Junction, VT: Chelsea Green.

Laverack, G. (2004). *Health Promotion Practice: Power and Empowerment*. Thousand Oaks, California: SAGE Publications.

Lees-Marshment, J. (2015) *The Ministry of Public Input: Integrating Citizen Views into Political Leadership*. London: Palgrave Macmillan.

Lefkowitz, B. (2007) *Community Health Centers*. New Brunswick, NJ: Rutgers University Press.

Leppo, K., Ollila, E., Peña, S., et al. (eds.) (2013) *Health in All Policies: Seizing Opportunities, Implementing Policies*. Helsinki: Ministry of Social Affairs and Health.

Lewis, M. J. (2003) *The People's Health. Public Health in Australia 1799–1950*. Westport, CT: Praeger.

Litman, T. (2013) "Transportation and public health." *Annual Review of Public Health* 34: 217–233.

Lleras-Muney, A. (2005) "The relationship between education and adult mortality in the United States." *Review of Economic Studies* 72: 189–221.

Lopez, G. (2016) "The US Justice Department will stop using private prisons," August 18, 2016, *Vox*. www.vox.com/2016/8/18/12536310/private-prisons-bureau-of-prisons (accessed May 18, 2017).

Lundberg, O., Dahl, E., Fritzell, J., et al. (2016) *Social Protection, Income and Health Inequities. Final Report of the Task Group on GDP, Taxes, Income and Welfare*. Copenhagen: WHO Regional Office for Europe.

Lundberg, O., Yngwe, M. Å., and Stjärne, M. K., et al. (2008a) "The role of welfare state principles and generosity in social policy programmes for public health: An international comparative study." *The Lancet* 372(9650): 1633–1640.

Lundberg, O., Yngwe, M. Å., Stjärne, M. K., et al. (2008b) "The Nordic Experience: Welfare States and Public Health (NEWS)." *Health Equity Studies* No 12. Stockholm: Stockholm University, Centre for Health Equity Studies (CHESS).

Mackenbach, J. P. (2011) "Can we reduce health inequalities? An analysis of the English strategy (1997–2010)." *Journal of Epidemiology & Community Health* 65: 568–75.

Maddison, S., and Carson, A. (2017) *Civil Voices: Researching Not-for-Profit Advocacy*. Melbourne: Probono Australia and Human Rights Law Centre, University of Melbourne.

Maggi, S., Irwin, L.G., Siddiqi, A., et al. (2005) "Analytic and strategic review paper: International perspectives on early child development." Geneva: Commission on Social Determinants of Health, World Health Organization.

Mahfuz, H. (2017) "How Turkey's citizens lost their rights." *New Internationalist* NI 508, December 2017, p. 15.

Majale, M. (2008) "Employment creation through participatory urban planning and slum upgrading: The case of Kitale, Kenya." *Habitat International* 32(2): 270–282.

Manandhar, D. S., Osrin, D., Shrestha, B. P., et al. (2004) "Effect of a participatory intervention with women's groups on birth outcomes in Nepal: Cluster-randomised controlled trial." *The Lancet* 364(9438): 970–979.

Marmot, M. (2004) *The Status Syndrome: How Social Standing Affects Our Health and Longevity.* New York: Times Books.

Marmot, M. (2015) "Inaugural address as WMA president." Moscow: World Medical Association.

Marmot, M. (2018) "Social causes of the slowdown in health improvement." *Journal of Epidemiology & Community Health* 72: 359–360.

Marmot, M., Allen, J., Goldblatt, P., et al. (2010) *Fair Society, Healthy Lives, the Marmot Review, Executive Summary: Strategic Review of Health Inequalities in England Post-2010.* London: Department of Health.

Marmot, M., Allen, J., and Goldblatt, P. (2010) "A social movement, based on evidence, to reduce inequalities in health." *Social Science & Medicine* 71(7): 1254–1258.

Marmot, M., Allen, J., Bell, R., et al. (2012) "WHO European review of social determinants of health and the health divide." *The Lancet* 380(9846): 1011–1029.

Matan, T. G., and Newman P. (2013) "A review of international low carbon precincts to identify pathways for mainstreaming sustainable urbanism in Australia." 7th State of Australian Cities Conference, Sydney, NSW.

Mayo, M., and Craig, G. (1995) "Community participation and empowerment: The human face of structural adjustment or tools for democratic transformation?." In G. Craig and M. Mayo (eds.), *Community Empowerment: A Reader in Participation and Development.* London: Zed Books, pp. 1–11.

McAfee, K., and Shapiro, E. (2010) "Payments for ecosystem services in Mexico: Nature, neoliberalism, social movements and the state." *Annals of the American Association of Geographers* 100: 579–599.

McCloskey, S. (2016) "The Sustainable Development Goals are toothless in the face of Neoliberalism: We need to pursue a new path to equality." *Sinergias—Diálogos Educativos Para a Transformação Social*, 4: 37–39.

McGlade, C., and Ekins, P. (2015) "The geographical distribution of fossil fuels unused when limiting global warming to 2 °C." *Nature* 517(7533): 187–190.

McKeen, J., and Wong, B. (2012) *The Illuminated Heart.* Gabriola Island, BC: Haven Institute Press.

McLeod, C. B., Hall, P. A., Siddiqi, A., et al. (2012) "How society shapes the health gradient: Work-related health inequalities in a comparative perspective." *Annual Review of Public Health* 33: 59–73.

McMichael, A. J. (2017) *Climate Change and the Health of Nations: Famines, Fevers and the Fate of Populations.* New York: Oxford University Press.

Melbourne City Council. (2017) "Participate Melbourne: 10-year financial plan." https://participate.melbourne.vic.gov.au/10yearplan (accessed March 8, 2018).

Mercer, R., Hertzman, C., Molina, H., et al. (2013) "Promoting equity from the start through early child development and Health in All Policies (ECD-HiAP)." In K. Leppo, et al. (eds.), *Health in All Policies: Seizing Opportunities, Implementing Policies.* Finland: Ministry of Social Affairs and Health, pp. 105–125.

Merry, J. (2013) "Tracing the U.S. deficit in PISA reading skills to early childhood: Evidence from the United States and Canada." *Sociology of Education* 86(3): 234–252.

Milanovic, B. (2016) *Global Inequality: A New Approach for the Age of Globalization.* Cambridge, MA: Harvard University Press.

Milio, N. (1986) "Multisectoral policy and health promotion: Where to begin?" *Health Promotion International* 1(2): 129–132.

Miller, C. (2014) "Citizen engagement in Australian policy-making." In C. Miller and L. Orchard (eds.), *Australian Public Policy: Progressive Ideas in the Neo-Liberal Ascendency.* Bristol, UK: Policy Press, pp. 333–350.

Mittlemark, M., Hunt, M. K., Heath, G. W., et al. (1993) "Realistic outcomes: Lessons from community based research and demonstration programs for the prevention of cardiovascular diseases." *Journal of Public Health Policy* 14(4): 437–462.

Monbiot, G. (2016) "The misinformation machine," December 1, 2016, *George Monbiot.* www.monbiot.com/2016/12/01/the-misinformation-machine/ (accessed May 2, 2018).

Mondragon. (2015) *Annual Report.* www.mondragon-corporation.com/wp-content/themes/mondragon/docs/eng/annual-report-2015.pdf (accessed May 2, 2018).

Moodie, R., Stuckler, D., Monteiro, C., et al. (2013) "Profits and pandemics: Prevention of harmful effects of tobacco, alcohol, and ultra-processed food and drink industries." *The Lancet* 381(9867): 670–679.

Moore, T., McDonald, M., and McHugh-Dillon, H. (2014) *Early Childhood Development and the Social Determinants of Health Inequities: A Review of the Evidence.* Parkville, Victoria: Centre for Community Child Health at the Murdoch Children's Research Institute and the Royal Children's Hospital.

Moughtin, J. C., Signoretti, P., and Moughtin, K. M. (2009) *Urban Design: Health and the Therapeutic Environment.* Oxford: Elsevier.

Moynihan, R., Doran, E., and Henry, D. (2008) "Disease mongering is now part of the global health debate." *PLoS Med* 5(5): e106.

Muradian, R., Arsel, M., Pellegrini, L., et al. (2013) "Payments for ecosystem services and the fatal attraction of win-win solutions." *Conservation Letters* 6(4): 274–279.

Murphy, R. (2015) *The Joy of Tax: How a Fair Tax System Can Create a Better Society.* London: Transworld.

Murray, R. B., Larkins, S., Russell, H., et al. (2012) "Medical schools as agents of change: Socially accountable medical education." *Medical Journal of Australia* 196(10): 653.

National Scientific Council on the Developing Child. (2016) "From best practices to breakthrough impacts: A science-based approach to building a more promising future for young children and families." Cambridge, MA: Harvard University.

Navarro, V., and Shi, L. (2001) "The political context of social inequalities and health." *Social Science and Medicine* 52: 481–491.

New Economic Foundation. (2018) "Health as a social movement: Theory into practice." http://neweconomics.org/2018/05/health-social-movement-theory-practice/?header=Latest (accessed May 9, 2018).

Newman, P. (2006) "Beyond peak oil: Will our cities and regions collapse?" *Res Publica* 15(1): 1–7.

NSW Department of Health. (2009) *Healthy Urban Development Checklist.* Sydney: NSW Department of Health.

OECD. (2014) "A new paradigm of rural innovation: Learning from and with rural people and communities." In *Innovation and Modernising the Rural Economy.* Paris: OECD Publishing. http://dx.doi.org/10.1787/9789264205390-7-en.

OECD. (2015) *Skills for Social Progress: The Power of Social and Emotional Skills.* OECD Skills Studies. Paris: OECD Publishing.

OECD. (2016a) *Education at a Glance 2016: OECD Indicators.* Paris: OECD Publishing.

OECD. (2016b) A New Rural Development Paradigm for the 21st Century: A Toolkit for Developing Countries, Development Centre Studies, OECD Publishing, Paris, https://doi.org/10.1787/9789264252271-en.

OECD. (2017a) *Health at a Glance 2017: OECD Indicators.* Paris: OECD Publishing.

OECD. (2017b) *Education at a Glance 2017: OECD Indicators.* Paris: OECD Publishing.

Ollila, E., Baum, F., and Peña, S. (2013) "Introduction to Health in All Policies and the analytical framework of the book." In K. Leppo et al. (eds), *Health in All Policies: Seizing opportunities, implementing policies.* Helsinki: Ministry of Social Affairs and Health, pp. 3–23.

Ortega, D., Ronconi, L., and Sanguinetti, P. (2016) "Reciprocity and willingness to pay taxes: Evidence from a survey experiment in Latin America." *Economia* 16(2): 55–87.

Ottersen, O. P., Dasgupta, J., Blouin, C., et al. (2014) "The Lancet-University of Oslo Commission on Global Governance for Health: The political origins of health inequity: Prospects for change." *The Lancet* 383: 630–667.

Oxfam. (2014) "Risk of reversal in progress on world hunger as climate change threatens food security." Oxfam media briefing, July 2014. Oxford: Oxfam International.

Painter, A. (2016) "A universal basic income: The answer to poverty, insecurity, and health inequality?" *BMJ* (Editorials): 355. doi: https://doi.org/10.1136/bmj.i6473

Pan American Health Organization. (2009) "Annual report of the director 2009: Progress in primary health care in the Americas." http://www1.paho.org/director/ar_2009/english/message.htm (accessed April 26, 2018).

Pape, M., and Lerner, J. (2016) "Budgeting for equity: How can participatory budgeting advance equity in the United States?" *Journal of Public Deliberation* 12: Issue 2, Article 9: http://www.publicdeliberation.net/jpd/vol12/iss2/art9

Parkes, M. W. (2010) "Ecohealth and Aboriginal health: A review of common ground. Evidence review prepared for National Collaborating Centre for Aboriginal Health." Prince George, B.C: National Collaborating Centre for Aboriginal Health.

Parks Victoria. (2017) "Healthy Parks Healthy People." YouTube, https://www.youtube.com/watch?v=oZp_8GPZ8-Y (accessed April 13, 2018).

Parkinson, G. (2017) "Tesla big battery officially switched on in South Australia," 1 December 2017, *Renew Economy.* https://reneweconomy.com.au/tesla-big-battery-officially-switched-on-in-south-australia-55285/ (accessed May 2, 2018).

Partenan, A. (2011) "What Americans keep ignoring about Finland's school success." *The Atlantic,* December 29. www.theatlantic.com/national/archive/2011/12/what-americans-keep-ignoring-about-finlands-school-success/250564/ (accessed May 9, 2018).

People's Health Movement. (2016) "12.7 Addressing the challenges of the UN Decade of Action for Road Safety (2011–2020): Outcome of the Second Global High-level Conference on Road Safety—Time for Results" (July 6). www.ghwatch.org/sites/www.ghwatch.org/files/WHA69_PHMCommentary4.pdf.

People's Health Movement. (2017) "WHO watch at the 70th World Health Assembly," May 24, 2017. http://www.phmovement.org/en/node/10667 (accessed June 8, 2017).

Perry, H. B., Zulliger, R., and Rogers, M. M. (2014) "Community health workers in low-, middle-, and high-income countries: An overview of their history, recent evolution, and current effectiveness." *Annual Review of Public Health* 35: 399–421.

Pickett, K. E., and Wilkinson, R. G. (2015) "Income inequality and health: A causal review." *Social Science & Medicine* 128: 316–326.

Pickett, K. E., and Wilkinson, R. G. (2017) "Immorality of inaction on inequality (Editorials)." *BMJ* 356: 1–2.

Piketty, T. (2014) *Capital in the Twenty-First Century.* Cambridge, MA: Harvard University Press.

Piquero, A., Farrington, D. P., Welsh, B. C., et al. (2008) "Effects of early family/parent training programs on antisocial behaviour and delinquency." *Campbell Systematic Reviews* 11, 2102–2105.

PlanH. (2017) "How Vancouver is making health and well-being everyone's business." https://planh.ca/resources/videos/how-vancouver-making-health-and-well-being-everyones-business (accessed July 5, 2017).

Pocock, B., Williams, P., and Skinner, N. (2012) *Time Bomb: Work, Rest and Play in Australia Today.* Sydney, NSW: NewSouth.

Pollock, A. M., and Roderick, P. (2017) "Open letter to Jeremy Hunt on the 69th anniversary of the NHS," July 5, 2017, *Huffington Post.* www.huffingtonpost.co.uk/allyson-pollock/jeremy-hunt_b_17390584.html (accessed April 13, 2018).

Popay, J. (2008) "Should disadvantaged people be paid to take care of their health: No." *BMJ* 337: 140–141.

Population Reference Bureau. (2017) "Human population: Urbanization." www.prb.org/Publications/Lesson-Plans/HumanPopulation/Urbanization.aspx (accessed June 23, 2017).

Pressman, J. L., and Wildavsky, A. (1984) *Implementation* (3rd ed.). Berkeley: University of California Press.

PricewaterhouseCoopers. (2016) "PwC Low Carbon Economy Index 2016." https://press.pwc.com/Multimedia/News-releases/All/pwc-low-carbon-economy-index-2016/a/0d616f0a-4f68-4e70-ad5f-38dacd8a59ca (accessed April 19, 2017).

Public Health England. (2017) *Spatial Planning for Health: An Evidence Resource for Planning and Designing Healthier Places.* London: Public Health England Publications.

Public Services International. (2017) "'Our water, our right,' Lagosians insist." www.world-psi.org/en/our-water-our-right-lagosians-insist (accessed May 18, 2017).

Puska, P., Vartiainen, E., Laatikainen, T., et al. (2009) *The North Karelia Project: From North Karelia to National Action.* Helsinki: National Institute for Health and Welfare.

Putland, C., Baum, F., and MacDougall, C. (1997) "How can health bureaucracies consult effectively about their policies and practices? Some lessons from an Australian study." *Health Promotion International* 12(4): 299–309.

Quebec. (2017) "Public Health Act." Quebec: Éditeur officiel du Québec, pp. 1–36.

Quiggin, J. (2010) *Zombie Economics: How Dead Ideas Still Walk Among Us.* Princeton, NJ: Princeton University Press.

Rasanathan, K., Posayanonda, T., Birmingham, M. and Tangcharoensathien, V. (2012) "Innovation and participation for healthy public policy: The first National Health Assembly in Thailand." *Health Expectations* 15: 87–96.

Raworth, K. (2017) *Doughnut Economics: Seven Ways to Think like a 21st Century Economist.* London: Random House Business Books.

Reddy, P. S. (2016) "Localising the sustainable development goals (SDGs): The role of local government in context." *African Journal of Public Affairs* 9(2): 1–15.

Rees, M. (2003) *Our Final Century: Will the Human Race Survive the Twenty-first Century.* London: William Heinemann.

Reeves, A., et al. (2017) "Introduction of a national minimum wage reduced depressive symptoms in low-wage workers: A quasi-natural experiment in the UK." *Health Economics* 26(5): 639–655.

REN21. (2017) "Renewables 2017 Global Status Report." Paris: REN21 Secretariat.

Renner, M., and Prugh, T. (2014) "Failing governance, unsustainable planet." In L. Mastny (ed.), *State of the World 2014: Governing for Sustainability*. Washington, DC: Worldwatch Institute/Island Press, pp. 3–19.

Republic of South Africa. (2015) "National integrated early childhood development policy." Pretoria: Government Printers. http://www.socdev.gpg.gov.za/Legislation/Documents/ECD%20Policy.pdf (accessed August 31, 2016).

Reynolds, C. (2011) *Public and Environmental Law*. Sydney: Sydney Federation Press.

Riccio, J., and Miller, C. (2016) *New York City's First Conditional Cash Transfer Program*. New York: MDRC.

Richardson, D. (2016) "Company Tax Cuts: What the Evidence Shows." Discussion paper. Canberra, ACT: The Australian Institute.

Robinson, M. (2006) "Budget Analysis and Policy Advocacy: The Role of Non-Governmental Public Action." IDS Working Paper 279.

Rockström, J. W., Steffen, W., Noone, K., et al. (2009) "A safe operating space for humanity." *Nature* 461: 472–475.

Roggema, R. (2012) *Swarming Landscapes: The Art of Designing for Climate Adaptation*. Advances in Global Change Research 48. Dordrecht: Springer Netherlands.

Roseboro, K. (2015) "Deceptive tactics used by industry-funded group to gain support for bill that would ban GMO labeling," July 20, 2015. https://www.ecowatch.com/deceptive-tactics-used-by-industry-funded-group-to-gain-support-for-bi-1882107465.html (accessed May 2, 2018).

Rydin, Y., Bleahu, A., Davies, M., et al. (2012) "Shaping cities for health: Complexity and the planning of urban environments in the 21st century." *The Lancet* 379(9831): 2079–2108.

Sahlberg, P. (2013) *Finnish Lessons 2.0*. New York: Teachers College Press.

Sahlberg, P. (2015) *Finnish Lessons 2.0: What Can the World Learn from Educational Change in Finland* (2nd ed.). Series on School Reform. New York: Teachers College Press.

Sainsbury, P. (2013) "Ethical considerations involved in constructing the built environment to promote health." *Bioethical Inquiry* 10: 39–48.

Sammons, P., Hall, J., Sylva, K., et al. (2013) "Protecting the development of 5–11-year-olds from the impacts of early disadvantage: The role of primary school academic effectiveness." *School Effectiveness and School Improvement* 24(2): 251–268.

Samons, R., Blanke, J., Corrigan, G., et al. (2015) *The Inclusive Growth and Development Report 2015*. Geneva: World Economic Forum.

Sanders, D. (2009) "Globalization, social determinants, and the struggle for health." In R. Labonte et al. (eds.), *Globalization and Health: Pathways, Evidence and Policy*. London: Routledge, pp. 334–340.

Sanders, D. (with Carver, R.) (1985) *The Struggle for Health: Medicine and the Politics of Underdevelopment*. London: Macmillan.

Sanders, M. R., Ralph, A., Sofronoff, K., et al. (2008). "Every family: A population approach to reducing behavioral and emotional problems in children making the transition to school." *The Journal of Primary Prevention* 29(3): 197–222.

Sarmiento, O. L., et al. (2013) "Bogotá, Colombia: A city with a built environment that promotes physical activity." In M. E. Bonilla-Chacín (ed.), *Promoting Healthy Living in Latin America and the Caribbean*. Washington, DC: World Bank, pp. 147–166.

Savage, M. (2018) "Richest 1% on target to own two-thirds of all wealth by 2030," April 7, 2018, *The Guardian*. www.theguardian.com/business/2018/apr/07/global-inequality-tipping-point-2030 (accessed April 30, 2018).

Schlosser, C. A., Strzepek, K., Gao, X., et al. (2014) "The future of global water stress: An integrated assessment." *Earth's Future* 2: 341–361.

Sengupta, A., Mukhopadhyaya, I., Weerasinghe, M. C., et al. (2017) "The rise of private medicine in South Asia." *BMJ* 357: j1482.

Sherwood, J. (2013) "Colonisation—it's bad for your health: The context of Aboriginal health." *Contemporary Nurse* 46(1): 28–40.

Shipan, R., and Volden, C. (2006) "Bottom-up federalism: The diffusion of antismoking policies from US cities to states." *American Journal of Political Science* 50: 825–843.

Shonkoff, J. P., Boyce, W. T. and McEwen, B. S. (2009) "Neuroscience, molecular biology, and the childhood roots of health disparities: Building a new framework for health promotion and disease prevention." *JAMA* 301(21): 2252–59.

Shonkoff, J. P., and Phillips, D. A. (2000) *From Neurons to Neighbourhoods: The Science of Early Child Development*. Washington, DC: National Academy Press.

Simons, M. (2017) "Journalism faces a crisis worldwide—we might be entering a new dark age," April 15, 2017, *The Guardian*. www.theguardian.com/media/2017/apr/15/journalism-faces-a-crisis-worldwide-we-might-be-entering-a-new-dark-age (accessed May 2, 2018).

Smit, W., Hancock, T., Kumaresen, J., et al. (2011) "Toward a research and action agenda on urban planning/design and health equity in cities in low and middle-income countries." *Journal of Urban Health: Bulletin of the New York Academy of Medicine* 88(5): 875–885.

Smith, M. K. (2000) "Adult education and lifelong learning: Southern critiques and alternatives." http://infed.org/mobi/adult-education-and-lifelong-learning-southern-critiques-and-alternatives/ (accessed October 30, 2017).

Smith, A. C., Holland, M., Korkeala, O., et al. (2015) "Health and environmental co-benefits and conflicts of actions to meet UK carbon targets." *Climate Policy* 16(3): 253–283.

Social Exclusion Knowledge Network. (2008) *Understanding and Tackling Social Exclusion: Final Report to the WHO Commission on Social Determinants of Health, from the Social Exclusion Knowledge Network*. Geneva: World Health Organization. http://www.who.int/social_determinants/knowledge_networks/final_reports/sekn_final%20report_042008.pdf?ua=1 (accessed April 27, 2018).

Solar, O., and Irwin, A. (2010) *A Conceptual Framework for Action on The Social Determinants of Health*. Social Determinants of Health Discussion Paper 2 (Policy and Practice). Geneva: World Health Organiszation.

Solomon, D. (2010) *The Priest*. New York Times Magazine, March 4. https://www.nytimes.com/2010/03/07/magazine/07fob-q4-t.html

South, J., Hunter, D. J., and Gamsu, M. (2014). "What Local Government Needs To Know About Public Health." *Need to Know Review* 2. London: Local Government Knowledge Navigator.

Standing Senate Committee on Social Affairs, Science, and Technology. (2001). "The health of Canadians: The federal role vol. 1, the story so far," March 2001, https://sencanada.ca/content/sen/committee/372/soci/rep/repocto2vol6-e.htm.

Starke. L. (2007) *State of the World: Our Urban Future. A Worldwatch Institute Report on Progress Toward a Sustainable Society*. New York: W. W. Norton.

Steffen, W., Broadgate, W., Deutsch, L., et al. (2015) "The trajectory of the Anthropocene: The great acceleration." *The Anthropocene Review* 2(1): 81–98.

Steffen, W., Grinevald, J., Crutzen, P., et al. (2011) "The anthropocene: Conceptual and historical perspectives." *Philosophical Transactions of the Royal Society A: Mathematical, Physical and Engineering Sciences* 369(1938): 842–867.

Stevenson, M., Thompson, J., Henrick de Sa, T., et al. (2016) "Land-use, transport and population health: Estimating the health benefits of compact cities." *The Lancet* 388(10062): 2925–2935.

Stigler, F. L., Macinko, J., Pettigrew, L. M., et al. (2016) "No universal health coverage without primary health care." *The Lancet* 387(10030): 1811.

Stiglitz, J. (2002) *Globalization and Its Discontents*. New York and London: W. W. Norton.

Stiglitz, J. (2012) *The Price of Inequality: How Today's Divided Society Endangers Our Future*. New York: W. W. Norton.

Stretton, H. (1972) *Ideas for Australian Cities*. Melbourne: Georgian House.

Stretton, H. (1999) *Economics: A New Introduction*. Sydney: UNSW Press.

Stuckler, D., and Basu, S. (2013). *The Body Economic: Why Austerity Kills*. New York: Basic Books.

Suhrcke, M., and Cookson, R. (2016) "Discussion paper on economics and health inequalities: Review of social determinants of health and the health divide in the WHO European Region." Copenhagen: World Health Organization.

Sylvester, T. (2017). "Native American groups vow to step up pipeline protests," August 2, 2017, *Newsweek*. www.newsweek.com/dakota-access-pipeline-keystone-pipeline-keystone-xl-native-americans-donald-554359 (accessed July 17, 2018).

Szreter, S. (1995) *Rapid Population Growth and Security: Urbanisation and Economic Growth in Britain in the Nineteenth Century. Population and Security*. Cambridge, UK: Centre for History and Economics, King's College.

Szreter, S. and Woolcock, M. (2004) "Health by association? Social capital, social theory, and the political economy of public health." *International Journal of Epidemiology* 33: 1–18.

Tax Justice Network. (2017) "Taxing corporations," May 25, 2017. https://www.taxjustice.net/topics/corporate-tax/taxing-corporations/

Tesh, S. N. (1988) *Hidden Arguments: Political Ideology and Disease Prevention Policy.* New Brunswick, NJ: Rutgers University Press.

Teves, O. (2012) "Protesters picket key tobacco show in Philippines," March 15, 2012, *Yahoo News.* http://news.yahoo.com/protesters-picket-key-tobacco-show-philippines-073230482.html.

The Australian Asbestos Network. (2017) "About." http://www.australianasbestosnetwork.org.au/australian-asbestos-network/ (accessed June 8, 2017).

The Economist. (2017) "Global liveability has improved for the first time in a decade." The Data Team, *The Economist.* www.economist.com/blogs/graphicdetail/2017/08/daily-chart-10 (accessed May 9, 2018).

The International Consortium of Investigative Journalists. (2017) "The Panama Papers." https://panamapapers.icij.org/ (accessed May 25, 2017).

The Right to Water and Sanitation. (2017) "Campaigns and civil society action." www.righttowater.info/rights-in-practice/advocacy/campaigns-and-civil-society-action/ (accessed July 17, 2018).

Thompson, R. M. (2017) "Is the Murray-Darling Basin Plan broken?" June 26, 2017, *The Conversation.* https://theconversation.com/is-the-murray-darling-basin-plan-broken-81613.

Thomsen, J. (2017) "Pittsburgh mayor fires back at Trump: My city will follow Paris agreement," June 19, 2017, *The Hill.* http://thehill.com/blogs/blog-briefing-room/news/335994-pittsburgh-mayor-fires-back-at-trump-my-city-will-follow-paris (accessed April 30, 2018).

Thow, A. M., Snowdon, W., Labonté, R., et al. (2015) "Will the next generation of preferential trade and investment agreements undermine prevention of noncommunicable diseases? A prospective policy analysis of the Trans Pacific Partnership Agreement." *Health Policy* 119(1): 88–96.

Tibinyane, A. (2017) "Namibia: Developing a national strategy on Health in All Policies." In V. Lin and I. Kickbusch (eds.), *Progressing the Sustainable Development Goals through Health in All Policies: Case Studies from around the world.* Adelaide: Government of South Australia, pp. 157–166.

Tolkien, J. R. R. (1996) *The Hobbit.* New York: Del Rey Books.

Torres, A., Sarmiento, O. L., Stauber, C., et al. (2013) "The Ciclovia and Cicloruta Programs: Promising interventions to promote physical activity and social capital in Bogotá, Colombia." *American Journal of Public Health* 103(2): e23–e30.

Townsend, M., Henderson-Wilson, C., Warner., E., and Weiss, L. (2015) *Healthy Parks, Healthy People: The state of the evidence 2015.* Melbourne: State Government of Victoria and School of Health and Social Development, Deakin University.

Tsouros, A. D. (2015) "Twenty-seven years of the WHO European Healthy Cities movement: A sustainable movement for change and innovation at the local level." *Health Promotion International* 30(S1): i3–i7.

Tudor-Hart, J. (1971) "The inverse care law." *The Lancet* 297(7696): 405–412.

United Cities and Local Governance. (2017) "Local Governance." https://www.uclg. org/en/action/decentralisation-governance (accessed June 19, 2017).

UNICEF. (2017) "Cuba: Statistics." https://www.unicef.org/infobycountry/cuba_ statistics.html (access July 17, 2018).

United Nations. (1945) "Charter of the United Nations and Statue of the International Court of Justice." San Francisco: United Nations.

United Nations. (2014) "Water for Life Decade: Water scarcity" (updated November 24). http://www.un.org/waterforlifedecade/scarcity.shtml (accessed November 10, 2017).

United Nations. (2016a) "The new urban agenda: Key commitments." October 20, 2016, Sustainable Development Goals. https://www.un.org/sustainabledevelopment/ blog/2016/10/newurbanagenda/ (accessed July 17, 2018).

United Nations. (2016b) *The World's Cities in 2016*. Data booklet. United Nations.

United Nations. (2017a) "Radical investments needed to meet global water and sanitation targets—UN report." http://www.un.org/apps/news/story. asp?NewsID=56558#.WgPrJo-Cy72 (accessed April 20, 2017).

United Nations. (2017b) "Sustainable development goals." https:// sustainabledevelopment.un.org/?menu=1300 (accessed June 30, 2017).

United Nations Development Programme (UNDP). (2014) "Global taskforce and regional governments for the post-2015 development agenda towards Habitat 111: Initial recommendations Habitat 111: Prepcom." New York: United Nations.

Unwin, A., and Yandell, J. (2016) *Rethinking Education: Whose Knowledge Is It Anyway?* Oxford: New Internationalist.

Victorian State Government. (2017) "Municipal public health and wellbeing planning." www2.health.vic.gov.au/public-health/population-health-systems/ municipal-public-health-and-wellbeing-planning (accessed July 5, 2017).

Virchow, R. C. (2006) "Report on the typhus epidemic in Upper Silesia." *American Journal of Public Health* 96(12).

Wade, R. H. (2017) "Global growth, inequality, and poverty: The globalization argument and the 'political' science of economics." In J. Ravenhill (ed.), *Global Political Economy*. Oxford: Oxford University Press, pp. 319–355.

Ward, K., Newman, J., John, P., et al. (2015) "Whatever happened to local government? A review symposium." *Regional Studies, Regional Science* 2(1): 435–457.

Waring, M. (1988) *Counting for Nothing: What Men Value and What Women Are Worth*. Wellington: Allen & Unwin.

Watts, N., Amann, M., Ayeb-Karlsson, S., et al. (2018) "The Lancet Countdown on health and climate change: From 25 years of inaction to a global transformation for public health." *The Lancet* 391: 581–630.

West, M. (2016) "Oligarchs of the Treasure Islands." https://www.michaelwest.com. au/oligarchs-of-the-treasure-islands/ (accessed May 9, 2018).

Weston, D. (2014) *The Political Economy of Global Warming: The Terminal Crisis*. Abingdon, Oxon: Routledge.

Whelan, J., and White, R. (2005) "Does privatising water make us sick?" *Health Sociology Review* 14(2): 134–145.

Whitehead, M. (1991) "The concepts and principles of equity and health." *Health Promotion International* 6(3): 217–228.

Whitehead, M., and Dahlgren, G. (1991). *Policies and Strategies to Promote Social Equity in Health*. Stockholm: Institute for Futures Studies.

WHO Global Health Observatory. (2018) "Density of physicians (total number per 1000 population, latest available year)," Global Health Observatory data. http://www.who.int/gho/health_workforce/physicians_density/en/ (accessed May 2, 2018).

WHO Regional Office for Europe. (2017) *What Is a Healthy City?* Copenhagen: WHO Regional Office for Europe.

Wilkinson, R. G., and Pickett, K. (2009) *The Spirit Level: Why More Equal Societies Almost Always Do Better*. London: Allen Lane.

Willis, P. (1977) *Learning to Labour: How Working Class Kids Get Working Class Jobs*. New York: Columbia University Press.

Winstanley, G. (1649) *The New Law of Righteousness*. UK: Giles Calvert.

World Bank. (2016) "Life expectancy at birth, total (years) 2015." https://data.worldbank.org/indicator/SP.DYN.LE00.IN (accessed February 28, 2018).

World Bank. (2018) "World Development Indicators." https://data.worldbank.org/products/wdi (accessed May 2, 2018).

World Health Organization. (1978) "Declaration of Alma-Ata." International Conference on Primary Health Care, September 6–12, Alma-Ata, USSR. http://www.who.int/publications/almaata_declaration_en.pdf?ua=1 (accessed July 17, 2018).

World Health Organization. (1986) "Ottawa Charter for Health Promotion, First International Conference on Health Promotion," November 21, Ottawa, Canada. www.who.int/healthpromotion/conferences/previous/ottawa/en/ (accessed August 18, 2017).

World Health Organization. (2010) "WHO Global Code of Practice on the International Recruitment of Health Personnel." Sixty-third World Health Assembly, WHA63.16 (May 2010). www.who.int/hrh/migration/code/practice/en/ (accessed May 2, 2018).

World Health Organization. (2011) "Rio Political Declaration on Social Determinants of Health," World Conference on Social Determinants of Health. Rio de Janeiro: Geneva CHE: WHO.

World Health Organization. (2014) *Global Status Report on Violence Prevention 2014*. Geneva: WHO.

World Health Organization. (2015a) "WHO Framework for Country Action across sectors for health and health equity: Selected case studies." Geneva: World Health Organization.

World Health Organization. (2015b) *Health in All Policies: Training Manual*. Geneva: World Health Organization.

World Health Organization. (2016) "Global monitoring of action on the social determinants of health: A proposed framework and basket of core indicators." Consultation paper. http://www.who.int/social_determinants/consultation-paper-SDH-Action-Monitoring.pdf?ua=1 (accessed July 17, 2018).

World Health Organization. (2018a) "Universal health coverage (UHC): Fact sheet." http://www.who.int/mediacentre/factsheets/fs395/en/ (accessed May 2, 2018).

World Health Organization. (2018b) Social Determinants of Health focussed monitoring. http://www.who.int/social_determinants/monitoring/en/ (accessed May 9, 2018)

World Health Organization. (2018c) "Ambient air pollution: A major threat to health and climate." http://www.who.int/airpollution/ambient/en/ (accessed January 11, 2018).

World Wildlife Fund. (2016) "International case studies for Scotland's climate plan, public transport, Zurich, Switzerland." Edinburgh: WWF.

Yang, X., Fei, T., and Wang, G. (2013) "Incorporating environmental co-benefits into climate policies: A regional study of the cement industry in China." *Applied Energy* 112: 1446–1453.

Yee, V., and Blinder, A. (2018) "National school walkout: Thousands protest against gun violence across the U.S." 14 March 2018, *New York Times*. https://www.nytimes.com/2018/03/14/us/school-walkout.html (accessed May 2, 2018).

Young, K. (1975). *Essays on the study of urban politics*. London: Macmillan.

Young, M., and Willmott, P. (1957) *Family and Kinship in East London*. London: Routledge & Kegan Paul.

Yunupingu, G. (2016) "Rom Watangu: An indigenous leader reflects on a lifetime following the law of the land." *The Monthly*. July. https://www.themonthly.com.au/issue/2016/july/1467295200/galarrwuy-yunupingu/rom-watangu (accessed July 17, 2018).

Zérah, M. H. (2009) "Participatory governance in urban management and the shifting geometry of power in Mumbai." *Development and Change* 40(5): 853–877.

Zeuli, K. A., and Cropp, R. (2004) *Cooperatives: Principles and Practices in the 21st Century*. Madison: University of Wisconsin Center for Cooperatives, A1457.

Zucman, G. (2017) "The desperate inequality behind global tax dodging." *The Guardian*, November 8. www.theguardian.com/commentisfree/2017/nov/08/tax-havens-dodging-theft-multinationals-avoiding-tax (accessed May 6, 2018).

About the Author

FRAN BAUM, PHD, is the Matthew Flinders Distinguished Professor of Public Health and Director of the Southgate Institute of Health, Society, and Equity at Flinders University. Professor Baum is a Fellow of the Academy of the Social Sciences in Australia, the Australian Academy of Health and Medical Sciences, and the Australian Health Promotion Association. She is a past National President and Life Member of the Public Health Association of Australia and a member and past Chair of the Global Steering Council of the People's Health Movement. She also served as a Commissioner on the World Health Organization's Commission on the Social Determinants of Health and has received several national competitive grants investigating aspects of health inequity. She has extensive experience teaching public health.

Index